To: Roger

From: Rhonda

Love You!!

# ELIJAH

## The Prophet of Confrontation

**Bible Biography Series**
**Number Three**

# John G. Butler

Copyright © 1994 by John G. Butler

Published by
LBC Publications
325 30th Avenue North
Clinton, Iowa 52732

*Printed in the United States of America*

ISBN 1-889773-03-4

*First printing 1991*
*Second printing 1994*
*Third printing 1997*
*Fourth printing 2000*
*Fifth printing 2002*

# Introduction

The Bible Biography Series is a series of twenty books written about Bible characters by John G. Butler. These books are expository studies of the Scripture. They are extensively organized and outlined, filled with Gospel lessons and practical applications of Scripture to every day life, written in easy to understand laymen's language, and theologically and morally they take a strong, old-fashioned, fundamentalist position which is increasingly unpopular but greatly needed in our day.

These books are very helpful to preachers in providing material for sermons and lessons on these Bible characters and texts. They will also be found to provide much instruction for the individual in his or her personal Bible study; and because of their organized structure, they are very adaptable to Sunday School classes and Bible study groups.

The twenty books of the Bible Biography Series consist of books on *Joseph, Jonah, Elijah, Elisha, Gideon, Samson, John the Baptist, Peter, Abraham, Lot, Paul, Moses, Joshua, Samuel, David, Nehemiah, Jacob, Hezekiah, Mordecai,* and *Ruth.*

The author, a native of Iowa, is a long-time, fundamentalist, Baptist minister who has been teaching and preaching the Word of God for over forty-five years with nearly thirty-five years of pastoral experience. He held pastorates in Williamsburg, Ohio; Detroit, Michigan; Chicago, Illinois; and Clinton, Iowa. He is also the author of the *Studies of the Savior,* a series of books about Jesus Christ.

# Contents

PREFACE ..................................................................9

I. THE WEATHER ...................................................11
(I Kings 17:1)
A. The Prophet of God
B. The Prince of Israel
C. The Prediction of Judgment

II. THE WADI ..........................................................45
(I Kings 17:2–7)
A. The Protection of His Life
B. The Provision of His Meals
C. The Preparation of His Heart

III. THE WIDOW ......................................................61
(I Kings 17:8–16)
A. The Perception of Duty
B. The Priorities of Duty
C. The Premiums of Duty

IV. THE WEEPING ...................................................77
(I Kings 17:17–24)
A. The Place of Trials
B. The Perplexity of Trials
C. The Product of Trials

V. THE WANDERERS .............................................93
(I Kings 18:1–20)
A. The Precept of God
B. The Problem of Obadiah
C. The Performance of Ahab

VI. THE WAVERING .................................................... 115
    (I Kings 18:21–40)
    A. The Preliminaries of the Contest
    B. The Proclamations of the Contest
    C. The Persuasions of the Contest

VII. THE WATER ........................................................ 140
    (I Kings 18:42–46)
    A. The Passions of the Flesh
    B. The Persistency of the Faithful
    C. The Pace of the Feet

VIII. THE WARRANT .................................................... 156
    (I Kings 19:1–8)
    A. The Persecution of Elijah
    B. The Pessimism of Elijah
    C. The Preservation of Elijah

IX. THE WILDERNESS ............................................... 176
    (I Kings 19:8–18)
    A. The Probing of the Question
    B. The Pedagogy of the Demonstration
    C. The Predictions of the Future

X. THE WICKED ........................................................ 192
    (I Kings 21)
    A. The Proposition of Ahab
    B. The Plot of Jezebel
    C. The Proclamation of Elijah

XI. THE WOUNDED .................................................... 213
    (II Kings 1)
    A. The Providence of Events
    B. The Practices of Unbelief
    C. The Pronouncement of Judgment

XII. THE WHIRLWIND ...............................................227
     (II Kings 2:1–12)
     A. The Pathway of Elijah
     B. The Parting of Elijah
     C. The Portrayal of Elijah

XIII. THE WRITING ....................................................245
     (II Chronicles 21)
     A. The Postscript of Service
     B. The Pursuit of Evil
     C. The Prophecy of Judgment

     QUOTATION SOURCES........................................259

# Preface

Elijah was a shock treatment, an exclamation point, a dynamic, no-nonsense personality. He saw things as only right or wrong, Jehovah or Baal. There was no middle ground with him, no toleration of evil. So with Spirit-led intrusion, he was ever confronting people about their sin. He confronted kings in their palaces and a vast crowd in the great contest on Mount Carmel. He sternly challenged idolatry with a strong sanctified scorn, and he fearlessly denounced leaders by announcing right to their face their death and the end of their dynasties.

Not only did Elijah speak out sternly and forcefully against evil, but he also dealt out deadly blows of Divine judgment. He prayed for and announced a devastating drought for Israel; he ordered four hundred fifty prophets of Baal to be slain at Mount Carmel; and he called down fire on one hundred two defiant soldiers. He was a deadly foe of evil.

While much of his recorded ministry reflects a man of stern, unbending nature, Elijah was not calloused. He was gentle enough to abide with a widow and her son for several years and compassionate enough to raise the widow's son from the dead. He was patient enough to train and inspire an Elisha and to encourage the training of young prophets.

Though "a man subject to like passions as we are" (James 5:17), Elijah excelled in dedication far beyond all of us; and his whirlwind trip to glory was a fitting crown for a life wholly given to serving God. If mankind would spend more time reading about Elijah than they do about the stars of their day and the heroes of their fiction, it would have a tremendous purifying effect. It would put backbone in their character, convictions, and performance. You cannot read Elijah honestly and come away without being inspired to new heights of holy living and service.

Godly men are seldom given much honor by their own generation. But truth, like cream, always comes to the top; and eventually the godly ones are given their due recognition. This was so true of Elijah. Despised and rejected by the multitudes in his lifetime, he, nevertheless, has been greatly honored over the years. In fact, few men have been honored over the years as Elijah has. We note here some of the honors given to Elijah.

*Scripture honors Elijah.* More is written of him in the New Testament than of any other prophet except Moses.

*God honored Elijah.* Elijah was one of two humans who did not taste death (Enoch was the other). And Elijah was one of two Old Testament saints (Moses was the other) who was on the mount when Christ was transfigured.

*Jews honor Elijah.* At the observance of the Passover, orthodox Jews leave the door open so that Elijah may enter if he should suddenly come. Also orthodox Jews reserve a vacant chair for Elijah at the circumcision of a child. And some Jews honor Elijah in that when lost goods are discovered and the owner cannot be found, they are set aide until Elijah comes to identify the owner.

*Geography honors Elijah.* A mountain in Greece is named after him.

*Mohammedanism honors Elijah.* Anyone acquainted with Mohammedanism knows of their great veneration for the prophet Elijah.

*Rome honors Elijah.* The Roman Catholic Church claims Elijah was the founder of the barefoot Carmelite order of monks. Such a claim is full of nonsense, as are many claims of the church of Rome; but nevertheless it does show esteem for Elijah.

*Music honors Elijah.* Felix Mendelssohn wrote a famous oratorio which he called "Elijah." Classical music lovers will especially remember the exceptional piece, "He watching over Israel," which is from this oratorio.

# I.
# THE WEATHER

### I KINGS 17:1

THE ENTRANCE OF Elijah in the Biblical record is abrupt, bold, and dramatic. Like a thunderbolt from the skies, Elijah suddenly appears on the scene and talks to King Ahab, the wicked king of Israel, about the weather. Talking about the weather is common conversation with people. But there was nothing common about the weather talk of Elijah before Ahab which is recorded in our text for this first chapter of our study of Elijah. A stern Elijah said that it was judgment time regarding the weather. He said a severe drought was coming to the land and would continue until Elijah decided to stop it. No rain, no dew, no moisture, nothing. Just the burning, searing, wilting sun day after day until Elijah called a halt to the torment. It was a bold and severe prediction about the weather which did not go over well with Ahab.

Though our text for this first chapter is only one verse, it certainly is filled with information, instruction, and drama. To further study our text, we will divide it into three parts. These three parts are the prophet of God (Elijah), the prince of Israel (Ahab to whom Elijah spoke), and the prediction of judgment (the message Elijah spoke to Ahab).

### A. THE PROPHET OF GOD

The first few words of our text give us some introductory information about Elijah. These words tell us the name, neighborhood, and nature of the prophet. Further on in the text we will learn some things about Elijah's calling, but we will consider that information later on when we get to that part of our text.

# Elijah

## 1. The Name of the Prophet

The name Elijah is a combination of the generic name for God ("El" from Elohim) and the name Jehovah ("jah" from Jehovah) the special Tetragrammaton name for God given to Israel. This combination of names makes Elijah's name mean Jehovah is God. The meaning of the name instructs us about three important things. They are the problem of the land, the person of the Lord, and the parents of the lad.

*The problem of the land.* The name Elijah was a most significant and appropriate name for Elijah's time and ministry. The great conflict of that day was whether Jehovah was God or Baal was God. Elijah's name, as well as his ministry, emphatically said Jehovah was God! But most of the people in Israel worshiped Baal instead Jehovah. This wicked Baal worship provoked the judgment of the drought which Elijah predicted. The conflict of Baal and Jehovah worship climaxed in Elijah's day on Mount Carmel when Elijah defeated the priests of Baal.

*The person of the Lord.* The name Elijah has New Testament ramifications, for in the meaning of the name it is an Old Testament testimony of the New Testament truth of the Deity of Jesus Christ. This truth is found in the fact that the Jehovah of the Old Testament is the Jesus of the New Testament (cp. Isaiah 43:11 with Luke 2:11). So Elijah's name carries some great messages. The name is good New Testament theology about God's Son as well as an Old Testament affirmation of Who is the Supreme God (Joel, the name of the prophet who authored one of the small books of the Old Testament, also means Jehovah is God—the Jehovah-Elohim parts are in reverse order compared to Elijah's name; but the meaning, of course, is the same).

*The parents of the lad.* Little is said in Scripture about Elijah's parents. But we learn much about their testimony for Jehovah in the name they gave their lad. The name said their testimony was courageous, continuous, correct, and conspicuous.

## The Weather

First, their *testimony was courageous.* It was courageous because of the popularity of Baal worship. With Baal worship so popular and also so intolerant of Jehovah worship, it would take great courage to name one's child "Elijah." But Elijah's parents had that courage. Elijah's parents were some of the few who remained true to Jehovah while most of Israel was given to Baal worship. Their courage to stand for Jehovah reflected great faith which had a great influence upon Elijah. How valuable are godly parents who have this kind of influence.

Second, their *testimony was continuous.* It was continuous because of the preservation of Elijah's life. As long as Elijah was alive, their testimony about Jehovah did not die but continued in him. All of us need a continuous testimony like that. Our testimony must shine more than just on Sundays. It must shine every day of the week. It must never die.

Third, their *testimony was correct.* It was correct because of the proclamation of the name. The name proclaimed that Jehovah was God. Elijah's parents had their theology straight—for they believed Jehovah, not Baal, was God. You cannot have a good testimony if your doctrine is not correct. We have some popular movements today which play down the importance of doctrine. But when doctrine is not important, your testimony ceases to be correct and valid. There would be no correct testimony for Elijah's parents unless the testimony said that Jehovah is God. Likewise there is no correct testimony today unless the testimony says that Jesus is God.

Fourth, their *testimony was conspicuous.* It was conspicuous because of the presence of Elijah. You cannot conceal a growing boy. He is going to be both visible and vocal. That would make his parents' testimony about Jehovah very conspicuous. Let our testimony for Christ be just as conspicuous. God does not want us to hide our testimony for Christ "under a bushel" (Matthew 5:15) but to put it where it will be seen and heard.

## 2. The Neighborhood of the Prophet

Our text says Elijah was a "Tishbite, who was of the inhabitants of Gilead." Elijah came from Tishbe of Gilead. Nothing is known of Tishbe, for there has never been a positive identification of a Tishbe in Gilead or anywhere else. That does not mean Tishbe did not exist, however. But while we know little of the town of Tishbe, we do know much more about the area of Gilead. Located just east of the Jordan River, Gilead was a hilly area that in some places was quite rugged and mountainous. While it was a generally fertile land so that crops and livestock could thrive in the area, it took much hard labor to make the land produce well because of the ruggedness of the land. Hence, it was not an area that tended to make a person soft and spoiled. Rather it was a place the produced real manliness which characterized Elijah. Joseph Parker said, "There was a wonderful similarity between the man [Elijah] and the region; stern . . . grand, majestic, and awful, were they both." Elijah was not raised in softness and ease. He was no wimp. He was all man. That kind makes the best servants of God. Softies do not make good prophets and preachers. They are flops at standing in the gap to stop evil. God does not call the lazy, indolent, and cream puffs into the ministry. He calls men into the ministry. The ministry is no place for the lazy, indolent, and cream puffs. We do not need prissy preachers! They are worthless.

**3. The Nature of the Prophet**

The abrupt, bold, zealous, and dramatic appearance of Elijah in our text reveals some of the nature of the prophet. First appearances in Scripture are often the key to what follows, and it was so in the case of Elijah. Other appearances of Elijah in Scripture are also characterized by abruptness, boldness, zealousness, and the dramatic. Elijah was not a passive, timid, mild mannered soul. It was his very nature to get to the point in a hurry, to flinch not at walking into danger, to be zealous, and to be dramatic in his actions. Elijah's nature fit his calling.

God always fits the man for the calling. If you do not possess the qualities needed for the call, God will give them to you if He calls you. Those who claim a particular call but evidence none of the needed qualities for the call are only pretending a call. God would not put a soft spoken, reticent man in the calling He gave Elijah. This calling only fit Elijah's nature.

## B. THE PRINCE OF ISRAEL

Ahab was the king of Israel during all but the last years of Elijah's ministry as God's prophet. That is why Elijah went to him with the prediction of the judgment upon the land, for Ahab was the prince of the people then. To take a detailed look into the person of Ahab, we will look at the country of the prince, the character of the prince, and the consort of the prince. All three were extremely corrupt which justified Elijah's prediction of great judgment upon the land via the drought.

### 1. The Country of the Prince

The country over which Ahab ruled and where Elijah spent most of his ministry was the northern part of the Jewish nation. Though it was called Israel, the name did not apply to all the Jewish nation then. It had applied to the entire Jewish nation until the split after King Solomon died. Then the northern part of the split was called Israel (also "Samaria," after its capital, and "Ephraim," after one of its tribes) while the southern part was called Judah. To further examine Ahab's country, we will look at the revolt, the rulers, and the religion of the country.

*The revolt of the country.* Ahab's country was the product of a revolt. Our text occurred around 900 B.C. which was about sixty years since the revolt had occurred which produced the tragic split of the Jewish nation into the southern and northern kingdoms. The revolt occurred right after Solomon died. It was one of the darkest times in Israel's history. Krummacher said the times were so bad, "It seemed as if Satan had transferred his residence from hell to earth."

Israel was a united kingdom under Saul, David, and Solomon. But those were to be the only kings who would rule over all the twelve tribes. Solomon's death signaled the end of a united monarchy and brought about the split of the kingdom into the northern and southern kingdoms. Had Solomon remained true to the Lord, there would have been no split in the kingdom. But in Solomon's latter years, he became consumed with the lust of the flesh and took unto himself hundreds of wives. Adding to this evil was the fact that he took these wives from nations and peoples from whom God had forbidden Israel to take wives. Then, to make matters worse, he allowed his many wives to turn his heart away from the true God to false gods. He went after "Ashtoreth the goddess of the Zidonians and after Milcom, the abomination of the Ammonites . . . Then did Solomon build an high place for Chemosh, the abomination of Moab, in the hill that is before Jerusalem, and for Molech, the abomination of the children of Ammon" (11:5,7).

The deterioration of Solomon's character brought about a great oppressiveness in his government. Bad morals and bad doctrine do not promote good conditions in any land. They eventually bring oppression, tyranny, and slavery. And sooner or later the oppressed will revolt. When Rehoboam came to the throne in place of his father Solomon, the elders of the land besought Rehoboam to ease up on the people, to have a more compassionate government, and to remove the heavy yoke from off the citizenry. But Rehoboam, strongly influenced by his evil peers (12:8–10), would not listen to the entreaties for a more compassionate government. Instead, he said he would be harder on the people than Solomon was. His total rejection of the pleas of the people for a less repressive government was met by a great revolt. Ten of the twelve tribes of Israel seceded from Rehoboam's rule and formed a new nation which was the northern kingdom generally called Israel. Only the tribes of Judah and Benjamin stayed loyal to Rehoboam, and they formed the southern kingdom called Judah.

This revolt was doomed to failure, however, even though it came about in opposition to gross injustice. It was doomed to failure because it tried to solve the problem of oppression without correcting the cause of oppression, namely, the moral and spiritual decline in the land. The people wanted to escape from the consequences of evil, but not from the evil itself. They cried for freedom while they pursued the sins which took away their freedom. But until people condemn and forsake their evil, they will not begin to escape the consequences of evil. We need to remember this fact, especially during election years. There is no real return to freedom until we clean up our doctrine and our deportment! We make a grave mistake to think some candidate will save us from our nation's problems when that candidate's doctrine is unsound and his morals and convictions are deficient. He may speak ever so eloquently and impressively against some of the problems of the land; but if he does not attack the evils which cause the problems, he will not bring true reform.

*The rulers of the country.* Ahab's country never had a godly leader. They had a total of 19 kings during their history, but all 19 were evil men. Elijah came on the scene during the reign of Ahab, their seventh king. A look at the first six kings which preceded Ahab will reveal the great moral and spiritual decline that took place as soon as the northern kingdom came into existence. When Ahab became king he only made the decline worse as we will see shortly. The six kings that preceded Ahab were Jeroboam, Nadab, Baasha, Elah, Zimri, and Omri.

*Jeroboam.* He started the northern split down a sinful path from which it never departed. He was a very wicked man. He did "evil above all [the kings which at that juncture would be Saul, David, and Solomon] that were before" him (I Kings 14:9). The Divine epitaph on his life was "Jeroboam, who did sin, and who made Israel to sin" (I Kings 14:16). Some 25 times that condemnatory phrase, "made Israel to sin," is said in the Bible of Jeroboam. Jeroboam corrupted the people by corrupting their religion. He made two calves of gold and led the people into worshiping them. Then he made priests "of the lowest of the people" (I Kings 13:33) which further corrupted their religion. The evil reign of Jeroboam over the northern kingdom lasted for 22 years. He was succeeded by his son Nadab.

*Nadab.* He reigned only two years; but they were evil years; for Nadab "walked in the way of his father, and in his sin wherewith he made Israel to sin" (I Kings 15:26). His short reign ended when Baasha assassinated him. Baasha then assumed the throne.

*Baasha.* He reigned for 24 years. His reign was a bloody reign. He killed all of Jeroboam's house and was in constant battle with the southern kingdom. Baasha also "walked in the way of Jeroboam, and in his sin wherewith he made Israel to sin" (I Kings 15:34).

*Elah.* When Baasha died, Elah, Baasha's son, succeeded him to the throne; but his reign, like Nadab's, was only two years. He was a worthless wretch because he was given to drink. This cost him his throne; for when he was on a drinking spree, he was assassinated by Zimri (I Kings 16:9,10), who was one of Israel's high ranking military officers.

*Zimri.* After murdering Elah, Zimri assumed the throne. But his reign as king lasted only seven days (I Kings 16:15). In those seven days, however, he left a dark trail of blood; for he killed all the house of Baasha so that no one of Elah's family could ever claim the throne again. But Zimri's conduct was rejected by the people; and under the leadership of Omri, the top military officer of the northern kingdom, an insurrection was made against Zimri. Seeing his chances of winning were nil, Zimri went into the king's house and set it on fire and died a suicide in the fire (I Kings 16:18).

*Omri.* Success in removing Zimri put Omri, the father of Ahab, on the throne. He reigned 12 years. In the first four years he was king over only part of the northern kingdom, for some of the people followed an upstart by the name of Tibni instead. After four years Tibni died, and this opened the door for Omri to rule over all the northern kingdom. Omri's reign continued the decline of Israel's character and leadership. The Scripture says Omri "did worse than all [the kings] that were before him" (I Kings 16:25). He was a wicked man and out-sinned his wicked predecessors. When he died his son Ahab became king.

## The Weather

With the evil examples of Ahab's predecessors as king, no wonder Ahab was such was wicked king.

*The religion of the country.* The political situation was not all that corrupted the land in Elijah's day. There was also great corruption from the religion of the land. Corruption from religion came when the worship of Baal replaced and cruelly suppressed the worship of Jehovah. The issue which Elijah raised at Carmel was which of these two religions is right? He said, "If the LORD [Jehovah] be God, follow him; but if Baal, then follow him" (I Kings 18:21).

To properly appreciate and understand the denunciation ministry of Elijah in the land of Israel, we will consider these two religions and how they differed.

First, the *worship of Baal.* Baal was a heathenistic, pagan god who was supposed to control rain and fertility. While over the centuries of heathen idolatry there seems to have been many Baals, the Baal worshiped in Israel during Elijah's day was considered to be the supreme male god. Ashtoreth (called Ishtar by the Assyrians, Astarte by the Greeks, and Venus by the Romans) was the supreme female divinity and was often associated with the religion of Baal. Where an altar to Baal was erected, it was common to find idol poles (sometimes called "groves" in the KJV) erected in honor of the goddess, Ashtoreth, who was considered the consort of Baal.

This religion of Baal was a morally rotten, vile, sensual, and cruel religion which made immoral sex acts a religious exercise. "Fertility rites played a large part in his worship. Licentious dances were prominent, and chambers existed for both male and female prostitutes" (Leon Wood). Baal religion vilely influenced the land by dropping the morals of Israel to incredible depths and destroying character en masse.

The cruelty of Baal religion was especially evident in its being very intolerant of the worship of Jehovah. It persecuted the worshipers of Jehovah with great violence. The land was filled with blood from the great oppression of the worshipers of

Jehovah by Baal religion. As we will see later, Ahab's wife Jezebel was the leader in this persecution of the worshipers of Jehovah. Being the daughter of Ethbaal, the great high priest of Ashtoreth (female counterpart of Baal) in Tyre, she was well acquainted with Baal religion and its bloody tactics. Her knowledge of this, coupled with her personality and corrupt character, made her a vicious and fanatical promoter of Baal worship and a bloody persecutor of the worshipers of Jehovah. Jezebel was so successful in slaying the prophets of Jehovah that several times Elijah complained to God that he thought he was the only one left of the prophets of Jehovah (I Kings 18:22, 19:10, 19:14).

The intolerance of Baal worshipers for Jehovah worshipers illustrates evil's habit of intolerance. Evil often seeks to be allowed and permitted on the basis of tolerance, freedom of expression, rights, equal time, etc. But once it gets a foothold, you can count on it changing its tune about tolerance and equal rights. It will be the sovereign, and any competitors will be cruelly battered into submission. Under Jeroboam, toleration for idolatry was strongly encouraged in the northern kingdom. He made the golden calves and put them in convenient locations so Israel did not have to go far to worship. After all it was "too much for you to go up to Jerusalem," he said (I Kings 12:28); so there must be toleration for some deviation from true worship. But toleration soon enabled evil religion to become the dominate religion; and when that happened, it was no longer toleration but totalitarianism.

The intolerance of evil for righteousness is seen on every hand in our day. Homosexuals talk tolerance today. They want equal rights; they want to be treated like everyone else. But that talk will end once they get in power. Genesis 19 shows us that fact. When homos dominate, they will persecute and oppress with cruel viciousness those who differ with them morally. Communism is the same way. As an example, in China during World War II the communists insisted on being included in the government. Finally they were allowed official recognition. Every one alive today knows what happened after that. Communism soon took over; and when it did, toleration ceased to exist for non-communists. Protesters for freedom, for other forms of government were machine-gunned down and run over by tanks. Hitler also gained power through the toleration of the Nazis by the other political parties in Germany. But when the Nazis got power, they bloodied the opposition into near extinction. Church troublemakers are also hypocrites in regard to toleration. They want their evil actions and unfaithful church members who are their friends tolerated, but they cannot tolerate a pastor or other church leaders they do not like.

Second, the *worship of Jehovah*. The worship of Jehovah was the religion that ought to have dominated in Israel. It was true, moral, and holy. It did not worship some stupid, man-made idol. It worshiped the one, great, and true God Who created the universe and all living creatures. But though this religion was the only right one and, therefore the best and the most blessed one of all, it was, however, the least popular one in Elijah's day. Persecutions had either eliminated its adherents by death or so intimidated those still alive, that few were left who would stand faithfully for Jehovah. God told Elijah that 7,000 had not bowed the knee to Baal (I Kings 19:18), but 7,000 is not very many when you consider the entire population of Israel was in the millions at that time.

Though Jehovah worship was so unpopular, it still produced, at that time, some of the greatest men ever to set foot on the earth. It produced Elijah, and few men compare to him. Also, late in Elijah's story, we will meet up with Elisha and Micaiah. What two tremendous prophets these men were! Centuries have come and gone since they lived, but not many have compared to them. Then there was Naboth, a farmer who was so loyal to the Word of God that he would not, even for a good price, sell his property to Ahab (I Kings 21). But in spite of the great characters produced by Jehovah worship, and in spite of the great character of Jehovah worship, the land was nearly unanimous in rejecting true religion. And this caused much trouble in the land. When true religion is unpopular, the church, the home, and the government are in big trouble. So Israel was in very serious trouble with God. Judgment was inevitable. The stern, condemnatory ministry of Elijah was the ministry Israel had coming to them for their religious condition. They were a sick people, and their religious preferences and practices invited and predicted great judgment upon the land.

The future well-being of a nation can be easily predicted by viewing the health of true religion in that nation. This means trouble for our nation. Mackintosh, writing back in the late 1800s, said, "We live in a time of more than usual barrenness and spiritual dearth. The state of the Church may well remind us of Ezekiel's valley of dry bones. We have not merely to cope with evils which have characterized by-gone ages, but also with the matured corruption of a time wherein the varied evils of the Gentile worlds have become connected with, and covered by, the cloak of the Christian profession." If Mackintosh thought things were bad then, what would he say today? The churches of our land are filled with sensualism, pagan music, a wholesale lack of moral standards, and a sick emotionalism all of which has more similarity to Baal worship than to Jehovah worship. And many churches who want to be identified as fundamental, Bible-believing churches cannot boast of being radically different, either. The influx of low moral standards (increasing acceptance of divorce, as an example), the popularity of "Christian" sex psychologists and their radio and writing programs, the wild bar room music sounds of "Christian Rock" heard more and more in church services, and the sensual costumes of star Gospel singers reflect more the character of Baal worship than they do Jehovah worship. All of this degradation says one thing—judgment is coming!

## 2. The Character of the Prince

We have already seen in passing that the character of Ahab was very decadent. Here we give some detailed attention to his bad character. We look especially at the extent of his degradation and some examples of his degradation.

## THE WEATHER

*The extent of his degradation.* Ahab was so bad that Scripture said he was worse than all the kings before him, and that included his father who had been worse than any of the previous kings. Twice the Bible records this fact of Ahab being more wicked than any of the kings who went before him: "Ahab the son of Omri did evil in the sight of the LORD above all that were before him" (16:30); and "Ahab did more to provoke the LORD God of Israel to anger than all the kings of Israel that were before him" (16:33). We noted earlier some of the great wickedness of the rulers who preceded Ahab to the throne. For him to be worse than all of them makes Ahab a terribly wicked man indeed. The extent of his wickedness was extremely great.

*The examples of his degradation.* Some of the wicked deeds of Ahab are recorded at length in Scripture. We will look at them in great detail later when we come to those Scriptures in our study of Elijah, for Elijah confronted Ahab about these evil. One great evil of Ahab recorded in Scripture was his continuous effort to hunt down Elijah to kill him (I Kings 18:10). Another evil of Ahab recorded in the Bible was his murder of Naboth who would not sell his vineyard to Ahab (I Kings 21). Scripture also informs us that Ahab was very supportive of the wicked Baal worship (I Kings 16:31,32). And one of the significant happenings recorded in the Scripture which emphasized how degraded Israel had become under Ahab was the rebuilding of Jericho during Ahab's reign. Just before Elijah is brought into the Scripture record, the Bible records that in Ahab's day "did Hiel the Bethelite build Jericho" (16:34). Jericho's walls tumbled down and were destroyed under the leadership of Joshua when Israel first entered Canaan. Joshua announced a Divine curse upon anyone who would rebuild Jericho. He said, "Cursed be the man . . . that riseth up and buildeth this city Jericho [Keil says the Hebrew indicates the walls specifically]; he shall lay the foundation thereof in his firstborn, and in his youngest son [that is, at the price of, at the loss of the life of his sons] shall he set up the gates of it" (Joshua 6:26). But in Ahab's day, the people had become either so ignorant of the Word of God or had developed so much defiance for it, that Jericho was rebuilt in spite of the awful curse pronounced on its rebuilding. Jamieson says, "The unresisted act of Hiel affords a painful evidence how far the people of Israel had lost all knowledge of, or respect for, the word of God." But neither ignorance nor defiance of the Word nullifies its truth and power, for Hiel was unable to escape the Divine curse for building the walls. He "laid the foundation thereof in Abiram his firstborn, and set up the gates thereof in his youngest son Segub, according to the word of the LORD, which he spake by Joshua" (16:34).

**3. The Consort of the Prince**

The cursed consort of Ahab was Jezebel his wife. She is one of the leading characters in the story of Elijah, and so we will note some details about this wicked woman here which will help us understand better the story of Elijah. We will note five significant things about Jezebel: she was the downfall of Ahab, the daughter of Ethbaal, the director of persecution, a danger to Judah, and a defiler in church.

*Downfall of Ahab.* One of the worst things Ahab ever did was marry Jezebel. The Scripture points this out as a most serious evil. "It came to pass, as if it had been a light thing for him to walk in the sins of Jeroboam the son of Nebat, that he took to [as] wife Jezebel the daughter of Ethbaal king of the Zidonians, and went and served Baal, and worshiped him" (I Kings 16:31). Ahab's marriage to wicked Jezebel was his great undoing. "There was none like unto Ahab, which did sell himself to work wickedness in the sight of the LORD, *whom Jezebel his wife stirred up*" (I Kings 21:25). In describing the wretched situation in Ahab's rule, Graham Scroggie said, "The land was ruled by Ahab: Ahab was ruled by Jezebel: Jezebel was under [controlled by] idolatry to Baal and Ashtoreth: and Baal and Ashtoreth were gods of blood [cruelty] and uncleanness." Ahab should never have married Jezebel. Her parentage should have been enough to cause him to stay far, far away from her; and, furthermore, the Scripture forbade Israelites to marry such people (Exodus 34:1–16, Deuteronomy 7:1–3, and Joshua 23:11–13). But Ahab scorned wisdom, as so many do when they get married, and married into great evil which ruined his life.

*Daughter of Ethbaal.* Jezebel's father was Ethbaal which was the big reason why Jezebel was so evil. Ethbaal (the name means "Baal is with him") "was originally the priest of the great temple of Astarte [Ashtoreth, the female counterpart of Baal] in Tyre. At the age of 36 he conspired against the Tyrian king . . . slew him, and seized the throne. His reign lasted 32 years, and he established a dynasty which continued on the throne at least 62 years longer." (F. C. Cook). Ethbaal headed up "the most wicked dynasty then in power" (Edersheim). His reign over the Sidonians (also known as the country of Phoenicia with its key cities of Tyre and Sidon) was a great curse to them. His involvement with Baal worship was the key to the great evil of his rule. And his influence upon Jezebel in the matter of Baal worship was the key to Jezebel's extremely unholy attitudes and conduct which made her the archenemy of all that was good and right.

*Director of persecution.* As we noted earlier, Jezebel was the big leader in the persecution of Jehovah worshipers. Being the daughter of Ethbaal she was well acquainted with Baal religion and its persecution tactics. Her knowledge of these evil tactics, coupled with her personality and corrupt character, made her a vicious, fanatical promoter of Baal worship and of the great persecution of the worshipers of Jehovah. She especially attacked the prophets of Jehovah to kill them (I Kings 18:13). And as we also noted before, she was so successful in slaying the prophets of Jehovah that several times Elijah thought he was the only prophet of Jehovah left (I Kings 18:22, 19:10, 19:14).

*Danger to Judah.* The curse of Jezebel was devastating upon the northern kingdom; but unrealized by most is that she also had a nearly disastrous influence upon the southern kingdom of Judah. Her daughter Athaliah married Jehoram who later became king of Judah. When Jehoram died, Athaliah's son Ahaziah became king. He was an evil king and was a good friend of his brother-in-law, Ahab's son, who was then king over the northern kingdom. This friendship cost him his life; for when Jehu waged war against Ahab's household and slew them, he also killed King Ahaziah, who was visiting Ahab's son (II Kings 8,9). This caused Athaliah, the daughter of Jezebel, to go into a rage. She destroyed all the royal seed of Judah, the southern kingdom, except for Joash, who was hidden from her, so she could reign over Judah (II Kings 11). Thus, she came close to destroying the seed of Christ! How great and guileful was the influence of Jezebel!

*Defiler in church.* We read of Jezebel in Revelation 2:20–23 as a type of those domineering women who often get in and defile the church. Like Jezebel, these women have a treacherous personality. They are immoral, usurp authority, and are self-appointed spiritual leaders ("calleth herself a prophetess" [Revelation 2:20]). They create all sorts of disturbances in the church and, if not stopped, will defile it, divide it, and destroy it. God has no place for these domineering women in the church. They are trouble every time. Oh, they may not appear to the naïve as evil people but rather as sweet Christian ladies. But such is not the real condition of their hearts. They are a defiled lot. Where you find a headstrong woman in a church who wants to run things, you will also find a defiled, evil, and wicked woman. God help our churches to discern these wicked women in their midst and to deal with them firmly and faithfully.

## C. THE PREDICTION OF JUDGMENT

Our one-verse text closes with the short but terse and condemning message which Elijah gave to Ahab which predicted judgment upon Israel in the form of a drought. The message said, "As the Lord God of Israel liveth, before whom I stand, there shall not be dew nor rain these years, but according to my word." Unlike our weather forecasters, Elijah was absolutely certain what the weather would be; and, furthermore, he would determine when the weather would change. No ordinary weatherman was he. But then Elijah was no ordinary man either.

It had to be some sight to behold when Elijah in rough peasant garb walked up uninvited to King Ahab and made his Baal-denouncing weather forecast about a drought of devastating proportions for Israel. It all happened so fast and so suddenly that before Ahab or anyone around him, if he was not alone, was able to react in rebutting or arresting Elijah, the great prophet had finished his stern pronouncement and was gone.

Elijah's short visit to Ahab signaled the beginning of the end for Ahab. Ahab had lived a very wicked life, had ruled Israel according to his evil passions; and seemed to be getting away with it. But no longer. The Divine whistle blower blew the whistle; and from then on Ahab was going to discover that "the way of transgressors is hard" (Proverbs 13:15).

To examine this prediction of judgment given by Elijah to King Ahab, we will note the preface to the prediction, the particulars of the prediction, and the prerequisite of the prediction.

## 1. The Preface to the Prediction

Elijah prefaced his weather forecast with a short, but important, introductory statement. The statement had two parts to it. It spoke of the Sovereign of Israel and the servant of Jehovah.

*The Sovereign of Israel.* "The LORD God of Israel liveth" was the first part of Elijah's message. It would get Ahab's attention at once. And if Jezebel was with Ahab, it would immediately inflame her wrath; for it declared two vital truths about Jehovah both of which were adamantly rejected by Baal worship, and hence by most of Israel and especially Jezebel. It said Jehovah (LORD) was Israel's God and that Jehovah was alive.

First, *Jehovah was Israel's God.* What a challenge this was to the worship of Baal, and what a rebuke and condemnation it was to Ahab and Jezebel. Elijah plainly and powerfully stated the basic and all important truth which Israel needed so desperately to be reminded of; namely, Jehovah, not Baal, was to be Israel's God. Baal worship, with Jezebel its vicious advocate, was endeavoring to eliminate Jehovah from Israel's theology. And it looked like the efforts were succeeding, too; for only 7,000 of all the millions in Israel had not bowed to this false theology. But Jehovah, not Baal, is the God of Israel and also of all the universe. Israel needed to bow down to that truth.

The issue in Israel in Elijah's time is the same issue that every age faces. The issue is who is your God? Who is going to rule your life? Who will be the Sovereign of the land? Will it be Baal or will it be Jehovah? Will it be a pagan idol or will it be the true and living God Who made heaven and earth? Will it be the god of the lust of the flesh, or will it be the God of holiness. Israel, in Elijah's day, had let sinful passions and practices become their god. Through Baal worship, they were really worshipping their own base desires. They had simply deified their wicked ways and made a religion of it.

Three thousand years later multitudes are still letting their evil passions rule their lives. They may not make an organized religion of their evil, but it is still the same thing as Baal being god, for they bow down to their passions and not to God Almighty. So many things are justified today on the basis of our fleshly appetites and desires. Few let the Word of God be the rule in their lives instead. So the issue is the same today; and we need more Elijahs to make clear Who is to be our God, our Ruler, and our Lord.

Second, *Jehovah was alive.* Elijah not only stated that Jehovah was Israel's Sovereign, but he also said that He was alive. Ahab and Israel needed this proclamation. The success and popularity of Baal had seemed to indicate that Jehovah was dead. After all, Jehovah was being openly mocked, despised, defied, and blasphemed; and yet no ill consequences seemed to come. Therefore, He must be dead. But how blinded the sinful heart is. It cannot discern the mercy of God properly. Here it interpreted the actions of His mercy as being a proof of His death or non-existence. At other times men interpret Divine mercy as an approval of evil. They will say, "If what I did was wrong then surely God would have punished me." Any delay in punishment is interpreted perversely as justification and exoneration of evil. Seldom do sinners see the delay in punishment as Divine mercy giving the sinner time to repent of his sin. But Elijah had come to straighten out Israel's thinking, and to correct their misinterpretation of Divine mercy. He announced that Jehovah is not dead, as they had thought and wished; but He is very much alive. That should have caused Ahab to shudder; but, as calloused by sin as he was, the proclamation only made him angry.

The announcement that Jehovah was alive was a direct attack upon Baal. He was nothing but an idol. Absolutely no life there at all. But Jehovah is vastly different. He is a living Person! How wonderfully this truth speaks of the great truth which is the foundation of the Gospel. It is the truth that Christ is alive! The Baals of men, such as Buddha, Mohammed, Confucius, and others are all dead; but Christ is alive. The cross seemed to end it all, but Christ still lives. The tomb overwhelmed the faith of those closest to Christ, but Christ came out of the tomb, and He is alive! Apostate religion scoffs at the literal, bodily resurrection of Christ. But their Baalistic theology is no match for the facts; for the Bible says, "He showed himself *alive* after his passion by *many infallible proofs*" (Acts 1:3). The angels told the defeated souls looking for Christ in the tomb, "Go . . . and tell . . . that he is risen from the dead" (Matthew 28:7). "The LORD God of Israel liveth," not Baal. What a great message; and yet, tragically, a message that is rejected by most people and to their eternal condemnation.

*The servant of Jehovah.* "Before whom I stand" was a phrase that said Elijah was the servant of Jehovah. From it we look at the calling of Elijah and the consecration of Elijah.

First, the *calling of Elijah.* Elijah's Divine calling as a servant of God was that of a prophet. Being a prophet said plenty about the evil condition of the land. Arthur W. Pink said, "God only sent forth . . . His prophets in a time of marked declension and departure of the people from Himself." Mackintosh adds, "The exercise of prophetic ministry in Israel, of old, was always a proof of the nation's decline." As with most prophets, Elijah's ministry was not so much predicting but indicting. His main task was to denounce sin and to point Israel to the right path.

Though greatly needed, Elijah's ministry of denouncing sin is never popular. It is always perilous for God's servant. A denouncer of sin will know much about rejection, about scorn, about mistreatment, and about persecution. He will seldom, if ever, be accredited by any religious group. He will walk alone. He will not be heeded by many but will be mostly ignored. And he will be continually spoken about in a negative way, not only by his foes, but even by his friends. This occurred repeatedly with Elijah, for both foes and friends spoke negatively of him. The widow of Zarephath spoke negatively of Elijah when she said, "Art thou come unto me to call my sin to remembrance, and to slay my son?" (I Kings 17:18). Obadiah spoke negatively of Elijah when he said, "What have I sinned, that thou [Elijah] wouldest deliver thy servant into the hand of Ahab, to slay me?" (I Kings 18:9). Ahab spoke negatively of Elijah when he said, "Thou . . . that troubleth Israel" (18:17) and "Hast thou found me, O mine enemy?" (21:20). Jezebel also spoke negatively of Elijah when she said, "So let the gods do to me, and more also, if I make not thy life as the life of one of them [slain prophets of Baal] by tomorrow about this time" (19:2).

Though the office he held by Divine appointment was a perilous office, Elijah, nevertheless, performed with excellence. He was more than a match for the evil of the day. No evil will ever exist but that God will raise up that which can overcome it. For every Ahab there will be an Elijah.

Second, the *consecration of Elijah*. The phrase "before whom I stand" reveals Elijah's great consecration in service. It tells us Whom he served and where he stood.

*Whom he served.* The phrase "before whom I stand" is a

phrase used in the Bible to refer to service. As an example, Deuteronomy 18:5 says, "The LORD thy God hath chosen him out of all thy tribes, to *stand to minister* in the name of the LORD." In Luke 1:19, the angel Gabriel speaks of himself as a servant of God when he says, "I am Gabriel, that *stands in the presence of God*, and am sent to speak unto thee." A servant stands before his master ready for orders. When Elijah said he stood before Jehovah God, he was informing Ahab that he was a committed servant of Jehovah.

"Before whom I stand" was a most logical statement for Elijah to make. He had just said Jehovah was God, and if He is God then He should rule in our lives. And how do we demonstrate this rule? By doing what He says to do—which is what service is all about. Many want to declare the doctrine that Jesus is Lord, but we notice that few follow up with Elijah's "before whom I stand" in their lives. We are top heavy on doctrinal statements today but very short on commitment-to-service statements. People in church readily sign great creeds; but when they are asked to sign their names on the dotted line for service, most of them get writer's cramp.

W*here he stood.* To stand before God not only speaks of your service, but it also tells us where you are standing, what your loyalties are, and on which side of the issue you stand. Elijah wasted no time in letting Ahab know that he, Elijah, was not on Baal's side. He was standing up for Jehovah. Elijah was about the only one in his day who seemed to be willing to let others know that he stood somewhere else than with Baal. When he walked into the opponent's stadium, where everyone was rooting for the home team, he still wore the colors and carried the pennant of his team. He still stood and cheered for his team no matter if everyone else was sitting down. That is not easy to do; but when it involves God, it is the only right thing to do. How do you stand in the world? Are you like a chameleon who changes color with the scenery? Are you afraid to let people know where you stand in regards to Jesus Christ and to right and wrong? Is the only place you are not afraid to live your conscience the private polling booth where no one sees you; or do you have enough spiritual fortitude to stand for righteousness in public, too? Many in the ministry employ subtle tactics to keep from taking a stand. Some avoid taking a position on issues by quoting this person and that person on both sides of an issue but never telling you where they themselves stand. They forget that God's men are not in the business of conducting a symposium; rather, they are to declare the truth; they are to declare what is right and what is wrong. Others in the ministry declare the truth; but they do it anonymously so they do not have to take a public stand. They will eagerly write the document, but they do not want to sign their name to it to declare their position and their loyalties. They are like a prominent member of a fundamental Baptist denomination who we know who had a sermon of his printed anonymously in the denomination's monthly magazine. He was a trustee of a college and feared some would be offended by his message and stop supporting the college. Hence, he would not be identified with the message. What cowardliness! And what made his cowardliness so bad was that he was not writing in a secular newspaper or magazine, where the enemies of God abound; but he was writing in his own denomination magazine. If you cannot stand up publicly in your church, where the sympathizers are, you certainly will not stand up well in the world where the enemy abounds! "If thou hast run with the footmen, and they have wearied thee, then how canst thou contend with horses?" (Jeremiah 12:5).

## 2. The Particulars of the Prediction

Elijah's weather prediction said, "There shall not be dew nor rain these years, but according to my word." This weather forecast was a message of judgment for the land of Israel. It gave a Divine sentence of judgment upon Israel for their wickedness, for their evil of going after Baal and all the attendant evils of Baal worship. To study this message of judgment, we will note the duration, the devastation, and the design of this judgment of the drought.

## THE WEATHER

*The duration of the judgment.* We must go to the New Testament to learn how long this drought lasted. Both Christ (Luke 4:25) and James (James 5:17) tell us it lasted three and a half years. A drought of that length would make itself felt in a very pronounced way. A shorter drought would be too easy to explain away and forget. But not a drought of three and a half years.

Because both dew and rain would stop, Ahab would know immediately that the drought was in effect no matter what time of the year Elijah came to him. If it was during the rainy season then, of course, it would stop raining. But if Elijah came during the dry season, Ahab would still know his message was true; for the heavy dews, which characterize the dry season, would stop (we will note more about the dews shortly).

An interesting feature of the duration of the drought was that Elijah would determine it. He said it would not dew or rain "but according to my word." Such a statement would make it very easy for Ahab to know if Elijah was a true prophet or a false one. It would be very easy to evaluate the integrity of Elijah's claims. And this is exactly what God wants. It is false religions and false prophets who clothe their predictions and sayings in ambiguity so that no matter what happens, they can claim vindication. Only truth dares to be so detailed and specific as this claim of Elijah was. Ahab and all Israel will know easily if Elijah was a presumptuous fraud or if he was indeed a prophet sent from God Almighty. So it was with Jesus Christ, too. The claims He made were stupendous. Hence, it was not difficult to discern if He was true or bogus. When He came out of the grave, it should have caused every critic to shut their mouth. But, of course, many critics are blind because they do not want to see; and no amount of proof, even the best of proof, will convince them. That does not discredit the proof, however, but will only intensify the judgment of the critics.

*The devastation of the judgment.* Three and a half years of no moisture meant tremendous trouble for the land. Israel experienced a "sore [severe] famine" (18:2) as a result. If Elijah had said that rain alone was going to stop—that is, it would still dew—the land, though hurt, would not have been so devastated. In the course of a year, Israel normally has a wet season of six months and a dry season of six months. The rainy season is October through March, and the dry season is April through September. The dry season is not totally dry, however; for during that time heavy dews come upon the land. Those dews are so heavy they often meant the difference between total barrenness of a land and a vegetation cover. And dew could keep a man alive, for collection of dew for drinking water has sometimes occurred in extreme situations. The importance of dew in Israel can be observed in the fact of it being used as a symbol of blessing. When Isaac gave the patriarchal blessing to Jacob, he said, "Therefore God give thee of the dew of heaven" (Genesis 27:28). Moses also mentions dew in his blessing which he gave to the tribes of Israel at the end of his life. He said of the tribe of Joseph particularly, "Blessed of the LORD be his land, for precious things of heaven, for the dew" (Deuteronomy 33:13). And God emphasized the blessed value of dew when He said of Himself, "I will be as the dew unto Israel" (Hosea 14:5).

So it was not just the lack of rain that would hurt Israel, but the lack of dew would really make the drought devastating. The land would suffer greatly. Elijah would see the brook Cherith dry up (I Kings 17:7), and grass would become so scarce that Ahab and Obadiah "divided the land between them" (I Kings 18:6) to look for grass for Ahab's horses and mules. But even worse would be the starvation and desolation of people. When Elijah went to Zarephath in Phoenicia (the famine was even felt severely in that land northwest of Israel), the condition in which he found the widow gives a picture of much starvation and death during the famine. It was no mild sentence from God, but a very devastating blow.

*The design of the judgment.* At least three important reasons can be cited for why this judgment of a drought was to come upon the land of Israel. It was designed first, to encourage repentance, second, to expose Baal, and third, to exalt Jehovah.

First, the judgment was to *encourage repentance.* When God smites and brings low, it is to lead man to repent of his evil. The pain of chastisement is to show man how wicked his deeds are and to encourage him to turn from his evil ways to paths of righteousness. So it was in the case of the judgment forecasted by Elijah. It was to cause men to see the evil of their ways in such a forceful manner that it would cause them to want to change their ways. This judgment of the drought plainly denounced Israel's idolatry—their worship of Baal. God had told Israel centuries before, "Take heed to yourselves, that your heart be not deceived, and ye turn aside, and serve other gods, and worship them; and then the LORD'S wrath be kindled against you, and he shut up the heaven, that there be no rain" (Deuteronomy 11:16,17). But in spite of God's warning, Israel did not view Baal worship and its associated evils as bad. To them it was very acceptable. They legalized it, propagated it, and approved it. But God did not! The drought said God condemned it severely. The drought made plain that Baal worship and its attendant evils were vile wickedness and worthy of severe judgment. The drought said God has different standards than Israel and the sooner Israel adopted His standards the better.

Some, of course, will complain about the severity of the judgment; but those who complain are always those who fail to see the enormity of the sin and its devastating effect upon people's well-being. Judgment is not cruel. God is not malicious and in unholy anger seeking to get His pound of flesh from those who will not bow down to Him. The Bible tells us judgment is a display of God's loving-kindness. In Psalm 107, the Psalmist speaks about Israel's waywardness and about God's judgment upon them as a result. In this Psalm the Psalmist calls the actions of God's judgment loving-kindness: "He turneth the rivers into a wilderness, and the watersprings into dry ground; A fruitful land into barrenness, for the wickedness of them that dwell therein . . . Whoso is wise, and will observe these things, even they shall understand the *loving-kindness* of the LORD"

(Psalm 107:33,34,43). Yes, God's chastening hand is an expression of His loving-kindness. "For whom the Lord loveth he chasteneth" (Hebrews 12:6). It is indeed an act of love to try to get people back on the right path. And the worse the evil is, the more severe the chastisement will have to be in order to make the proper correction.

God, therefore, is not to be faulted and accused of cruelty in bringing the drought upon the people. Furthermore, neither is Elijah to be criticized for preaching judgment. To preach judgment is not being hateful, hardhearted, uncompassionate, and unloving. Rather, it is the act of a faithful minister who loves his people enough to take the risk of being hated and abused for preaching judgment in order to try to save the people from their evil ways. The preacher who refuses to indict sin and proclaim judgment upon it is the preacher who lacks love for his people!

Second, the judgment was to *expose Baal*. Baal, being the god of fertility, was supposed to be especially strong in the area of rain and good crops. When rain and dew stopped in the land, the people would beseech Baal to bring rain. But Baal would be unable to do that. The longer the drought persisted, the more powerless Baal would be shown to be. It would show he had no influence, no power to do anything at all about the rain. Particularly would Baal's powerlessness be shown in that Elijah, Jehovah's prophet, said that he, Elijah, would decide when the drought would end. Baal's prophets would not be able to end the drought, for Baal could not give them any power. The prophets of Baal would doubtless be under great pressure to do something about the drought, especially as the drought became increasingly severe, but they could not. This exposing of Baal would climax on Mount Carmel when Elijah would challenge the prophets of Baal to show what their god could do, and he in turn would show them what Jehovah could do.

God uses judgment to expose our false creeds if we will not heed more gentle admonition about them. And we have plenty of false creeds and philosophies today which invite Divine judgment. We do not call them by such names as Baal anymore, of course. Hedonism, Atheism, Existentialism, Humanism, or Freudianism are some of the contemporary names for Baal. Carnality, worldliness, greed, homosexuality, or drunkenness are probably more descriptive, howbeit less flattering, names for these false gods and philosophies of ours. But whatever the names, they are all the same. We depart from God's ways; and the arguments we have for so doing become our creeds of life and that which determines our lifestyle. We foolishly think these sinful creeds justify doing things which God Almighty opposes. Like Israel, we forsake God in preference for the gods we have made with our own minds and hearts. But then God pulls out the rug from under us and sends us some much deserved judgment. This quickly exposes the folly of our evil creeds and philosophies and shows them to also be powerless to help us through a crisis. They are powerless to give us hope when all things fail us, powerless to solve our problems, powerless to give us satisfaction, powerless to give us a meaningful life, and powerless to give us comfort and assurance when we face death and eternity. The false prophets (often called professors, psychologists, psychiatrists, scientists, politicians, or celebrities) of these creeds and philosophies have no answers for the most important questions of life. They cannot end the worst drought of all, the drought of man's soul, which can dry up every interest, every hope, every pleasure, and every profit in life.

Third, the judgment was to *exalt Jehovah.* Baal was being honored in the land, not Jehovah. The judgment of the drought was designed to reverse that practice. It would honor Jehovah's ways, and it would honor Jehovah's word. It would show His holy way as the only acceptable way, and it would show His Word as true. Let us look at these two things in more detail.

The *honor of Jehovah's ways.* Jehovah's ways were being despised, forsaken, and mocked as a result of Baal worship in the land. Baal worship promoted the vilest of morals. It honored gross unholiness. But Divine judgment would emphasize that the holy ways of God were the best ways, the only acceptable ways. And it would show that Baal's ways were destructive ways. If mankind does not honor God's holy ways by obedience to them, he will one day honor them as a result of judgment. And from the looks of things, the only way our land will honor the holy ways of God is through judgment; for our land is certainly not honoring God's holy ways through obedience.

The *honor of Jehovah's Word.* God had said that if Israel departed from His ways, He would bring drought to the land (Deuteronomy 11:16,17). Israel had for many years departed from Jehovah, but so far no drought. The forecasted drought, however, would show that Jehovah's Word was not null and void. It would validate the Word and thus give great honor to Jehovah; for when a person's word is proven true, it greatly honors that person.

People will always complain about God's judgment, but the noble designs of Divine judgment invalidates any criticism of judgment. We've examined three designs of this judgment of the drought, and all three more than justify the infliction of the land.

## 3. The Prerequisite of the Prediction

Why was Elijah sent to Ahab? Why was he chosen for the task of declaring God's anathema upon Israel's sin? Was it because he had some impressive degrees earned at some famous seminary? Was it because he was a star athlete (which, unfortunately, gets many in our pulpits today)? Was it because he had a large church? Was it because he was the head of some important ministerial council in the land? No, it was none of these reasons, though these reasons seem very important to mankind. Rather, God sent Elijah to Ahab because Elijah was studied up, prayed up, cleaned up, and stirred up. There may have and doubtless were also some other reasons, but these four reasons especially stand out in importance. Elijah had the important qualifications for service for God.

We worry too much about opportunities. We need instead to concern ourselves about qualifications. You get studied up, prayed up, cleaned up, and stirred up; and you will have a job in God's vineyard—you can count on that! Christ complained that

## THE WEATHER

the "laborers are few" (Luke 10:2). The reason for that problem is that few are studied up, prayed up, cleaned up, and stirred up.

*Elijah was studied up.* Elijah knew the Word of God well. He had obviously studied it much. The message Elijah gave Ahab—"there shall not be dew nor rain these years"—was rooted and grounded in the Scriptures. Elijah's message said what God's Word said. It said that if Israel was going to "serve other gods and worship them [as they were doing then] . . . then the LORD'S wrath [will] be kindled against you, and he [will] shut up the heaven, that there be no rain" (Deuteronomy 11:16,17) and that "It shall come to pass, if thou wilt not hearken unto the voice of the LORD thy God, to observe to do all his commandments . . . The LORD shall make the rain of thy land powder and dust: from heaven shall it come down upon thee, until thou be destroyed" (Deuteronomy 28:15,24).

The Word of God was a great motivator and mover of Elijah. As an example, when Elijah was praying on Mount Carmel for fire to fall on the altar, he said, "Let it be known . . . that I have done all these things at thy word" (I Kings 18:36). A true prophet of God spoke and acted as the Word of God decreed, not as the world dictated. Therefore, he must know the Word of God well. He must be a man of the Word. You cannot be a man of God if you are not a man of God's Word. And you most certainly cannot be God's spokesman to declare His message if you do not know His Word. Yet, we have a good number of men who claim to be preachers but who know little of the Word of God, spend little time in study of it, and whose sermons (not surprisingly) are nothing but chaff though they may be very entertaining to the audience.

Being a man of the Word of God meant Elijah spoke a message of authority. Any message that is based on the Word of God will be authoritative. It will not be a message of uncertainties, but of finalities. It will be a message filled with strong conviction. Elijah was not guessing about the drought he forecasted. He was informing Ahab that it was coming—no ifs, ands, or buts about it. His message was based on what God said, and there is no higher authority. We need messages of this authority today. Messages without this authority will do us no good at all. They will not solve problems, give good direction, or deliver souls. Our messages must be from the Word of God if they are to be valid and worthy of declaring.

I was warned as a young man not to take "too much Bible" in college if I was going on to seminary because I would get enough Bible in seminary. My response to that warning is that I am not aware that one can get "too much Bible." The idea that one can get "too much Bible" is ludicrous and originated in hell with Satan. It is the same wicked thinking that fears getting "too holy." Any person who is afraid of getting "too much Bible" will be of little use for God.

*Elijah was prayed up.* We learn in the New Testament that Elijah was prayed up. Elijah "prayed earnestly that it might not rain, and it rained not on the earth by the space of three years and six months. And he prayed again, and the heaven gave rain" (James 5:17,18). Elijah prayed fervently ("earnestly") and frequently ("prayed again"). This praying was done in private. It was not ostentatious public praying done to impress people with his pious language and form. There are times when one must pray in public (Elijah did so at Mount Carmel), but where we examine a man's prayer life is in his private praying. There Elijah truly excelled. He was prayed up. And God uses much those saints who are prayed up.

Some have criticized Elijah for praying for the rain to stop and thus bringing upon the land and people much hardship and suffering. On the surface it does sound like cruel praying. But it was not cruel praying. Matthew Poole said, "This prayer of his was not . . . malicious, but necessary, and (all things considered) truly charitable; that by this sharp and long affliction, God's honor . . . might be vindicated, and the Israelites . . . might hereby be awakened to see their own wickedness . . . and the necessity of returning to the true religion." F. B. Meyer said, regarding the charge of the prayer being terrible, "Was it not more terrible for the people to forget and ignore the God of their fathers and to give themselves up to the licentious orgies of Baal and Astarte?" Elijah prayed according to the Word of God. So it was a good prayer regardless of what critics may say. He was only asking God to do what God had promised to do if His people went after idolatry. He was praying for the rod of God's chastisement to do its work. His prayer was to have the knife of the surgeon cut into the body of the sick nation and cut out the evil to spare the life of the nation. Yes, the nation will suffer, but it is for their own good. And you will note that God answered the prayer, and that says something about the excellent character of the prayer which Elijah prayed.

*Elijah was cleaned up.* In the New Testament James confirms that Elijah was indeed cleaned up. He was indeed a "righteous man" (James 5:16), for James said, "The effectual fervent prayer of a righteous man availeth much" (Ibid.) which Elijah's prayer did which says much about Elijah's righteous living. As one reads the Old Testament narrative about Elijah, one will have no difficulty seeing that Elijah was an outstanding righteous man. Elijah did not have even a smudge of Baal on him. He had not bowed his knee to Baal. He would not compromise one iota with Ahab. He did not go to ministerial meetings with the prophets of Baal. He was like Elisha his successor who was described as a "holy man of God" (II Kings 4:9).

God has instructed His servants to "be ye clean, that bear the vessels of the LORD" (Isaiah 52:11). As a young boy I would sometimes get to help mother set the table for a meal. But before I started setting the table, Mother would inevitably ask, "Are you hands clean?" That was the qualification that had to be met to help set the table. It is the same with God. If you want God to use you, get cleaned up. Today the ministry is plagued by a shocking number of men who are defiled through and through. Divorce is not uncommon among ministers. Immoral escapades are becoming more frequent with preachers.

Lying, stealing, and cheating are found as often in ministers as they are found in the congregation. However, you cannot clean up others if you are dirty yourself. The foul lives of ministers have made a mockery of their preaching and the testimony of their churches. Integrity has been replaced by infidelity and the devil rejoices at all this foulness. Oh, let God's men be clean men. They may be despised, ridiculed, unpopular, and rejected by people—that will not hurt their ministry. But if they are defiled—that will ruin their ministry for God and bring great dishonor to God.

*Elijah was stirred up.* If you are studied up, prayed up, and cleaned up—you will be stirred up! You will be stirred up against sin. The reason many folk are so apathetic regarding sin is because they do not get into the Word much, do little praying, and live defiled lives. Nothing kills zeal against sin as fast as failure in these three areas does. And failure in these areas abounds today which is why few are stirred up about the evil.

From Elijah's life, we learn that being stirred up against sin means you will be fervent, bold, and unpopular.

*Fervent.* When one is stirred up against sin, he will speak out with much passion and earnestness against it. Elijah certainly did just that when he gave Ahab the weather forecast. His message to Ahab was no casual speech and should not have been. Sin flooded the land and needed an earnest, fervent denunciation. It was not time for mild messages on mischief but stirring sermons on sin. So Elijah gave Ahab a fervent, dynamic declaration that shook the palace and the empire.

The Apostle Paul was another man who was stirred up about sin and as a result spoke out fervently against it. This is seen, as an example, in his reaction to the idolatry in Athens. "Now while Paul waited for them at Athens, his spirit was stirred in him, when he saw the city wholly given to idolatry. Therefore disputed he in the synagogue with the Jews, and with the devout persons, and in the market daily with them that met with him" (Acts 17:16,17). Then later Paul made an earnest speech to the

Athenians in the Areopagus (Acts 17:19) exposing the folly of idolatry and exalting the true God. Unlike Paul or Elijah, many professing Christians could walk down the streets of Athens or across the land of Israel without being stirred up in the slightest against the evil of the idolatry. They are so apathetic about sin that instead of being stirred up by all the evil before their eyes, they would admire the art work of the idols and grandeur of the temples of idolatry. Today so much apathy exists in the church that folk cannot get stirred up much about any sin either in their lives or in the lives of others. They can watch sin on TV by the hour and never be stirred in the slightest. No wonder the church has so little effect on society in our time.

We could use a lot more fervent preaching against sin like Elijah's preaching to Ahab in our pulpits today instead of the weak, soft, and compromising messages we get on sin. There is not much fervency in word or deed from most preachers regarding sin. Few seem to be stirred up about sin. If a preacher does get fervent in denouncing sin, some church member is sure to admonish him to be more temperate and loving. But God does not use folk for His work who are not stirred up. He sends an Elijah who is really stirred up about evil.

*Bold.* It took much courage for Elijah to come out of the backwoods into the presence of a godless king and declare to his face the message that he did. It took much courage to declare that Jehovah, not Baal, was God; that he, Elijah, was Jehovah's servant; and that the weather was going to turn sour and remain that way until he, Elijah, decided to change it. Elijah took his life in his hands that day, for he walked into the lion's den and bearded the lion. What boldness! What courage! But you can expect that from one who is stirred up against sin because he is studied up, prayed up, and cleaned up.

If you would declare God's message in a wicked generation, you will have to have great courage. If you lack that courage, you will quickly capitulate to evil, water down your message, be selective in the sins you denounce (you will denounce only those sins which do not affect your congregation), and adjust your ways to please the crowd instead of Christ. But courage will be your portion when you get stirred up for God against evil in the way you ought. So many people can get stirred up about a host of matters in the world—most of which do not matter and have nothing to do with eternity—but few get stirred up enough about evil that they gain a holy boldness to confront it and fight it.

*Unpopular.* Being stirred up about sin will not endear one to mankind, but it can make one very unpopular in fact. Elijah became a hunted man because he was stirred up against sin. The prophets of old were despised and persecuted and some were slain because they were stirred up about sin in Israel. And some pastors have been run out of their churches by the congregation because they were stirred up about sin in their church. But popular or not, if you want to be God's servant, you better get stirred up against sin.

The gauntlet has now been thrown down by Elijah. Baal worship is being challenged as it has not been challenged before in Israel. And Ahab and Jezebel will watch helplessly as an opponent of Baal worship controls the weather and makes a mockery of all that pertains to Baal.

# II.

# THE WADI

### I KINGS 17:2–7

AFTER ELIJAH COMPLETED his assignment of going to King Ahab and declaring to him the judgment of the drought, God gave Elijah another assignment. This next assignment ordered Elijah to "Get thee hence, and turn thee eastward, and hide thyself by the brook Cherith [the Hebrew word translated 'brook' means wadi, which is a watercourse located in a valley or ravine that is often dry except during the rainy season], that is before Jordan" (v. 3).

There is plenty to do in God's service, and God will always have an assignment for you. He will reveal it plainly, too. Of course, you must fulfill previous assignments before you will be granted new assignments. "God does not grant fresh revelations until there has been a compliance with those already received" (A. W. Pink). If you are confused about the will of God for today, it may be a result of your having not obeyed the will of God yesterday.

This new assignment for Elijah did not have the excitement of the previous one, but it was just as obligatory. Being sent to the palace to see the king was something special. There was prestige, position, and publicity in going to the king. Going to Cherith was just the opposite. But obligation in service is not determined by the excitement, status, popularity, or convenience of a task but by the Word of God. Too many, however, are more obligated to sentiment, glory seeking, personal ease, and fleshly excitement than they are to the Word of God. They are not interested in the "Cherith" assignments of God's Word which have to do with their daily lifestyle and governs what they eat and drink and where they live. Therefore, such folk seldom, if ever, know what it is to be in the will of God and to possess the choice blessings of doing His will.

Doing this assignment was very essential to Elijah's own personal well-being. Doing any assignment can be said to be essential to one's well-being, but this assignment was especially so with Elijah. God would provide for some very important needs for Elijah in this assignment. How important then it is for him to obey. And obey he did! "He went and did according unto the word of the LORD" (v. 5). He went to Cherith as directed and thus obtained the blessings God intended for him. And his obedience was prompt. He did not wander around enjoying the sights of Samaria before heading for Cherith; but when God commanded, Elijah promptly obeyed. And it was a good thing he promptly obeyed; for his needs were urgent, very urgent. And what were those essential needs Elijah had which would be met by going to Cherith? They were the protection of his life, the provision of his meals, and the preparation of his heart. His life was in jeopardy, he needed the sustenance of daily bread, and he needed spiritual instruction and nourishment to refresh him from past service and to prepare him for future service. We, too, may have very urgent needs, needs which we may not even be aware of, but needs which can and will be met only by prompt and complete obedience. How important it is then that we respond to God's commands with dedication and dispatch.

## A. THE PROTECTION OF HIS LIFE

God ordered Elijah to "hide" by the brook Cherith. The word "hide" means "to lie hid, to hide oneself . . . to conceal something from anyone; to guard" (Wilson). In order to protect his life, Elijah was to conceal himself from the public eye. He was to lie low and keep out of sight.

There are two things we want to note about this protection. First, we will note the necessity of this protection. Second, we will note the judgment in this protection.

## The Wadi

**1. The Necessity of This Protection**

Elijah's message to King Ahab, which greatly honored Jehovah and greatly dishonored Baal, did not inspire honors from the king or from most of Israel. To use present day terminology, the king did not make Elijah chaplain of the palace; nor did the Rotary Club give him the "man-of-the-year" award; nor did the ministerial association of Samaria invite him to speak at their monthly luncheon. No, his message provoked great anger, as messages against sin usually do. And in Elijah's day this anger could turn violent very quickly. "Because of the temper of the time, any man who took such a daring stand of faith in God was marked for liquidation" (W. Phillip Keller). King Ahab was so upset with Elijah that when the predicted drought came, he went to great lengths to find him. Obadiah, one of Ahab's servants, related this fact to Elijah when he said, "There is no nation or kingdom [around Israel], whither my lord hath not sent to seek thee" (I Kings 18:10). And Obadiah gave further evidence of Ahab's great venomous zeal to find Elijah by disclosing that when a nation or kingdom said Elijah was not in their land, Ahab "took an oath of the kingdom and nation, that they found thee not" (Ibid.). Elijah was at the top of the "most wanted list." He was considered by Ahab to be the one who "troubleth Israel" (I Kings 18:17). Therefore, Elijah needed special protection for his life. He needed to be concealed from evil men. Had Elijah remained in public, he would have been apprehended and either had his life threatened to make it rain again or else killed outright for being the blame for the drought.

Obedience to God often provokes more hatred than honor from men. The soul that dares to follow the Lord faithfully will be exposed to hatred, scorn, ridicule, oppression, and criminal meanness. Try being an Elijah in character and in loyalty to God; and you, too, will be hunted and sought out for mistreatment. And you, too, may suffer privation and tough times sequestered in a lowly, obscure "Cherith" while your enemies enjoy acceptance with the people and more affluent surroundings and circumstances. But only a fool would argue that it is better to be accepted and honored by a godless populace than to be lying low in some wilderness haunt like Cherith.

Protecting Elijah's life was necessary if Elijah was going to keep serving the Lord as God desired. In this there is an important lesson. God is ever trying to protect His own from death dealing blows to their service. We are not to give Satan undue advantage in opposing our service. Our declaration of commitment to God riles Satan greatly. He will do all he can to stop our service, cancel our commitment, and destroy our dedication. Therefore, how important to listen to God regarding such things as where to live, what to eat, and whom to be with. Failure to obey God's orders can end our abilities and opportunities to serve. We may have to miss out on the "goings on" at times in order to stay fit and able for His service. But unless we go to Cherith where protection is provided for future service, we will never make it to Mount Carmel or any other place where we can, by our service, bring great honor to God.

## 2. The Judgment in This Protection

The method used to protect Elijah's life—concealing him from the public eye—was a form of judgment for Israel. God could have protected Elijah by other means and still have left him in public so people could hear his messages. But God did not do that. Protection came by concealment. This means the people could no longer hear his important messages, his warnings, and instructions. Taking this away from the people would really hurt the people, for they desperately needed the ministry of Elijah. But they were not going to get it for some time. They had despised their spiritual opportunities—such as having a prophet of God in their midst—and now in judgment God will take away their spiritual privileges.

It is a great curse upon any nation when God hides His preachers from them. The presence of a man of God in society is an extremely vital need of society. Therefore, when God takes His ministers away, it is a terrible judgment. We think it is very important to the welfare of a community to have a physician in the community, and indeed it is. But how much more important is it to have a true man of God in the community. The physician gives help for the physical needs, but the preacher gives help for one's spiritual needs. And the spiritual needs of man are his greatest, most important needs of all. But if we despise our spiritual blessings and opportunities—such as having a man of God in our midst—God will take them away from us. The Psalmist speaks of this in Psalm 74. In verses 7 and 8, he first tells of the people forsaking God when he says, "They have cast fire into thy sanctuary; they have defiled by casting down the dwelling place of thy name to the ground. They said in their hearts, Let us destroy them together; they have burned up all the synagogues of God in the land." Then, in verse 9, he records the results of forsaking God, "We see not our signs; there is no more any prophet, neither is there among us any that knoweth how long." Another Psalm speaks the same truth when it says, "As he delighted not in blessing, so let it be far from him" (Psalm 109:17). God, speaking through Moses, warned the Israelites of this peril of forsaking Him. He said if Israel forsook Him, "I will hide my face from them" (Deuteronomy 32:20). The same message is repeated in the Gospels, "They took counsel together for to put him [Jesus] to death" and so the consequences were, "Jesus therefore walked no more openly among the Jews" (John 11:53,54). If you do not want the blessing, God will oblige you and take it away.

Does not this truth explain why so many pulpits in our land are so barren of good spiritual food? Of course it does. People have for too long shown little interest in spiritual blessing. If the preacher's sermon goes a bit long, they fume and fuss as they prefer their all-Sunday-afternoon sports' shows and beer commercials on TV to a few extra minutes of spiritual instruction from God's Book. So God, in His justified wrath, has emptied pulpit after pulpit of men who could preach with excellence; and now about all you get from the Sunday sermons are husks.

During World War II, a British newspaper editorial sounded forth the same message of the loss of spiritual blessings and opportunities through disrespect of them. It said, "We have been a pleasure-loving people, dishonoring God's day . . . We have preferred motor travel to church going—now there is a shortage of motor fuel. We have ignored the ringing of church bells calling us to worship—now the bells cannot ring except to warn us of invasion. We have left our churches half-empty when they should have been well filled with worshippers—now they are in ruins . . . The money we would not give to the Lord's work—now is taken from us in higher taxes and the high cost of living. The food for which we refused to give God thanks—now is unobtainable. The service we refused to give God—now is conscripted to our country. Lives we refused to live under God's control—now are under the nation's control."

Treat Elijah right or Elijah will be hidden; and his ministry, which could be such a tremendous blessing to the land (it could bring the much needed rain in Israel's case and prevent the terrible drought), will be unavailable. It was a costly time for Israel when Elijah was hidden away by a secluded wadi lest the people slay him. And it is costly for any people when they do not honor their spiritual blessings whatever these blessings may be.

## B. THE PROVISION OF HIS MEALS

The second thing God provided for Elijah at Cherith was his meals—his food and water. God promised that the ravens would feed him there, and God told Elijah to drink of the brook there. God is not unmindful of our daily needs; and He provides for them, too. "Behold the fowls of the air . . . your heavenly Father feedeth them. Are ye not much better [more valuable, more important to God] than they?" (Matthew 6:26).

### 1. The Food

"I have commanded the ravens to feed thee there . . . the ravens brought him bread and flesh in the morning, and bread and flesh in the evening" (vv. 4,6). The source, stipulation, and schedule of the supply of food is stated in these verses; and they are most instructive.

## The Wadi

*The source of the supply.* God would work a miracle in supplying the food. He would command ravens to be the caterers for Elijah. From a human standpoint, ravens would certainly not be the most likely or appealing creatures to bring one his food. They were scavengers, considered an unclean animal in the law of Moses (which meant you could not eat them), and were thought to be an omen of misfortune, tragedy, and death. T. DeWitt Talmage, describing the unlikeliness of the raven to provide men with good food, says of the raven, "It was a bird so fierce . . . that we have fashioned one of our most forceful and repulsive words out of it—ravenous. That bird has a passion for picking out the eyes of men and animals. It loves to maul the sick and the dying, It swallows, with vulturous gurgle, everything it can put its beak on; and yet all the food Elijah gets for six months or a year, is from the ravens."

God still uses ravens at times to supply the needs of His own. The ravens may not be literal birds; but they are sources, which in human thinking, are very unlikely to be of any help in meeting the needs of the saints. God is not limited in sources from which He can meet our needs. If we do not receive from some expected source, God will provide from the unexpected. Sometimes God's cupboards are in strange places. But all of this keeps our eyes on God as the primary source of our supplies rather than on the means which God uses. And keeping our eyes on God greatly encourages our faith, especially in times when circumstances seem so negative and our needs are so great. Too often, if our circumstances are unfavorable and we see no human help nearby, we despair and conclude God is handcuffed and cannot help us. But not so! He can command the unlikely, even the ravens, to feed us if He so desires. Our sources of help are as unlimited as God's power. Banks, credit unions, and savings and loan institutions may fail; but God never fails. People whom we counted on to help us may betray us, but God never betrays us. When those whom we believed generous unexpectedly become miserly in their performance, then count on God to make those whom we know to be selfish and miserly to suddenly become unusually generous. God can make men, as well as animals, to act contrary to their natural dispositions and supply the needs of His own. The ravens will feed us if necessary.

The fact that ravens fed Elijah was a great indictment upon Israel. It was a shocking testimony to the sad state of affairs in their land. Here a great man of God, one of their greatest prophets, is so unwanted and unprovided for that God must use birds to feed him. How one treats God's servants is a most revealing reflection of one's relationship with God. And how you treat God's servants will dictate how God treats you. Israel, or any people, will pay for their delinquency in failing to take care of God's man. So no wonder the blessings of God are so few and meagerly in many churches. These churches half starve their pastor and treat him like a tramp. Then they have the audacity to think God will bless the church. We have yet to see any healthy, thriving church that is miserly in regards to their pastor!

*The stipulation of the supply.* "I have commanded the ravens to feed thee *there*" (v. 4). God will supply our needs but not without some responsibility upon our part. To experience the fulfillment of God's promises requires a faith which leads to obedience. "Elijah must comply with the Divine behest if he was to be supernaturally fed . . . God will not put a premium on either unbelief or disobedience" (A. W. Pink). Elijah's responsibility is found in the word "there" in our text. If Elijah wants to experience the miracle and have his meals provided, he must go to God's "there"; or he will starve to death. "There" is where God's will is, and it is in God's will where the promise will be realized. "There" is the stipulation of the supply.

When we are where God wants us to be, we will see God working for us in wonderful ways The complaint of many saints regarding their spiritual lack and disappointments is only a confession of their disobedience. They would not go "there" in obedience to the will of God. Their marriage, their job, their church situation, and other circumstances are all so unsatisfying to

## The Wadi

them. But they should not be surprised or complain. God promised Elijah that the ravens would feed him at Cherith, not in Samaria or Jerusalem or Bethlehem or Tishbe.

*The schedule of the supply.* Twice daily the food was delivered to Elijah. "The ravens brought him bread and flesh in the morning, and . . . in the evening" (v. 6). The schedule of supply promoted Elijah's character and faith.

First, *character*. Elijah was not furnished with luxuries but with what he needed and no more. He was not even given three meals a day but just two. No coffee breaks, either. Such a schedule demanded and encouraged character. But many in our land would think it impossible to live such a Spartan lifestyle in regards to food. And it is only a disgrace when we see professing Christians waddling into church, grossly overweight, couch potatoes who seldom, if ever, practice any discipline in terms of physical appetite. Such folk do not make good soldiers of Jesus Christ. They have not learned the first thing about denying self (Matthew 16:24). It would be interesting to see how large an increase would occur in a church's weekly offering intake if the membership began to exercise some character and godly discipline about fleshly appetites and passed along to the Lord's work the savings in grocery expense.

Second, *faith*. The schedule of supply indicates the ravens never brought Elijah more than enough for one meal. He was not able to store up food for the future. While that is not necessarily evil (we wisely store up a summer's harvest for the winter months), there is a lesson here on trusting God from day to day. Too often when we get a surplus, we trust it rather than God. The desire for surplus often leads to hoarding, too. Man prefers to trust in a full cupboard rather than in a faithful God. Talmage said, "You know as well as I that the great fret of the world is that we want a surplus—we want the ravens to bring enough for fifty years . . .[but] We had better be content with just enough." We like surplus, but God likes faith and often arranges our circumstances and supplies so it requires daily faith.

## 2. The Water

"Thou shalt drink of the brook . . . and he drank of the brook" (vv. 4,6). Elijah's water supply was the wadi. We note two things about this water supply. It was not miraculous, and it was not forever.

*It was not miraculous.* God did not work a miracle to supply water for Elijah. He worked a miracle to provide the food but not the water. God does not work miracles unless they are necessary. God does not work miracles which would tend to make people lethargic, lazy, and irresponsible. God is not running a welfare program like our government which subsidizes sloth and promotes disinterest in energetic effort. Neither is God in the entertainment business performing miracles as a sideshow for the church. It is the flesh that prays for miracles when miracles are not necessary. Therefore, if your car is in need of gas and you can easily drive to a gas station and "fill'er up," then you had better drive to the gas station and get your gas. To pray for a miracle to fill the gas tank is absurd and a mark of laziness and folly. The same holds true regarding physical needs, too, although this is not nearly as discernible to some as the gas and car illustration. If you are sick and can get to a doctor for help and medicine which will promote your health, you have no business praying for a miracle. Many healing campaigns are nothing but the flesh wanting some excitement.

God may work a miracle and send ravens, but do not let that blind you to the command to drink from the brook. It was necessary to work a miracle regarding Elijah's food in order to keep Elijah's hideout unknown to his enemies. But water flowed right by him at Cherith; and if he wants water, he will get it without a miracle; or he will be disobedient to God and die of thirst.

*It was not forever.* Again the lack of the miracle with the water is seen in that the "brook dried up, because there had been no rain in the land" (v. 7). God did not work a miracle to keep the brook flowing. Streams do dry up. Christians must be prepared for sources to dry up. But we must not confuse the drying up of a source with the drying up of God's help or power. All that the drying up of the wadi signified, as far as God's help was concerned, was that God will now use a different source to supply Elijah with his need. "Why does God let them dry up?" asks F. B. Meyer; and then he answers, "He wants to teach us not to trust in His gifts but in Himself."

This is the same lesson we learned about the source of Elijah's food. Sources vary so that we will keep our eyes on God, not the earthly source. So jobs are not forever, sources of income may end, friendships may wither away, popularity may dry up quickly (as John the Baptist discovered), and health may evaporate because of the heat of some illness. But drying brooks are not an indication of God forsaking us. They only indicate that God is changing the source of His help. It is a hard lesson to learn and a difficult situation to experience. But God takes most of His own through a brook-drying experience sometime in life, if not many times; for it provides a great opportunity to grow in faith, to keep our eyes focused better on God Who is the primary source of our supplies.

## C. THE PREPARATION OF HIS HEART

God not only supplied Elijah's physical and material needs at Cherith; but He also supplied his spiritual needs there, too. Elijah had spiritual needs, as well as physical and material needs, which must be supplied if he was going to continue his service for the Lord. God not only takes care of our body, but He also takes care of our soul. Both need care. But we get so concerned about physical and material needs that we often forget our greatest needs are spiritual. Furthermore, we do not seem to discern the needs of the soul nearly as well as we discern the needs of the body. Few would miss perceiving Elijah's need of physical protection and of such things as food and water. But not many recognize that Elijah also had great spiritual needs. His spiritual heart needed considerable preparation for the future if he was to continue his fight against the evils in the land. Cherith was not just a hideout for Elijah. It was also a place of preparation for his heart.

We will consider three important spiritual needs of Elijah which were met at Cherith. They were the need of solitude, humility, and patience.

## 1. The Need of Solitude

Scripture exhorts us to "Be still, and know that I am God" (Psalm 46:10). In order to do that, we will have to get alone, apart from the noise and clamor of the crowd; so we can listen to God speak. F. B. Meyer said, "We cannot exorcise the devils which possess men, unless we have first entered into our closets and shut our doors, and spent hours of rapt communication with God. The acquisition of spiritual power is impossible, unless we can hide ourselves from men . . . in some deep gorge, where we may absorb the power of the eternal God." C. H. Mackintosh said, "Our time of training in secret must far exceed our time of acting in public."

Cherith provided Elijah with an excellent situation for solitude, for there he would be alone and also away from the noise of public life. His days would not be marked by countless duties and interruptions which would hinder meditation and contemplation. He had time to think, to pray, and to meditate on the Word of God. How valuable, then, was this solitude. Thankfully, he did not spend all this solitude at Cherith watching TV. Too many saints would have done just that—or, since there was no TV there, they would have (because they are so sick spiritually) complained about nothing to do.

All men need a time alone with God. No, this does not sanction the extremes of hermit lifestyles; nor does it approve of the monkey business of monks and their monasteries. Solitude is not forever. It is not the end, but it is a means to the end. It is a refueling station, a time to prepare the heart for the future when one deals with the public.

Great men of God in the Scripture had notable times of solitude. Moses spent forty years on the backside of the desert to

## The Wadi

become equipped to lead Israel out of Egypt. David spent much time alone in the wilderness with his sheep, but it was a profitable time for he learned lessons in his solitude which made him the great man he was. John the Baptist spent much of his life alone in the wilderness before he became the herald of Christ. Paul spent some time alone in Arabia before getting started on his missionary work. And John the apostle was for a time secluded on the Isle of Patmos, but out of that seclusion came the great book of Revelation.

Let us learn from this need of solitude and practice it in our own lives. Find a place where you can get alone daily with God. You may have to look hard to discover the place, but it is worth the search. A farmer may have to find it in his barn; some may have to park their car along the side of the road in order to get alone. But you need that time alone to spend with God in His Word and in prayer. It gives strength, perspective, guidance and help as few things do.

**2. The Need of Humility**

Serving in high places is perilous business. It can quickly foster pride in the best of souls. Heights can bring on dizziness which bring serious falls. When God puts one in a high place, He will often send some humility in order to promote the spiritual equilibrium of those serving there. Cherith was a humble place. It was a brook, not a big river. It was a crude wilderness haunt, not a castle. It was secluded from the fawning attention of men. No one could live at Cherith, as Elijah did, and get puffed up for long. Even the food and water arrangements would be humbling.

But how important for Elijah to experience this humble circumstance. He needed it. He had just come from a sterling performance before the king. He had done something no one else had dared to do. What courage, what fidelity, what dogmatism, what a message, what a performance! Even his worst enemies would have to admire the performance though they hated the message. So pride could easily come to Elijah from that occasion. But God quickly stopped any attack of pride Elijah might have experienced by sending him to Cherith.

Pride was a far worse enemy than any that could slay him physically. Cherith would protect him from that as well as from those who would murder him. Elijah needed the humbling of Cherith or he would be rendered useless for future service. His grand performance before the throngs on Mount Carmel could not have occurred if he had been filled with pride. Before God exalts, He first humbles; and Elijah was going to be very exalted at Mount Carmel. Therefore, he needed this prior humbling to make him fit for Carmel.

Are you chaffing at some humbling situation in your life? Has God kept you from the high honors of men and allowed you to receive their scorn instead? Are you stuck in some secluded, obscure Cherith where few, if any, are able to see your talents and applaud and praise you? Do not despair, but rather thank God that He has spared you from the pit of pride. Your usefulness to God is not dependent on your station in life or on the honors of man, but it is very dependent on your willingness to walk humbly before God at all times. If God has kept you in the lowly, it may have spared you far more spiritual disaster than you could ever realize. Enjoy the quietness and the scenery at Cherith. Delight in God's care for you and do not envy those who are basking in the sunlight of the accolades and honors of men. Your day is coming; and when it does you will have the character to survive, something few people do.

## 3. The Need of Patience

Evil does not promote patience. If one lives in an extremely evil day, as did Elijah, he will need to give extra attention to the matter of cultivating patience. The Psalmist addresses this problem when he says, "Rest in the LORD, and wait patiently for him; fret not thyself . . . because of the man who bringeth wicked devices to pass . . . For evildoers shall be cut off, but those who wait [who have patience] upon the LORD, they shall inherit the earth" (Psalm 37:7,9).

## THE WADI

It is not easy to be patient when one sees evil succeed. And it was succeeding extremely well in Elijah's day. But patience is a must if evil is to be opposed successfully. So God provides in Cherith a place where Elijah could grow in patience so that Elijah would be better equipped to oppose the evil of his day—especially on that great day on Mount Carmel. He really needed patience there; and he really evidenced it there, too, thanks, in part, to his Cherith experience.

Elijah learned patience in several situations at Cherith. He learned it in forced inactivity, and he learned it in the drying up of the wadi.

First, he learned patience in inactivity. At Cherith he was forced into a period of inactivity. This would be very hard to endure for a man of Elijah's nature. He was a man of action. Inactivity would tax his patience to the extreme. But such an exercise on his patience would help it to grow stronger. There was going to be much waiting ahead for Elijah before his great encounter at Carmel. So he needed much patience to wait God's time. Failure to wait God's time would have been disastrous to his work.

Second, he learned patience in the drying up of the wadi. If Elijah was going to survive, he needed a new source of water. When should he start looking for one? When should he leave Cherith and go where water was available? The right thing to do, which he did, was to wait on God for further instructions. But you will note that God did not instruct him to move until the wadi was completely dried up. What patience it took for Elijah to stay put and not move when he saw that stream of water get smaller and smaller each day. Many would have taken things into their own hands and moved long before Cherith dried up completely. But such impatience would have produced a parched corpse on some desert of self-will. Elijah had been sent to Cherith by God's orders, and so he was duty bound to stay there until God said otherwise. And he did, which resulted in great blessing; for as we will learn later, God finally gave him orders to move to Zarephath where he would be provided for in another wonderful way.

How important to patiently wait for God's orders. How tragic to not wait. King Saul is an illustration of this tragedy (I Samuel 13:8–13). Samuel had instructed Saul to wait till Samuel came to offer the burnt offering. But Saul did not wait. Circumstances became pressing, and he took things into his own hands and offered the burnt offering himself. But it cost him greatly. The kingdom rule was taken out of his family.

Saul is not alone in suffering great loss for not waiting on God. Many others have lost a kingdom of blessings because they would not wait for God to direct, choose, or decide. Pressing circumstances, drying brooks, and hard times have been used as excuses to depart from the Word of God as the authority in life. In fleshly impatience, decisions regarding one's job or marriage or other situation have often been made on the basis of fleshly reasoning, not on the basis of Divine orders. And like Saul, disaster sets in. God's blessings are aborted. The rewards of waiting on the Lord are forever lost.

This patience must not be confused with procrastination. Procrastination, just like impatience, is fleshly rebellion, too. Impatience runs ahead of the Lord; but procrastination lags behind. Either one is wrong. But patience will keep in step with God. And keeping in step with God is so very necessary if we expect to serve God faithfully and obtain God's best in life.

Elijah's time at the Wadi Cherith was a memorable one. How good was it that he followed God's instructions to go there. But Cherith is not a permanent residence. When God accomplished His plan for Elijah at Cherith, He ordered Elijah elsewhere for more waiting, more learning, and more serving.

# III.
# THE WIDOW

## I KINGS 17:8–16

ELIJAH FACED A great crisis. He was out of water. The brook Cherith, his sole water supply, had dried up. It had dried up as a result of the lack of rain. The drought, which had come upon the land of Israel because of their Baal worship and its attendant evil practices, was making its effect felt very acutely throughout the entire land. Though a great prophet of God, Elijah was not exempt from the suffering and privation which the drought brought to the land. Good people suffer, too, when a land is being judged for its sin. "None of us liveth to himself" (Romans 14:7); and when we sin it causes others, even the innocent, to suffer.

About a hundred miles northwest of Elijah's location at Cherith was the town of Zarephath. It was located on the coast of the Mediterranean Sea in the land of Sidon (general area of Phoenicia) which bordered Israel. It also was affected by the drought that had come upon Israel, for the drought had reached beyond the borders of Israel into neighboring lands. In that town was a widow who was nearly out of food because of the dire conditions in the land. A widow would be among the first and foremost to suffer privation in a drought, for her resources were generally much less than that of most people. Because of her great need, she, like Elijah, faced a life and death situation. They both needed help, and in a hurry, if they were going to survive. And help was available, too. It was available from God. But it would only be obtained through obedience to Divinely prescribed duty. Obedience to their God-given duty would bring the two together to witness the wonderful miracle-working power of God on their behalf.

Obedience to duty is always the best way to obtain help from God. Crises can be conquered, difficulties can be surmounted, problems can be solved, and great needs can be met if we will do what God commands. But, alas, so few obey. So few do their duty. So instead of conquering, they are conquered; instead of surmounting difficulties, they are overcome by difficulties; instead of solving problems, they only make their problems more complex; and instead of having their needs met, their needs only become greater.

With the subject of duty so prominent in the text before us, we will consider in this chapter the perception of duty, the priorities of duty, and the premiums of duty in the life of the prophet Elijah and also in the life of the widow of Zarephath.

## A. THE PERCEPTION OF DUTY

The Apostle Paul said, "Be ye not unwise, but understanding what the will of the Lord is" (Ephesians 5:17). How very important is that exhortation, and how very important to seek and to know the will of God for our lives. Some are not so sure we can always perceive the will of God, our Divine duty. But such doubt is only the voice of disobedience speaking, for you can indeed perceive your Divine duty. And our text will help us in this matter of knowing the will of God. From it we will learn three important truths about perceiving our Divine duty. First, we perceive it in Scripture—our duty is revealed to us in the Word of God. Second, we perceive it in season—our duty is always revealed on time. Third, we perceive it in segments—our duty is revealed to us step by step.

### 1. Duty is Perceived in Scripture

Elijah watched the brook dry up before he moved. He waited at Cherith until "the word of the LORD came unto him, saying, Arise, get thee to Zarephath" (vv. 8,9). The will of God for Elijah was revealed to him by the Word of God. But Elijah

## The Widow

was not alone in this experience. The widow in Zarephath also had her duty disclosed to her by the Word of God. We note this fact in verse 9 where we read, "I [God] have commanded a widow woman there [Zarephath] to sustain thee" (v. 9).

If you wish to perceive your duty, if you want to discover the will of God for your life, and if you would check your life to see if it is in accordance with God's will, then you must go to the Word of God. It is the one infallible guide regarding God's will. What we call the will of God in our life must conform to the Word of God, or it is not the will of God. Many, who want us to think they are doing God's will, are acting contrary to the Word of God which means they are not in the will of God no matter how much they may insist they are. Such folk often think they are in the will of God because of some good feeling or emotion which they are experiencing at that time. They do not determine the will of God by the Word of God; hence, they will have great difficulty perceiving accurately the will of God for their lives.

Those who are the most persistent in doing the will of God are those who make the Word of God prominent in their lives. Elijah certainly was faithful to God's will; but we are not surprised; for, as we noted in a previous chapter, the Word of God was very prominent in his life. And it is very prominent in the whole story of Elijah recorded in Scripture. As an example, the phrase, "the word of the LORD," or a similar one is found repeatedly in the story of Elijah (cp. I Kings 17:2,5,8,16,24; 18:1,31,36; 19:9; 21:17,28; and II Kings 1:17).

Today very few people give the Word of God much place in their lives. Even churches are that way. The teaching and preaching of the Word is not the main emphasis of the church program of many churches. Rather, it is recreation, socials, and the like that are the main emphasis of these churches. So no wonder people are increasingly ignorant of the will of God. No wonder the policies, standards, and doctrines embraced by the churches are so worldly. And no wonder that a pastor who wants to follow the Word of God in leading a church will often experience much opposition from his congregation because they do not know the will of God regarding the church and its program and policies.

## 2. Duty is Perceived in Season

Failure to perform one's duty is never because God was late in revealing what that duty was. God is always on time. Both in Elijah's life and in the widow's life, this fact is most salient. God spoke to Elijah in adequate time when the brook dried up and Elijah was in need of another source of water. Elijah did not die of thirst. If he had been like many of us, he would have worried about where he was going to get water and have wondered if God was going to give him directions in time. But we need not be concerned about God being late. He was on time. He knew Elijah's need; and when it was time, He revealed to Elijah what he was to do.

God also spoke to the widow in adequate time. When she had come to the last of her supplies, then God spoke to her. She was preparing her last meal when the Word of the Lord came to her, through Elijah, telling her what to do. She did not starve, as she was anticipating (v. 12); for God came in time.

Those who are attuned to the Word of God will often testify that just when they needed to make some important decision or faced some special temptation or trial, a particular passage of Scripture was especially impressed upon their mind, and it became a ready guide for their conduct. That helpful Scripture may have come to their attention in daily devotions, or it may have come through a sermon heard at church. How important, then, to be faithful in our daily study of the Word and in our attendance at church. The very passage of Scripture and the very message from the Word which we need at that moment is waiting for us. We have seen folk miss church who soon thereafter fail in doing the will of God in an area that we dealt with in the very sermon we preached when they missed church. Had they been in church, they would have heard the message from the Word which would have been so very timely for their life's situation. We have seen this happen enough times that we really fear for folk who miss church services. If God's preacher is preaching under the guidance of the Holy Spirit, his messages will be most timely whether he realizes it or not at the time he is preaching. They will fit the needs of the congregation.

Yes, God is faithful. He will reveal His will on time. But if we are going to know His will on time, we must be faithful to listen to what He has to say in His Word.

**3. Duty is Perceived in Segments**

Another prominent aspect in the revealing of the duty of Elijah and the widow was that their duty was revealed to them a step at a time. Elijah was ordered to Cherith by God's Word. But when ordering him to Cherith, God did not tell him that the next step was Zarephath. It was not until the brook dried up and it was time to move on that God revealed his new assignment. So it was with the widow, too. When Elijah, as God's spokesman, declared her duty, he did not declare it all at once. First, it was "Fetch me . . . a little water" (v. 10); then after she started for the water, it was "Bring me . . . a morsel of bread" (v. 11); and then after that, it was "make me . . . a little cake" (v. 13).

F. B. Meyer said, "God's servants must learn to take one step at a time . . . God does not give all the directions at once, lest we should get confused; He tells us just as much as we can remember and do. Then we must look to Him for more; and so we learn, by easy stages, the sublime habits of obedience and trust." Lieutenant Al Collins, a favorite Navy Chaplain of mine, said in one of his Bible classes that the will of God is like the headlights of an automobile in that they give enough light so we can see far enough ahead to drive safely, but they do not show the whole road ahead of us. It was an illustration I have never forgotten, for it describes so well the practice of God in leading us step by step. God generally shows us only what we need to know at the time. We do not need to know about tomorrow's duty until tomorrow comes. Therefore, concentrate on today's revealed duty and perform it well; and then when tomorrow comes, you will be given tomorrow's assignment.

Having the will of God revealed step by step exhorts us to spiritual stewardship, for it is the habit of God not to reveal tomorrow's will unless we have done today's duty. If Elijah had not gone to Cherith, he would not have learned of God's orders for him to go to Zarephath. Had the widow not followed her orders each time, she would not have received further orders. The Prophet Jeremiah also experienced this truth in a very conspicuous way. God spoke to Jeremiah and said, "Arise, and go down to the potter's house, and there I will cause thee to hear my words" (Jeremiah 18:2). Jeremiah was already hearing God's Word in that text. But if he wanted to know more, if he wanted to get further revelation, he had to obey his present duty. He did obey, and as a result, he then heard more from God. That is the key to learning our duty. You obey each step, and you will not miss a step in knowing the will of God. Be a good steward of your present duty, and you will know your future duty.

## B. THE PRIORITIES OF DUTY

Unless duty has top priority, it will frequently be left undone. Divine duty needs to be respected. It is God's orders and God's will for our lives. Therefore it has precedence over any other duty. Nothing must usurp its prior place in life. And nothing did usurp the priority of Divine duty in the lives of Elijah and the widow. They put duty ahead of their situations, ahead of self, and ahead of their senses. They did not let circumstances, selfishness, or fleshly reasoning keep them from doing their duty.

### 1. Duty has Priority over Situations

Elijah's circumstances certainly did not encourage doing what God told him to do. Yes, the drying brook would encourage going elsewhere for water but not to the town of Zarephath. Zarephath was only eight miles from Sidon, the city of Ethbaal who was the head of "the most wicked dynasty then in power" (Edersheim), the leader of Baal worship, and the father of Jezebel. Therefore, if Elijah is going to obey God, he must go right into the back yard of his enemies. Dangerous is hardly the word for it. The flesh would call it suicidal. J. Hammond says, "His feeling [about leaving Cherith to go to Zarephath] would be something like that of David's men, 'Behold, we be afraid here in Judah: how much more then if we come to Keilah' (I Samuel 23:3). Of all hiding places, that would seem to him to be the most to be dreaded. How can he escape detection there?"

Furthermore, God ordering Elijah to Zarephath meant Elijah must make a journey of about a hundred miles or more. Great difficulty would be encountered making such a trip with the famine in full swing; and in traveling that many miles, it would be difficult to keep himself from being detected. So Elijah's situation certainly did not encourage doing his duty. How easy would it have been for him to have let the danger and difficulty of his situation have priority over his duty. But he did not. He demonstrated what we all need to do: give first place to our Divine duty regardless of how contrary our circumstances are.

The widow also had circumstances which would seem to far outweigh her duty in importance. Her Divine duty was to take care of Elijah. But how could she take care of Elijah when her situation was so desperate? Her supplies consisted of only food enough for one meal for herself and her son. "I have . . . but an handful of meal in a barrel, and a little oil in a cruse; and, behold, I am gathering two sticks, that I may go in and dress it [prepare it] for me and my son, that we may eat it, and die" (v. 12). Hardly does her poverty seem compatible to her duty. Her circumstances would say she was the one who needed help, not the one to give help.

But her poverty was not the only difficult situation that faced her in keeping Elijah. Keeping Elijah was also a very dangerous thing to do. He was a much wanted man, and those who harbor wanted men are subject to great peril. She would be risking her life to keep Elijah.

Yes, the widow's situation really opposed her duty; and she, like Elijah, could have easily let her situation keep her from doing her duty. Few would have criticized her if she had. But regardless of her circumstances, she still gave priority to her Divine duty; otherwise she never would have done it.

How often we evade doing the will of God by some situation excuse. The slightest difficulty or least danger seems sufficient to cancel duty for most. We do not want to have to put out any effort, be inconvenienced, take any risks financially or otherwise, or subject ourselves to any suffering to do the will of God. If our Divine duty does not come on easy street, we skip it. But doing our duty is not to be secondary to favorable conditions. It is to have priority regardless of what our situation is.

**2. Duty has Priority over Self**

A self-centered person will not do his duty well, if at all. Self cannot reign if duty is to be done. Elijah certainly had to put his own concerns about self in the background in order to obey the Lord and travel to Zarephath which was located in an area very hostile to him personally. But in our text, the most conspicuous display of unselfishness is seen in the widow of Zarephath. She was especially challenged as to whether self or duty had priority. She was first challenged when Elijah asked her for a drink of water when he first spoke to her. She was busy at the time getting things together to fix a meal for herself and her son. She was also nearly overwhelmed with the sorrow because her future seemed so bleak. She thought death by starvation was imminent for her and her son. But she put her concerns and burdens of self aside and immediately went after a drink for Elijah; all of which showed considerable unselfishness.

But the biggest challenge, however, as to whether self or duty would come first, occurred when Elijah said to her, "Make me thereof a little cake first" (v. 13). Elijah's request was for her to give him the last bit of meal instead of her and her son eating it. What a severe test for self. Even the best of unselfish people would struggle here. And the famine would make this challenge even more difficult. "Famine brings out selfishness in hideous shapes [cp. II Kings 6:28,29]" (*The Biblical Illustrator*). But the widow passed the test with flying colors. She was not a selfish woman. She gave Divine duty priority over self.

W. Phillip Keller said, "We know nothing about genuine self-giving and self-sharing until our own self-survival is literally put on the line. Such a thought terrifies most of us!" How true. But the widow of Zarephath did it. Her own survival was involved in giving to Elijah. "The woman was asked for all she had, and she gave it!" (Joseph Parker). Self must not have priority or much duty to which God calls us will never be performed. Many who are out of the will of God have their own selfishness as the chief cause of their delinquency.

Lest anyone misinterpret Elijah's request as selfishness on his part, we hasten to point out several facts which will exonerate Elijah from any selfishness in making his request for the cake. First, Elijah, as God's prophet, was speaking only what God instructed him to say. It was "according to the word of the LORD, which he spake by Elijah" (v. 16). And what God, through Elijah, was saying to the widow was to give to God first. Second, Elijah, being God's prophet, was simply God's representative through whom she would give to God. The challenge to the widow was to give to God first, even if it was her very last bit of food. She would fulfill the challenge, her duty, by giving to Elijah.

The widow is not the only one who is to give to God first. We all have this duty. I. M. Haldeman said, "In asking the woman to care for him first as the representative of the Lord, Elijah was acting in the line of the Divine principle. The law is that God shall be first." This is the same message of Christ in Matthew 6:33: "Seek ye first the kingdom of God, and his righteousness." But few do. As an example, people who get behind in their tithe or do not give at all have not begun to practice this priority. Self is the crippling priority in these people's lives.

### 3. Duty has Priority over Sense

Fleshly rationale often opposes doing our duty. But human reasoning, ever so honored by an unbelieving world, is never to have priority over God's commands. God's commands may not always make sense to our intellect; though in fact they are the most logical things to do because they are God's commands. But failure to fully understand the reason for our duty does not diminish the responsibility for doing it.

Human reasoning would certainly have argued against the duty of the widow and that of Elijah. When the widow was told that if she gave first to Elijah her meal and oil would not run out, human reasoning would have argued that "She had neither precedent nor example for such an act and for such a hope" (James Smith). When Elijah was told to go to Zarephath, human reasoning would have argued that it was surely strange to go to Zarephath instead of to some secret hideout far from Israel and her friends, especially such an unholy ally as Ethbaal of Sidon. Furthermore, human reasoning would have told Elijah that a widow was the last person in the world who could sustain him. And when he got to Zarephath, that reasoning would appear to be even more justified. Not only was she a widow, but she was also in poverty and down to her last meal! Has God made a mistake? Is God stupid? Both Elijah and the widow could have easily said, "Yes." Human reasoning would certainly say, "Yes," to those questions. But so much for human reasoning. As the context shows, the widow took care of Elijah very well; and Elijah's safety was never in jeopardy. Human reasoning may sound ever so wise and good, but it is no match to God's commands! And we must never give it priority over God's commands.

We are not asked to understand God's commands; we are only asked to obey them. We need no other reason to do them than that they are His commands. However, a great host of church members in fundamental, Bible-believing churches, who, therefore, ought to know better, protest doing their duty today by saying it is unreasonable, will not work, cannot be done, and is not practical. They make these excuses sound so intellectual, scholarly, humanly logical, and respectable. Their disobedient mind becomes a master in reasoning which opposes God's will. So women are not keepers at home but seek the job market for themselves and a host of baby sitters and day-care centers for their children. Others show more interest in Sunday overtime work than in Sunday church services. Also, divorces are permitted, yea, even encouraged; and divorced persons remarrying are likewise sanctioned and encouraged. And abortions, buying of lottery tickets, social drinking, benevolence towards homosexuals, cinema attendance, and the renting of x-rated videos is increasing. All this in contrary to Divine duty prescribed in the Scripture. But human reasoning cleverly argues in opposition and is too often given priority over duty. If duty, however, is to be done, it must always have priority over human reasoning. "Thus saith the Lord" is the final authority regarding duty.

## C. THE PREMIUMS OF DUTY

The blessings for doing our duty are many. Giving priority to Divine duty does not short-change anyone. The prospects, to the human eye, may not seem very encouraging when duty is first assigned. But that only tests our faith. It does not take away from the premiums received for doing our duty.

We will consider three wonderful blessings, three great premiums, which we can anticipate when doing our duty. They are the providence of God, the power of God, and the provisions of God. These blessings should be a real encouragement to doing our duty.

**1. The Providence of God**

The Apostle Paul said, "We know that all things work together for good to them that love God, to them who are the called according to his purpose" (Romans 8:28). This verse promises Divine providence. God will work everything out. Circumstances will be wonderfully arranged, planned, and ordered by God. It is a great promise, but it is definitely not for everyone. Many glibly quote this verse when troubles come and say, "Everything will work out in the end." But that is not true. Everything may not work out in the end. Circumstances may not dovetail beautifully for you. This promise is only for those who do their God-given duty. It is for those who "love God" and who are "called [and thus living] according to his purpose [His will]." They are doing what God has told them to do. And one of the premiums for doing your Divinely assigned task is that beneficial providence will be your portion.

Elijah certainly experienced this blessing in a wonderful way in our text. When God ordered him to go to Zarephath, He said, "I have commanded a widow woman *there* to sustain thee" (v. 9). Now notice what happened when Elijah obeyed. "So he arose and went to Zarephath. And when he came to the gate of the city, *behold, the widow was there*" (v. 10). What providence! The world would say it was a lucky coincidence. But what does the ungodly, unbelieving world know about Divine providence? Nothing! But those who do the will of God will know plenty about the providence of God. It is a valuable and blessed premium for those who will do their Divine duty.

The widow also experienced wonderful providence in her life because of doing her duty, particularly the duty of preparing for that supposedly last meal. Pink says, "Let it be duly noted that his woman did not fail to discharge her responsibility . . . Instead of giving way to utter despair, sitting down and wringing her hands, she was busily occupied gathering sticks for what she fully believed would be her last meal. This is not an unimportant detail, but one which we need to take to heart . . . Discharge your responsibility to the very end, even though it be in preparing for your final meal. Richly was the widow repaid for her industry. It was while she was *in the path of duty* (household duty!), that God, through His servant, met with and blessed her." She would have missed this wonderful providence of the meeting with Elijah had she not been doing her duty!

Scripture gives us many other instructive illustrations of how people experienced the blessing of the providence of God because they did their Divine duty. Abraham's servant was sent to Haran to find a bride for Isaac. When the servant arrived in Haran, the first woman he met at the well was the very woman who would become Isaac's bride. The servant's comment on this wonderful providence was, "I being in the way, the LORD led me" (Genesis 24:27). Yes, indeed, he was in the way of doing his duty; and so providence worked for him in a wonderful way. Mordecai did his duty and exposed an assassination plot aimed at King Ahasuerus. On the eve of Mordecai's planned hanging on the gallows by wicked Haman, the king had insomnia. So since he was awake, he commanded his servants to read to him from the record of his administration. In the reading he heard about the deed of Mordecai. As a result he had great honors done to Mordecai which kept Mordecai from the gallows. The providential insomnia resulted in saving Mordecai's life (Esther 6). What a choice blessing for simply doing one's duty! Another incident of providence in Scripture involved Peter and John preparing for the Passover for Christ and the disciples. When Peter and John asked Christ, "Where wilt thou that we prepare?" (Luke 22:9), Christ answered, "Behold, when ye are entered into the city, *there* shall a man meet you, bearing a pitcher of water; follow him . . . And he shall show you a large upper room furnished; there make ready" (Luke 22:10,12).

You, too, can experience this blessed benefit of doing your Divine duty. Be where you are supposed to be, do what you are supposed to do, and you will discover God ordering providence for you. The widow will be at the gate just as you arrive. Rebekah will be at the well to water your camels. The king will have insomnia on the eve of your planned execution by Haman; and thus, you will be spared the gallows. When sent to find a place for observing the Passover, you will meet a man just as you enter the city; and he will show you where you are to have the Passover. God decrees it. Providence will work for you when you faithfully do your duty.

## 2. The Power of God

Elijah told the widow to do her duty, which was to give to God first; and she would witness the power of God working a miracle on her behalf. We note the work of God's power and the wisdom of God's power in this case.

# Elijah

*The work of God's power.* "The barrel of meal shall not waste [be used up], neither shall the cruse of oil fail, until the day that the LORD sendeth rain upon the earth" (v. 14). The widow "went and did according to the saying of Elijah . . . And [as a result] the barrel of meal wasted not [was not used up], neither did the cruse of oil fail" (vv. 15,16). Every day during the remaining two years or more of the famine, she (and also Elijah, for he had done his duty in coming to Zarephath and so would share with the widow in this experiencing of the power of God) saw the power of God at work. Her barrel of meal never ran out; the cruse of oil never ran out. She could dip in the barrel for meal, and there would always be some no matter how much she took out. She could tip the cruse of cooking oil to pour from it, and oil would always flow from it. Amazing! Only the power of God can do that. And it is a predictable premium for all who will do their Divine duty.

A number of saints in every age can testify of this miracle in their lives. Some, as an example, have given of their money so sacrificially that it appeared they would not have enough left for themselves to live on. But then the miracle began. God worked mightily for them. He either cut their expenses to match their income ("I will rebuke the devourer for your sakes," Malachi 3:11), or He stretched their income to cover their expenses ("Give, and it shall be given unto you; good measure, pressed down, and shaken together, and running over" [Luke 6:38]). And sometimes that extra income came from most unexpected sources. God's power is available to the obedient, to those who do their assigned tasks.

*The wisdom of God's Power.* The miracle which occurred in the widow's home demonstrates a great truth about the power of God; namely, God's power is never displayed apart from God's wisdom. Spurgeon said, "Why did not God given her a granary full of meal at once, and a vat full of oil instanter? I will tell you. It was not merely because of God's intent to try her, but there was wisdom here. Suppose He had given her a granary full of meal, how much of it would have been left by the next day? I question whether any would have remained. For in the days of famine men are sharp of scent, and it would soon have been noised about the city, 'The old widow woman who lives in such-and-such a street has a great store of food.' Why, they would have caused a riot, and robbed the house, and perhaps have killed the woman and her son. She would have been despoiled of her treasure, and in four and twenty hours the barrel of meal would have been as empty as it was at first, and the cruse of oil would have been spilled upon the ground." Leon Wood has some similar observations on this subject. He said, "This manner of miracle was for good reason. It was necessary that it work this way if Elijah's presence was to remain unnoticed. Borrowing of jars from neighbors would have invited attention, and so would a pantry full of meal. Such news would soon have spread as far as town officials, and then word would have been taken to Ahab. With the miracle working as it did, there was no reason for people to wonder. They would have thought that the widow's improved economic condition was because she had a paying boarder." God can, in His wisdom, display His power in such a way that the faithful saints will see and receive it fully; but the unbelieving world about them will be completely uncognizant of it.

### 3. The Provisions of God

"She and he, and her house, did eat many days" (v. 15). Elijah had great needs when he left Cherith. He needed water and food and a place to stay. The widow of Zarephath had great needs, too. She did have water (water would not be a problem at Zarephath, for the wells there would be supported by the nearness of the sea which would help maintain the water table), and she had a house, but she did not have food. However, Elijah's need of provisions and her need of provisions were both taken care of when the two of them attended faithfully to their Divine tasks, for that is another wonderful premium for doing our duty.

The church at Philippi experienced this blessing, too. Paul

said to them, "My God shall supply all your need according to his riches in glory by Christ Jesus" (Philippians 4:19). The reason he promised God would provide for them was that "your care of me hath flourished," and "ye sent once and again unto my necessity" (Philippians 4:10,16). The saints at Philippi saw their duty and did it. Their reward for faithfully attending to their duty was to have their provisions supplied by God.

Elijah and the widow give quite a lesson to all of us about how to solve our problems. Maybe you are in the midst of a multitude of troubling circumstances which threaten to undo you. You grope for answers and do not know which way to turn. If that is your situation, then do as Elijah and the widow did—do your God-given duty regardless. When you do, you will see things clear up in a way you may not have believed could have happened. God will begin to work on your behalf, and one day you will suddenly realize that all those problems, which you thought were impossible to be solved, have been solved, and your great needs have been marvelously provided in spite of your circumstances. How did it all happen? Were you a genius and devised some fantastic formula for success? No, you simply obeyed your heavenly orders; you did your Divine duty. And it was the key to your being a victor in life instead of a victim.

# IV.

# THE WEEPING

## I KINGS 17:17–24

WITH THE MIRACLE of the multiplying of the meal and the oil continuing daily, Elijah and the widow and her son were getting along wonderfully despite the famine that raged all around them. Then one day the tranquility of their situation was painfully interrupted. "And it came to pass after these things, that the son of the woman, the mistress of the house, fell sick; and his sickness was so sore [severe], that there was no breath left in him" (v. 17). A trial, a great fiery trial, came upon both Elijah and the widow. Tears would flow freely and especially from the widow. The heart-rending sobs of a deeply sorrowing woman would once again be heard in that humble abode. She, who had lost a husband to death, now loses not just a son but her only son. A heavy trial indeed.

Much is recorded in Scripture about trials, and nothing will help us so much as the Bible regarding trials. A good example of how helpful the Bible is on the subject of trials will be found in this passage of Scripture before us. In this passage on the great trial of the death of the widow's son, we will consider the place, the perplexity, and the product of trials.

### A. THE PLACE OF TRIALS

Trials can be and should be expected in any place in this life. No age, location, circumstance, or spiritual advancement will exempt us from trials. In spite of this fact, however, we still are frequently surprised when trial comes. There are some places we just do not expect trials to occur. But the case of Elijah and the widow demonstrate that trials show up in these unexpected places, too. They experienced their trial in the place of obedience, service, blessing, and previous trial.

## 1. The Place of Obedience

Elijah and the widow were walking obedient lives. As we noted in our previous chapter, both had been tested quite severely about obeying the Lord. And they had passed those tests with flying colors. Elijah had faithfully obeyed the Lord about going to Zarephath, even though it was a dangerous spot for him personally. The widow had faithfully obeyed the Lord about giving food to Elijah instead of having it for herself and her son. Yet, in spite of their noble obedience, they now experience a tremendous trial in the sudden death of the widow's son.

We normally think that if we live right, we will be exempt from afflictions. Obedience does indeed eliminate many unnecessary trials, for there are many troubles which simply come upon us because we have been disobedient. These trials we would escape if we would not rebel against the Lord. But even when we follow Him faithfully, we will not escape all trials. No one was more obedient than Christ, yet He suffered afflictions as none other. And the Psalmist says, "Many are the afflictions of the righteous" (Psalm 34:19). Yet, as Phillip Keller said, "People, somehow, are given to believe, either through wrong teaching or false preaching, that if they put their confidence in Christ; if they are obedient to His commands; if they act in forthright faith, all will be well for the rest of their days. They conclude somehow that they will automatically be exempted from the tragedy and turmoil of their times."

It is very important for us to realize that the obedient are not exempt from trials, for it will keep us from making wrong and injurious conclusions and decisions when trials come. For one thing it will keep us from concluding that it does not pay to do right. The devil would love to have us make that conclusion. Whenever we suffer affliction on the path of obedience, he is right there to make that charge. However, when we understand that the righteous experience trials, not for their demise but for their good, we will be encouraged to stay on the path of obedience and not quit it as the devil says to do.

Also, it is important for us to know that the obedient suffer trials so we do not conclude that trials always indicate evil in our lives. Trials have a tendency to make the conscientious think they are more evil than others if they are suffering more troubles than those around them. But as J. Urquhart said, "Affliction is no more proof of wrath [God's punishment for evil] than is the farmer's plowing of his field. To him, with his eye upon the future harvest, it is only the needful preparation of the soil." In the same vein Matthew Henry said, "Extra ordinary afflictions are not always punishment for extra ordinary evils but sometimes the trial of extra ordinary graces."

## 2. The Place of Service

Elijah, as God's prophet, had given his whole life to being God's servant. In Zarephath he was where God told him to be and doing what God said to do. He was a most faithful servant of God. The widow was also serving the Lord. Ever since Elijah had come to town, she had provided him room and board. This service required much extra work and was a risk to her life if Elijah's enemies discovered he was boarding in her house. But faithful and gallant service for the Lord did not stop either Elijah or the widow from experiencing a heart breaking trial. The widow's son still died even though both were serving with excellence.

Sometimes we tend to think that giving ourselves to service for the Lord should exempt us from troubles and trials. But those serving faithfully are going to have afflictions. The devil will see to that if no one else does. Serving well will upset the devil. You are working against his program, and he does not take that lightly. Therefore, he will endeavor to make it miserable for you. When you serve the Lord, you are going to a battle, not to a picnic. To experience trial, even though serving faithfully, should be no more of a surprise to the servant of God than for the soldier boy to experience battle and enemy gunfire in a time of war. Elijah and the widow were opposing the evil forces of the devilish religion of Baal. It is not surprising that they suffered troubles. Rather, we should probably be surprised they did not suffer more troubles.

## 3. The Place of Blessing

Elijah and the widow were living amidst great blessing. Every day they experienced the blessing of the meal and oil multiplying. On every hand the famine was taking its toll, yet they were doing very nicely because of the great blessings of God upon them.

Sometimes such abundance of blessing causes one to think trial is forever in the past tense. Like David, we often say, "In my prosperity I said, I shall never be moved" (Psalm 30:6). It is easy to forget trial when blessing comes. And God is gracious to make our blessings so great at times that it often does wipe out the grief and the cares of previous troubles. As Joseph said when he named his first-born son Manasseh, "God . . . hath made me forget all my toil [troubles of the past]" (Genesis 41:51).

Blessing, however, does not exempt us from trial. In fact, great blessing may often be needed to prepare us for some great trial in the future. Arthur Pink says, "It often happens that God exercises His people with the heaviest trials when they have been the recipients of His richest blessings . . . Having tasted experimentally of the Lord's goodness, they are better fitted to meet adversity." Elijah and the widow had been witnessing a daily miracle for some time. That provided preparation for them to face this great trial which would require another miracle. The same thing was true with Joseph and Mary in the New Testament. They had received great blessing in the gifts from the Wise Men. But those gifts prepared Joseph and Mary to face victoriously the severe trial which came to them when they were forced to flee to Egypt because of Herod's murderous designs upon the Christ Child. Joseph and Mary were poor and would

# The Weeping

have been in quite a fix trying to flee to Egypt in their poverty. But those gifts of the Wise Men gave them plenty to pay the expenses of their trip to and their sojourn in that foreign land.

Another encouraging truth about experiencing trial in the place of blessing is found in the fact that trial brings blessing. As we will note later, trials are a source of great blessing. We would not want the blessings we have to cancel out future blessings, and neither does God. So trials often come to those who are experiencing great blessing in order to increase their blessing. Surely we should not complain about that fact.

## 4. The Place of Previous Trial

Lightening does strike in the same place twice. Both Elijah and the widow had known much about rugged trials before this one. Elijah had the trial of being Ahab's enemy and, therefore, being a much sought after man. He also had the trial of going to Cherith and of watching the brook dry up. Then he had the trial of going to Zarephath, a difficult trip and a place of much personal danger. The widow had faced much severe trial in the loss of her husband, in the poverty of widowhood, and in the famine which at one time threatened to starve her and her son to death. One would, therefore, think that Elijah and the widow had gone through enough rough times. But no, they are again in the midst of a painful trial.

Is God cruel to keep subjecting them to trial? No, a thousand times no! The value and validity of this place of trial is illustrated by the habit of a lapidary. The better the stone, the more he subjects it to polishing on the grindstone. Stones which do not have good character are tossed aside by the discerning lapidary after a little time on the grindstone. But stones with character and real promise are put to the grindstone again and again to bring out their beauty and luster and to greatly increase their value. Hence, when trial comes again and again to the godly, it says plenty about their great character, about their great esteem to God. It does not say God has it in for them. It more likely says they are very special to God.

## B. THE PERPLEXITY OF TRIALS

Trials often perplex as did this trial. The two main questions trials cause us to ask concern cause and conduct. First, why did the trial come (cause)? Second, what do we do now (conduct)? The trial here will help answer these questions.

### 1. The Cause of the Trial

Both the widow and Elijah groped almost frantically for causes of the trial. And in their haste they drew some very erroneous conclusions. The widow pointed her finger at both her tenant (Elijah) and her transgression as possible causes. Elijah pointed his finger at God. So the lodger, the lady, and the Lord were all under suspect as being the cause of the trial.

*The lodger is blamed.* The widow first tried to blame Elijah for the trial. She said, "Art thou come unto me to call my sin to remembrance, and to slay my son?" (v. 18). Being acquainted with the fact that Elijah had called for a drought for the land because of the sin of the people in worshipping Baal, the widow, in her anxiety, concluded that Elijah had discovered some sin in her and was now calling for God to judge her, too, by slaying her son. But this was a most unwise and ungrateful accusation and did not take into consideration all the facts. Phillip Keller said, "When suffering or sorrow suddenly engulfs us like a flood, we often quickly forget the goodness of our friends, our family, even our God. In self-pity and hurt we lash out against whoever is near at hand. We heap abuse upon husband or wife, parent or child, friend or neighbor . . . in the tirade innocent bystanders bear the brunt of our abuse." If we do not look immediately to God for answers, the pain of trial can cause us to be most unkind and unreasonable in casting blame upon others.

*The lady is blamed.* Elijah in ordering the judgment would be part of the cause in the widow's mind, but not all the cause; for she suspected her sin was the root cause of the trial. The Bible does not report what this particular sin was which the widow had in mind, but it makes no difference what it was. She simply felt it was at the bottom of the trial; and she, therefore, was somehow to blame for this severe trial.

This charge, while still not right in her case, was a more noble charge than blaming Elijah for her trial. It showed some godly character in her. The godly are more likely to attribute their troubles to sin than the ungodly. Arthur Pink says, "It is at this very point that the difference between an unbeliever and a believer so often appears. When the former is visited with some sore trouble or loss, the pride and self righteousness of his heart is quickly manifested by his, 'I know not what I have done to deserve this: I always sought to do what is right; I am no worse than my neighbors who are spared such sorrow—why should I be made the subject of such a calamity?' But how different is it with a person truly humbled. He is distrustful of himself, aware of his many shortcomings, and ready to fear that he has displeased the Lord."

The widow was to discover that her second accusation was not true either and that trial does not necessarily mean the afflicted one has sinned. Sometimes the accusation is true, however, and we need to examine our hearts carefully in this matter. But we must not morbidly conclude that every trial is judgment for one or more of our sins.

*The Lord is blamed.* Elijah in his desperate seeking for a cause wondered if God was perhaps to blame for the problem. He questioned if God was acting justly in His actions towards the widow. He said in his prayer, "O LORD my God, hast thou also brought evil [adversity] upon the widow with whom I sojourn, by slaying her son?" (v. 20). Arthur Pink said, "This dark dispensation occasioned a real testing of Elijah's faith. God is the God of the widow and the Rewarder of those who befriend His people, especially who show kindness to His servants. Why, then, should such evil now come upon the one who was affording him shelter?"

It is a habit of human nature, and even in the best of people, to blame God when troubles come. Elijah, to his credit, did not charge God as crudely and rudely as many do. His prayer, though it blamed God, was more of a puzzled question about God's behavior than an outright charge of God's failure. But the world is not so nice. They blame God for everything they can. From illness to war to poverty, the world foolishly and unjustifiable blames God for their problems while conspicuously ignoring their own blame. They ignore the devil as a cause, too. We need to ponder more the book of Job and see how often the devil inflicts. He seems to get very little blame for troubles, and yet he is a great instigator of evil. And as we pointed out earlier, he is definitely going to be on the attack against those who are battling against his work, such as Elijah and the widow were.

Yes, trials raise many questions. How they perplex us at times. In fact, the perplexity is sometimes a trial in itself. Especially at the commencement of the trial do we find the trial strange and difficult to understand. But Peter said, "Beloved, think it not strange concerning the fiery trial which is to try you, as though some strange thing happened unto you" (I Peter 4:12). Though they seem so strange to us at times, they are not strange to God; for God has good reasons for allowing them. We may not always be able to discover the reason this side of heaven, but that should not stop us from pursuing the reason. We at least need to pursue the reason long enough to see if the trial is for chastisement. That reason we must know, or the chastening trial will be of no avail; and we will, therefore, be setting ourselves up for another and more severe disciplinary trial. We have enough trials without adding to them unnecessarily, so we need to examine every trial from the chastening standpoint.

If chastisement is not the cause, we can rest assured God has other good reasons. Often times we suffer trials not because of some particular sin but simply to improve our graces, to gain more spiritual strength, faith and wisdom. And trials are given to glorify God, too. That truth was especially pointed out in John 9 regarding the blind man. When the disciples asked Christ whose sin caused the blindness, He said it was not sin at all; but the blindness occurred "that the works of God should be made manifest in him (John 9:3)." Some may complain that it is cruel of God to make us suffer in order that He might be glorified. But we must remember Christ also suffered greatly for us that we might be glorified through salvation for all eternity. If God Incarnate suffered so much for our glory, we certainly have no right whatsoever to complain if we are asked to suffer a little that He might be glorified. In fact, that gives our trial great meaning, justification, and consolation to have as its purpose the glory of God.

Yes, God has reasons for every trial. and they are always good reasons. Learning that truth well will help us to experience our trials victoriously.

## 2. The Conduct in the Trial

What should we do now? That is one of the most common questions during a trial. And it is a very important question, too; for what we do in a time of trial has much to do with whether the trial makes or breaks us. Too often our conduct when trial comes only aggravates the situation. The widow lashing out sharply at Elijah is an illustration of that sort of conduct. But she is not alone in reacting to her trial in such a way as to make matters worse. Many when beset with trial go to the bottle to try to drink away their troubles. Others endeavor to drug their senses to numbness hoping that will help them through the trial. Still others try to cope with their trials by losing themselves in an endless round of pleasures, many of which are unvirtuous. But all these fleshly expedients are of no avail. They only worsen the trial.

Elijah, however, though very upset by the trial, did know what to do. Elijah said to the widow, "Give me thy son. And he took him out of her bosom, and carried him up into a loft, where he abode, and laid him upon his own bed. And he cried unto the LORD" (vv. 19, 20). Elijah took the problem to the Lord in prayer. That is one of the best things we can do when trial comes. Sometimes it may be all we can do, but that does not limit us in getting help in trial. What would really limit us is if we could not pray—even if we could do a host of other things. "God is our refuge and strength, a very present help in trouble" (Psalm 46:1); and we need to seek His help in prayer in time of trouble. When trial first hits us, we may be very perplexed, very upset, and very troubled in mind, body, and spirit. But if we will only take the matter to the Lord, we will get help—and better help than anywhere else. He will clear up our thinking, work mightily on our behalf, and give us victory in our trial.

Elijah's prayer is a good primer on how to pray in time of trouble. He prayed earnestly, specifically, boldly, and privately.

*He prayed earnestly.* Twice the Scripture says he "cried" unto the Lord (vv. 20, 21). This was not passive praying, routine reciting of a prayer book, or a lifeless repeating of stale requests from a prayer notebook. This was real, earnest pleading with God. It is the only way to pray in time of trial. We should at least pray as earnestly as the trial is earnest.

*He prayed specifically.* "Let this child's soul come into him again" (v. 21). The request was specific about what it wanted—life. It was specific about who it was for—this child. If you have a specific problem, be specific when you take it to the Lord. Specific requests will receive specific answers, and how blessed are specific answers.

*He prayed boldly.* Elijah asked for the resurrection of the lad when he prayed, "Let this child's soul come into him again" (v. 21). What a great request that was! Significantly, he did not base this request on examples of the past, for this resurrection was the first one recorded in Scripture! He simply based it on the greatness of God which He had learned about in His Word.

Great boldness is a combination of great faith in God and great esteem of God's power. Thus to pray boldly honors the Lord. Sometimes our prayer requests dishonor God because they make God look so weak and puny. But Scripture exhorts us

## The Weeping

to "Come boldly unto the throne of grace, that we may obtain mercy, and find grace to help in time of need" (Hebrews 4:16). Trials are certainly a time of need and are, therefore, a time to pray boldly.

*He prayed privately.* Elijah went to his own room to pray for this lad. "He took him out of her bosom, and carried him up into a loft, where he [Elijah] abode, and laid him upon his [Elijah's] own bed. And he cried unto the LORD" (vv. 19, 20). Praying with others has its place and value. But private prayer is generally where we can do our best praying. Free from inhibitions of what others will think or say about how we pray, and free from any prayer hindering self-consciousness which is often present when praying with others, we can in private prayer really get down to business with God. We need to develop a good, personal, private prayer life whether we can pray in public or not. Having a good, private prayer life gives one a great advantage in dealing with one's trials.

Elijah had some great perplexities about the trial, but he was not perplexed about what to do when faced with a trial. He knew one should take the trial to the Lord and tell Him about it. You are always headed on the right path in the time of trial when you take it to the Lord and tell Him your problem.

The disciples of John the Baptist, like Elijah, are a great illustration of this action of taking one's troubles to the Lord. When John was beheaded, "his disciples came, and took up the body, and buried it, and went and told Jesus" (Matthew 14:12). "Went and told Jesus" was the best thing they could have done.

We may feel we want to tell a host of other people our troubles, and that is not necessarily wrong, but we do our best when we tell the Lord about our trials. Many whom we tell our troubles to, unlike the Lord, will not be able to help us at all. But, in fact, they may, by their comments, actions, and suggestions, only make things worse. Many psychologists and psychiatrists fall in that category. They are generally the most overrated people on the block. But going to the Lord and telling Him your troubles is never a risk. He will not make things worse but will only make things better.

## C. THE PRODUCT OF TRIALS

Trials, regardless of why they come, can produce great blessings for us if we react to them properly. Some blessings can only be obtained through trial. The butterfly must experience the trial of struggling through the small aperture of a cocoon if its wings are to gain strength to fly. People often must experience the trial of an operation in order to regain their health. The athlete's slogan of "no pain, no gain" also says trial is often the only way to benefits. And the greatest benefit and blessing of all, our salvation, was made possible only through the great trial of suffering by our Savior. Therefore, if we were to be exempt from trials, we would miss many blessings.

Elijah and the widow gained many great blessings from this sore trial of the death of the widow's son. The trial produced the blessings of life, joy, opportunity for service, proof of profession, and spiritual knowledge. Choice blessings indeed. Of course, the carnal mind may not value these blessings. All it sees is the material. But those who know that spiritual blessings are the greatest blessings of all will quickly recognize that this trial brought tremendous blessing to both Elijah and the widow.

### 1. The Trial Produced Life

"The LORD heard the voice of Elijah; and the soul of the child came into him again, and he revived" (v. 22). Trial seemed to bring death; but in the end it brought life—and life more abundantly. When the lad was sick, he was alive: but it was not quality life. However, when he was resurrected, he certainly had life more abundantly!

Trial is often a great reviver. As an example, we get stale, languid, and dead in spiritual interest. Then God sends a trial that drives us to prayer and into the Word of God; and lo and behold, we get revived! Our spiritual interests take on new life, new energy.

## The Weeping

The greatest life giving trial was the trial of Calvary which Christ experienced. From the agony of death on the cross, in that great affliction upon Christ, came resurrection life for the soul of man. "I am come that they might have life, and that they might have it more abundantly" (John 10:10), Christ said. But little did anyone realize then that this great life would only come to man through the greatest trial of all. And little do any of us realize that trial produces life. But it does, and what hope this gives to those going through trial.

**2. The Trial Produced Joy**

It is hard to imagine the tremendous joy which must have swept over the widow when Elijah brought her son back to her and said, "See, thy son liveth" (v. 23). Some translators justifiably put an exclamation point after "liveth," for joy demands it. I do not know how you can make that statement without an exclamation point. The raising of the widow's son from the dead would cause Elijah and the widow to overflow with great joy.

James said, "Count it all joy when ye fall into divers [various] temptations [trials]" (James 1:2). When Peter spoke to the saints about their trials, he said, "Rejoice . . . happy are ye" (I Peter 4:13,14). Admittedly, it takes a very strong eye of faith to see the joy in trials when the trials first descend upon a person. Our troubles often seem to take away completely any hope of future joy. But regarding trials, joy is the promise of Scripture, both in exhortation and example. What an encouragement this is to the tried! What a different perspective this gives of trials than our usual view of them.

**3. The Trial Produced Opportunity for Service**

Sometimes we pray that God will use us more, but we seldom anticipate Him answering the request through trial. And yet our troubles frequently open doors for service. The trial of the death of the widow's son gave Elijah an opportunity to serve in a great way. And what a service he performed for God and this widow in his taking the widow's son and praying for him to have his life restored! However, he never could have served in the capacity he did had it not been for this excruciating trial.

The Apostle Paul found trials to be open doors for getting out the Gospel to more people He said, "I would ye should understand, brethren, that the things [his many trials] which happened unto me have fallen out rather unto the furtherance of the gospel; so that my bonds in Christ are manifest in all the palace, and in all other places" (Philippians 1:12,13). Paul gave another exhortation about trials producing opportunity for service when he said, "Who comforteth us in all our tribulation, that we may be able to comfort them which are in any trouble, by the comfort wherewith we ourselves are comforted of God" (II Corinthians 1:4). Experiencing a trial makes it possible for us to help others in trial. It opens a door of service for us. So if you want to be busy in service for God, do not be surprised if you experience many trials. They qualify you to serve and give opportunity to serve in many ways.

We need to emphasize here that when opportunity to serve presents itself, we are to be good stewards of such opportunities. Elijah certainly was. When trial gave him opportunity to serve, he served with great dedication. This is especially seen in "he stretched himself upon the child three times" (v. 21). He gave his "body, soul and spirit . . . to this great work of reviving. There are many who pray for reviving who would not stretch their little finger to lift a soul out of the ditch of sin. In 'stretching himself' he gave himself wholly to the work" (James Smith).

### 4. The Trial Produced Proof of Profession

Elijah's identity as a man of God was confirmed by this trial. The widow said at the end of the trial, "Now by this I know that thou art a man of God" (v. 24). This statement did not mean the widow had been in serious doubt about Elijah's identity. She had seen plenty of evidence in the daily miracle and in Elijah's lifestyle to show his identity as a man of God. But this trial simply verified it. It proved it beyond a shadow of a doubt.

## The Weeping

Do you claim to be a Christian? To the world it may be just so many words until they see how you act under the stress of trial. They may not openly challenge your claim to being a Christian, for they can see your different lifestyle. But trial is a special test, a very severe test, the real proving grounds of our profession of faith. Anyone can act nice in good times; but when troubles come, it is a different story. This is where Christianity should really show up. So if you have been praying to be a better testimony before your friends, neighbors, and relatives, it just may be that God will send you some troubles. For your afflictions will give you an opportunity to be a testimony for Christ in a very forceful, clear, and unmistakable manner. And the world needs to see more sterling examples of Christianity in this dark age of compromise and frauds.

### 5. The Trial Produced Spiritual Knowledge

This benefit of the trial we see especially in the widow. Because of the trial she was able to say to Elijah, "Now by this I *know* that thou art a man of God, and that the word of the LORD in thy mouth is truth" (v. 24). She had gained some valuable spiritual knowledge from this trial. First, she had gained the knowledge of knowing who was a true servant of God which is invaluable knowledge especially when so many frauds abound who fleece the faith and finances of the ignorant. Second, she had gained the knowledge of the veracity of the Word of God which is vital knowledge to have if one is going to grow in faith. You may have your head crammed full of all sorts of knowledge, but very little of it will be as valuable as the knowledge this widow gained from her troubles.

Trials are a classroom of extraordinary value. They teach us important truths, vital truths, practical truths. So much schooling today does nothing of the sort. Sometimes the only way we will ever learn important truths is through trials. David said, "It is good for me that I have been afflicted, that I might learn thy statutes" (Psalm 119:71). What a great justification that is for our afflictions.

Trials are not a waste; they are not a loss; they are not a mistake. As we have just noticed in the products of the trial for Elijah and the widow, trials produce some of the greatest blessings man can ever possess. It is definitely not easy to perceive this at the time of the trials, of course. In fact, during trials it is very difficult to see anything positive coming from them. But that only gives us opportunity to demonstrate more faith in God's Word. His Word gives us many exhortations and examples of the results of trials in life. If we ponder and meditate more on these exhortations and examples, we will react better in our trials and secure more valuable blessings from them.

The meaning of the name "Zarephath" is most fitting for Elijah and the widow in their experiences there; for the meaning emphasizes what we have observed about trials in this chapter; namely, trials are good for us, they help us, they bless us, and they strengthen us in the most important areas of life. J. Hammond said, "The name points to furnaces or workshops for the refining of metals." Robert Jamieson said, "The etymology of the name indicates that it was a place for smelting metals." Arthur Pink adds that the name Zarephath means "refining" and comes "from a root that signifies a crucible—the place where metals are melted." So Zarephath, according to these meanings, was a place associated with refining. For Elijah and the widow, Zarephath was certainly a place of refining. God put their faith in the fiery furnace of trials. It looked at times like the fire would destroy their faith. But like the work of smelting furnaces upon metal, the fire through which God put their faith did not destroy their faith but rather refined it, purified it, made it stronger, better, and more valuable. Elijah and the widow were better people as a result of the trial.

# V.

# THE WANDERERS

## I KINGS 18:1–20

ELIJAH'S WARFARE WITH Baalism is now coming back to center stage. After his initial confrontation with King Ahab and the declaration of the devastating drought, Elijah went into hiding at Cherith and then Zarephath. During the time of his hiding, the focus was on the personal experiences of Elijah. Now it is back to the great contention he has with Baal worship.

Elijah, the good soldier that he was, did not make any moves until his great General, Jehovah, gave orders to move. And the orders to leave Zarephath to go and confront Ahab again did not come until "after many days . . . in the third year" (v. 1). "In the third year" indicates that Elijah had stayed over two years in Zarephath, probably about two and a half years. With the drought lasting three and a half years (Luke 4:25), he then must have sojourned at Cherith for approximately a year. The long stay in inactivity would tax Elijah's patience to the limit. And he may have done some chafing at the bit during the three and a half years of hiding, for Elijah was a man of action. But he wisely submitted to God's orders regarding staying at Zarephath and did not leave Zarephath until the command came from God to do so.

"There was a sore [severe] famine in Samaria" (v. 2) indicates that the three and a half years of drought really hurt the land. Surrounding nations appeared to have also suffered considerably from this dry spell; but Samaria (another name for the northern kingdom which was also called Israel and Ephraim), the nation with whom God had His main contention at the time, received the brunt of the famine. Desolation would thus be on every hand. Rich pasture land would be turned into brown, burned out grass which was good for nothing. Plowed fields would be baked, stone-hard, and without crops. Brooks and rivers would be mostly dried up, and the vegetation which thrives by them would be dead or dying. Skeletons of animals would be everywhere, and what animals were alive would be nothing but skin and bones. But the great tragedy would be the terrible condition of the people. Famine kills; so death would abound among mankind. What survived, with few exceptions, would be emaciated bodies, struggling from one day to the next to stay ahead of the grim reaper.

The devastating conditions of the land, brought on by the famine, was the rod of God upon a nation that had deserted Him in wholesale fashion for the rotten religion of Baal. The drought was to bring Israel to their senses and back to Jehovah. And it did have a purifying effect; for as we will see in a later chapter, the people were conditioned to now listen to the entreaty of God's prophet and to turn against the prophets of Baal. The nation was not ready to listen to Elijah when he first confronted Ahab. The nation was prospering materially then and deeply involved in the pleasures of the flesh through Baal worship. But now, with the nation nothing but a wasteland as a result of the famine, the people are more ready to listen to God's prophet. Therefore, the time is now ripe to openly attack Baalism with death dealing blows. So Elijah is ordered back to the land, back to the conflict, and back to confrontation with Baalism.

Upon arriving back in the land of Israel, Elijah first meets up with two government officials. One is Ahab the king, the one whom Elijah is especially ordered by God to see. The other is Obadiah, the governor of Ahab's house (v. 3), a very high government position ("probably the second man in the kingdom" [Maclaren]; "third ruler in the kingdom" [J. Hammond]). When Elijah meets these men, they were wandering over the land looking for grass for Ahab's horses and mules. They present a very pathetic picture in that after three and a half years of devastating drought, two of the highest government officials of the land are engaged in nothing better than trying to find some grass for dumb animals. Their wandering about the land looking for grass evidences that they had been doing a lot of wandering in the past few years—wandering far from God and far from their responsibility of caring for the nation.

In this study of Elijah's meeting with these two wanderers, we will consider the precept of God—which ordered Elijah to see Ahab; the problem of Obadiah—whom Elijah encountered when on his way to see Ahab; and the performance of Ahab—the worst king Israel had experienced up to this time.

## A. THE PRECEPT OF GOD

Elijah's orders to leave Zarephath to go see Ahab were short and plain. God said, "Go, show thyself unto Ahab, and I will send rain upon the earth" (v. 1). We will look at three things about this Divine precept: the requirement of the precept, the reinforcement for the precept, and the response to the precept.

**1. The Requirement of the Precept**

"Go show thyself unto Ahab" was the requirement of God's precept for Elijah. This command was exactly opposite the one he received just after his first confrontation with Ahab. That command said "hide" (17:3) thyself. This one says "show" thyself. The former called for seclusion from the public eye; the latter called for manifestation. One shuns the public eye; the other seeks it. One withdraws from the conflict; the other pursues it.

So often the orders of "hide" and "show" are in sharp contrast to what the flesh wants at the time. When Elijah was ordered to Cherith to "hide" himself, it was a time when the flesh would have much impetus to want to "show" itself. Elijah was fresh from a daring, dramatic, and successful encounter with Ahab; and the natural desire of the flesh at that heady moment was not to go "hide" but to stay in sight and bask in the public eye. Public achievement seldom breeds a desire for seclusion! The flesh wants to stick around and sign autographs and receive accolades and other fawning attention of the admiring public. But such experiences are too frequently breeders of ruinous pride. Go "hide" is the best command then.

When the command comes to "show" oneself, it will generally come when the desire to "show" oneself is all but gone. After three and a half years in seclusion, Elijah would now have some good reasons to not want to "show" himself. For one thing his personal danger had increased considerably, for the famine had made him notorious in the eyes of his enemies Ahab and Jezebel. Also, Elijah would be leaving the comforts of his Zarephath circumstances where, because of a continuing miracle, his daily meals were no problem in spite of the famine. Leaving Zarephath to "show" himself meant having to scavenger for food in a land devastated by famine. Go "show" thyself would have little appeal at this time for Elijah.

God is most wise in when He gives His orders to us. He knows that the flesh wants the limelight for self-exaltation. But service for the Lord cannot be rendered well when self-glory is a prominent motivation. Therefore, God will often order our service so the flesh cannot glory. Thus when opportunity is great for the flesh to seek personal glory, He will "hide" us in obscurity lest we be ruined by self-glorying. But when it is time to "show" ourselves, He will have the circumstances so arranged that opportunity and desire for self-exaltation will be minimal.

## 2. The Reinforcement for the Precept

The command to "show thyself" was reinforced with a promise from God which said, "I will send rain upon the earth" (v. 1). The drought was going to end. It was a blessed promise! It would fulfill what Elijah had said when he first spoke to Ahab; namely, "there shall not be dew nor rain these years, *but according to my word*" (I Kings 17:1). Elijah, because he was in communion with God, would be the one who would say when it was going to rain or not rain, for God would reveal it to him so he could predict it.

Elijah had a tough assignment. But God gave inspiration,

help, and encouragement for fulfilling the assignment by giving him the promise of rain. Krummacher said, "Elijah, on this arduous path of faith, which directed him to Ahab, was supported by the promise, 'I will send rain upon the earth.' He could therefore thank God and take courage." Without that promise, the task of confronting Ahab would be much more difficult, if not impossible. But now, with the promise of rain, Elijah's past prediction to Ahab about his (Elijah's) controlling the weather would be reinforced and thus give Elijah great confidence and great encouragement for obeying the present precept.

Previously Elijah had also been encouraged to do God's commands by being given Divine promises. His orders to go to Cherith were accompanied by the promise, "I have commanded the ravens to feed thee there" (17:4). And the command to go to Zarephath was given with the promise, "I have commanded a widow woman there to sustain thee" (17:9). Elijah experienced in these promises what all will experience; that is, when God commands He accompanies the command with a promise which is to help inspire and enable obedience to the command.

Do your commands look hard and impossible? If so, then look for God's gracious promises to encourage obedience, to reinforce your compliance with the command. If God says, "Get thee out of thy country, and from thy kindred, and from thy father's house, unto a land that I will show thee" (Genesis 12:1), it will be accompanied by the promise, "I will make of thee a great nation" (Genesis 12:2). If God orders you to Egypt to speak to Pharaoh and to the Israelites about leaving Egypt, and you fear you cannot speak, God will give the promise, "I will be with thy mouth, and teach thee what thou shall say" (Exodus 4:12). If you are commanded to "Go ye . . . and teach all nations" (Matthew 28:19), and you fear going into the hostile world with a Gospel message many will reject and often with violence, then listen for the promise which says, "And, lo, I am with you always" (Matthew 28:20). If we pay attention, we will discover every command comes with adequate promises to greatly encourage us to obey.

## 3. The Response to the Precept

Elijah was given a command, and he was given a promise to encourage obedience to the command. So how did Elijah respond? As soon as God ordered him to "show thyself unto Ahab" (v. 1), we read that "Elijah went to show himself unto Ahab" (v. 2). What a noble response; what great obedience!

Going to Ahab this second time would be much harder to do than the first time. Pink said, "If much boldness had been required when he was called upon to announce the awful drought, what intrepidation was needed for him to now face the one who sought him with merciless rage." But increased difficulty does not diminish one iota the responsibility to obey. And Elijah, to his great credit, obeyed promptly regardless of the worsening of the situation. Joseph Parker said of this act of obedience, "The Lord said, Go, and Elijah went! Not, Elijah objected; Elijah reasoned; Elijah pointed out the difficulties; but simply Elijah went." Elijah obviously kept his eye on the promises more than on the problems.

Oh, that all of us so obeyed the Lord. But too often we are prone to argue, to point out the difficulties, to offer a myriad of excuses, and to suggest alternatives; God's promises notwithstanding. You would think, by the way many folk talk—and that includes a host of professing Christians—that God's commands are nigh unto impossible to obey, that they are impractical, outdated, and even absurd. But all such talk is only the talk of unacceptable rebellion; it is not the talk of acceptable reasoning. If God's orders are there, our obligation to obey is also there.

Military men are trained to obey at all times, no matter what the situation, so that no battle condition will be met with hesitant or rebelling men. Such would be disastrous to the winning of a war. So it is in spiritual matters, too. The General knows what to do. It is up to us to obey instantly, earnestly, and fully when given our orders.

## B. THE PROBLEM OF OBADIAH

On his way to see Ahab, Elijah encountered Obadiah. Obadiah

"was the governor of his [Ahab's] house" (v. 3); but in spite of his high position in wicked Ahab's government, he is said by Scripture to have "feared the LORD greatly" (Ibid.). Thus, Obadiah has been an enigma for ages. "Obadiah stands in Scripture as one of the most baffling and bewildering of all characters" (Phillip Keller). "It is startling to find such a man as Obadiah occupying so influential a position at Ahab's court" (F. B. Meyer). "There are few things in these books of Scripture more surprising and suggestive than the position of Obadiah in the palace of Ahab" (J. Hammond).

Some Bible commentators denounce Obadiah completely. Others exonerate him completely. But we do not believe either position is totally correct, for Obadiah was both right and wrong. Some things he did were very good, but other things he did were very bad. Some deeds should be commended, but others must be condemned.

## 1. He is to be Commended

To wholly condemn Obadiah is to ignore some plain statements of Scripture. The Scripture says he "feared the LORD greatly" (v. 3); and when Jezebel was killing the prophets, he "took an hundred prophets, and hid them by fifty in a cave, and fed them with bread and water" (v. 4). So he feared Jehovah and favored the prophets. Two commendable deeds. Let us look at them in more detail.

*He feared Jehovah.* To say Obadiah "feared the LORD greatly" indicates he was not a Baal worshipper. Baal worship was predominant in Israel during Obadiah's time. With few exceptions most people worshipped Baal. Therefore, the pressure to worship Baal would be great. Obadiah may even have been threatened at times in an effort to coerce him into worshipping Baal. False religion, in contrast to true religion, is notorious for this tactic of using force to gain worshippers. But regardless of the times, Obadiah did not worship Baal. This is most commendable indeed.

## Elijah

*He favored the prophets.* Jezebel burned with a hellish hatred for Jehovah's prophets and spilled their blood throughout the land. But she was not able to slay them all. Elijah escaped, of course, and others escaped too—some by the work of Obadiah. "For it was so, when Jezebel cut off the prophets of the LORD, that Obadiah took an hundred prophets, and hid them by fifty in a cave, and fed them with bread and water" (v. 4). Obadiah saved the lives of a hundred prophets of Jehovah. That was no trivial act! It required much courage, effort, and expense. He deserves high marks for this saving of the prophets. Any time you befriend a true prophet of God, you are to be commended. God takes special notice on how you treat His preachers. "Touch not mine anointed, and do my prophets no harm" (Psalm 105:15) tells us that fact.

So Obadiah does have some positive marks, some very good marks, in fact, on his report card; and these cannot be denied. But the bad marks cannot be denied either, and he had plenty of them which we will consider next.

### 2. He is to be Condemned

Those who wholly commend Obadiah cannot seem to get away from the statement that Obadiah "feared the LORD greatly"; and no matter how Obadiah acts later, they simply will not condemn him. We must remember, however, that though Obadiah "feared the LORD greatly," it does not mean he lived a spotless life or even a consistently good life. As an example, Lot is spoken of as being "just" and "that righteous man" and having a "righteous soul" (II Peter 2:7,8); but no one will be so foolish as to say everything Lot did was right. Nor will they be so foolish as to look upon Lot as basically a good man. Lot was a compromiser, he was carnal, and he was corrupt. Lot preferred the company of homosexuals to the company of godly Abraham. And Lot committed incest with both his daughters. That certainly is not commendable! It is to be condemned and ardently! "Righteous" or not, Lot behaved despicably much of the time.

So it was with Obadiah. Though Scripture says in one place

# The Wanderers

that he "feared the LORD greatly," we find much in Scripture elsewhere which does not commend him but rather condemns him. Our text condemns him in his employment with Ahab and in his excuses for not obeying Elijah.

*His employment.* Obadiah's job had him working with the wrong people and doing the wrong thing.

First, he worked with the *wrong people.* He was the "governor of his [Ahab's] house" (v. 3). Ahab and Jezebel were very, very wicked people. Obadiah's job called for him to work with them and keep company with them. To be in their presence in good graces and especially to be acceptably employed by them in a high, vital position would create some definite character problems. For one thing Obadiah would have to muffle his witness. He "could only have continued in this position by keeping silent as to his religious allegiance" (Leon Wood). Furthermore, he could not cry out in holy protest of their evil ways. To do so would have cost him his job and perhaps even his life. This silence, therefore, made him "an accomplice with Ahab and Jezebel in their diabolical deeds, for silence gives both consent and tacit endorsement to any action it does not oppose" (Phillip Keller). Thus Obadiah is to be strongly condemned. He had no business being so closely associated with Ahab and Jezebel. His job was one no follower of Jehovah should touch. It would be like a Christian being the right hand man of the beer magnate Augie Busch, or like a believer being a close associate of the notorious gangster Al Capone. These jobs are totally incompatible to being a Christian. You cannot work these jobs without compromising your Christian beliefs.

Some may insist that Obadiah was no different than Daniel and Joseph who both also held high government posts in governments run by men we would not call godly. But about the only similarity between these two men and Obadiah is that they were all three Jews. After that there is little, if any, similarity in their situations. Daniel and Joseph obtained their positions because of their testimony for God which was accepted by the kings who appointed them to their high office. And these kings, unlike Ahab and Jezebel, did not oppose Jehovah worship as ardently as Ahab and Jezebel. Several times in Daniel's experience, the king did indeed make laws which temporarily opposed Jehovah worship. But you will note that during one of those times, Daniel went to the lions' den rather than compromise his religious convictions. Obadiah did nothing of the sort! He was not a Daniel or a Joseph in character, and he did not have the employment situation Daniel and Joseph did, either. His employment by Ahab cannot be justified by Daniel's and Joseph's position in government.

Second, he was doing the *wrong thing*. This is not surprising, for he was employed by the wrong people. Obadiah was wandering about the countryside trying to find grass for Ahab's horses and mules which was certainly wrong in terms of priority. Rather than hunt for grass for dumb animals, even if they were important to Israel militarily, the important task at hand ought to be addressing oneself to the cause of the famine so that the famine could be stopped. Vance Havner said, "Obadiah was out . . . looking for grass when he should have been praying for rain and calling men to repent and return to God. Sin was the trouble then as it is today, and when men turned to God the showers fell. What a waste of time then . . . trying to find a little grass when the real trouble is politely ignored!"

We also need to note that it was unscriptural for Israel's kings to have horses, for Deuteronomy 17:16 decreed that the king of Israel "shall not multiply horses to himself." But Ahab did, and so did a lot of the other kings. That does not justify disobedience to the Word of God, however. The Word said no horses. Therefore, to be engaged in trying to save horses was Scripturally wrong no matter how many kings had horses. Yes, Obadiah was definitely in the wrong employment; and he deserves nothing but severe condemnation for it.

*His excuses.* When Elijah met up with Obadiah, he told Obadiah, "Go, tell thy lord, Behold, Elijah is here" (v. 8). Immediately Obadiah began making excuses why he should not obey Elijah's orders to inform Ahab of Elijah's whereabouts. This shirking of duty really condemned Obadiah, and what added to the condemnation is that Obadiah is not recorded as offering any objections to doing service for wicked Ahab when he was told to go hunt for grass for dumb animals; even though such a task, as we have just noted, was the wrong thing to be doing. No wonder Elijah told Obadiah that Ahab was "thy lord" (v. 8). Obadiah may have wished to make it appear that Elijah was his lord (v. 7), but in his actions it was Ahab. Like many professing Christians, Obadiah wanted folk to think he was submitting to God; but in fact, his actions said otherwise, and rather pronouncedly, too.

We note four of Obadiah's excuses. They have to do with acquittal, accusation, allegiance, and achievement.

First, *acquittal*. Obadiah began his excuses with a bit of self-righteous conceit. He said, "What have I sinned, that thou wouldest deliver thy servant into the hand of Ahab, to slay me?" (v. 9). Obadiah's question meant he did not think himself guilty of any sin which merited the severe chastisement of this supposed death errand. He would acquit himself of such a charge. Elijah was not charging him with any sin, but Obadiah's used his acquittal as a convenient excuse. In principle, it said he was too good for the job, and Elijah should not to risk such a good men on such a risky job. But the excuse exposed Obadiah's lack of dedication, for the job did in fact demand a good man.

Second, *accusation*. The worst excuse of all in Obadiah's arsenal was the excuse which accused God of being untrustworthy. Obadiah actually questioned the integrity of God. He described God as tricky and deceitful. He said to Elijah, "It shall come to pass, as soon as I am gone from thee, that the spirit of the LORD shall carry thee whither I know not; and so when I come and tell Ahab, and he cannot find thee, he shall slay me" (v. 12). What a corrupt view of God! It was a most blasphemous statement about God. How untrusting Obadiah was of God. How greatly the accusation condemns Obadiah.

Obadiah's view of God certainly reflected the influence of Baalism upon him. He had been around Baal's people so long and listened to them so much that he began to think Jehovah was like Baal. Baal was indeed considered capable of deceit and trickery, and so Obadiah thought Jehovah God was likewise.

Many professing Christians are like Obadiah. Because of their too close relationship with the world they talk and think like the world. You cannot keep close company with the ungodly without being defiled. You cannot watch the trash on TV (is there much else on TV?) without being defiled. You cannot fraternize with a materialistic, humanistic world and not defile your thinking. Separation may seem too much for most saints, but the fact is you either separate from the world or you will be defiled, for "evil communications [company, crowd] corrupts good manners" (I Corinthians 15:33).

This unholy fraternizing with the world has corrupted many churches, too, just as it affected Obadiah's religious thinking. Many church programs, services, doctrines, and policies reflect the thinking of the world much more than they reflect the teaching of the Word. They reveal that the membership is too close to unholy men and not close enough to a holy God.

Third, *allegiance*. Obadiah's third excuse was to proclaim his life long allegiance to Jehovah. "I thy servant fear the LORD from my youth" (v. 12). This is such a sick statement, for it comes right after he had just accused Jehovah of being tricky and untrustworthy. How hypocritical are the people who offer excuses for service. If Obadiah had truly feared God all these years, then this should make him eager to serve God by going after Ahab as Elijah has ordered. Allegiance is not an exemption from serving but an expectation for service.

Those who are quick to boast of their faithfulness are often those who lack faithfulness. When churches or schools or other groups keep telling you they are standing where they have always stood, it is a good indication they are not standing there; for if they were still standing there, they would not have to keep telling you the fact—you could easily see it was so.

Fourth, *achievement*. The last excuse Obadiah offered was his achievement of hiding one hundred prophets. He said, "Was it not told my lord what I did when Jezebel slew the prophets of the LORD, how I hid an hundred men of the LORD'S prophets by fifty in a cave, and fed them with bread and water?" (v. 13). This obnoxious boasting was another sick excuse. Instead of being an excuse, it ought to be a reason for his serving. If he has done so gallantly in the past, this should make him a good choice to inform Ahab of Elijah's return to the land. But as with some of the previous excuses, what should have been a reason for service was used by Obadiah as an excuse not to serve.

Pride never encourages service for the Lord. Though it boasts of past service for the Lord, the boasting is seldom done to show one's qualification for future service; but it is often a pitch to gain exemption from service instead. One sees this is some church members. They like to boast about how much they have done in the past. But do not be so naïve as to think this boasting is an indication they are wanting to do more service. Their boasting, besides seeking self-exaltation, says they have done their part (and gallantly, they want you to know); now let others do the work. But we need to remember that one's present spiritual condition is not determined by what we did in the past but by what we are willing to do in the present.

Obadiah had done a notable deed in saving the prophets, but he overrated it, and it was small compared to Elijah's deeds. If anyone could do some boasting, it would be Elijah. He lived in the midst of miracles and was even instrumental in raising one from the dead! Let Obadiah do something of that caliber. But Obadiah evidenced no knowledge of Elijah's exploits; and he was so self-centered, he thought his deed so great that surely someone would have told Elijah. Mackintosh said, "His hiding the prophets seems, in his estimation, to have been such a remarkable thing that he wondered if all had not heard it." Generally those who do the least boast the most. And those who are not living for God as they ought will be the first to tell you that they are really doing great things for God. Such boasting, however, is nothing but a cover-up for their compromising ways. And so Obadiah is greatly exposed and condemned here.

Obadiah may indeed be commended for some things he was and did; but he can also be condemned (and even more so) for what he was and did. He was not a good example of what a Christian ought to be. He was like Lot, who thought he could play both sides of the street. He lived a double standard. He tried to serve both Ahab and God, but such a stand is impossible. Jesus said, "No servant can serve two masters; for either he will hate the one, and love the other; or else he will hold to the one, and despise the other" (Luke 16:13). Those who try serving both Ahab and God will end up favoring the ungodly over the godly every time. So Obadiah was more willing to submit to Ahab than Elijah. He complained more of sacrifice in doing God's work (running an errand for Elijah) than he did in doing the devil's work (hunting grass for Ahab).

Obadiah does not impress us at all. And Obadiah did not seem to impress Elijah very much either. Spurgeon says, "I suspect that Elijah did not think very much of Obadiah. He does not treat him with any great consideration, but addresses him more sharply than one would expect from a fellow-believer." Obadiah finally did run the errand for Elijah, howbeit reluctantly. Obadiah had a long ways to go before his faith would burn within him and produce the prompt and enthusiastic obedience to God's service that Elijah exhibited.

We never hear of Obadiah again. He was no champion saint who would be found helping out Elijah at Mt. Carmel or exhorting his fellow Israelites to come back to Jehovah. Curiosity would like to know what happened to Obadiah. Experience and Obadiah's past would suggest he continued working with Ahab. And Obadiah's boasting would suggest he may have tried later to glory in the fact of his meeting with Elijah and in his carrying the news to Ahab that Elijah had finally been found.

## C. THE PERFORMANCE OF AHAB

Summoned by Obadiah, Ahab stopped his search for grass for

his horses and mules and came to met Elijah. Of the meeting of these two men, Matthew Henry said, "We have here [in] the meeting between Ahab and Elijah, as bad a king as ever the world was plagued with and as good a prophet as ever the church was blessed with."

Ahab was a detestable character. He was one lousy king and man. His character was corrupt through and through. He does not perform well in life to say the least. Our text gives us some details regarding Ahab's performance—of which little is complimentary. We will study his performance in his administration of his kingdom, in his accusation of Elijah, in his arraignment by Elijah, and in his assignment from Elijah.

## 1. The Administration of Ahab

Ahab, as king, did not administer his government well at all. We note two aspects of his administration which manifest his poor performance. He was insensitive of the needs of the people, and he was inept in solving the problems of the nation.

*He was insensitive.* After three and a half years of famine which had made Samaria into a wasteland, Ahab's great concern was not for the food problems of his people; but rather he was more concerned about food for his horses and mules. He was more concerned about his horses and mules dying from the famine than he was about the people dying. It is true that these horses and mules were something more than a few pleasure riding animals. They were vital to the military. Some were used, of course, for government officials to ride on during special government doings. But most of the horses and mules assembled by kings were for military purposes. They were for the cavalry and for the chariots. But to give them priority over the needs of his people was still very wrong. F. B. Meyer said, "It was this famine that brought out the true character of Ahab . . . his one thought was about the horses and mules of his stud; and his only care was to save some of them alive . . . what selfishness is here! Mules and asses before his people!"

Ahab's insensitiveness to his people's needs reminds us of the communist nations of our time. They, too, put more emphasis on maintaining their military might than upon solving the food problem of their own people. Such rulers only see the people as pawns to be used, not as people to be served. Human life means little to them. They will starve their people, impoverish them, and send them to battle capriciously, grossly insensitive of their lives and needs. And this spirit of Ahab is not limited to government leaders. It is also seen in the man who must have his smokes, his drinks, his gambling, and his fun and games even if it means his family has to go without food and clothes. It is seen in the woman who must have the abortion regardless of what it does to the baby's life. It is seen in the drug pusher and bartender who care little about the lives they are destroying but only about the money they rake in from their evil businesses. It is the hardness of heart which comes from forsaking God.

Ahab's greater concern for his animals than his people also reminds us of the fact that in time of spiritual sickness there is often a greater concern for animals than humans. Paganism, such as in India, protects livestock to the extent that it lets people starve to death instead of giving them meat from the protected livestock that wander about the country. In our country the animal rights movement is so zealous in protecting animals that it would stop a great source of food for humans and prevent testing for many health problems. Also in our country we have the Endangered Species Act which is so ridiculous in its priorities of protecting all sorts of animals that it has put thousands of people out of jobs for nothing more than the protection of such animals as an owl. All of this does not show the intelligence or compassion of people but the spiritual degeneration of people. It is simply an indication of how far we, like Ahab, have gotten away from God.

*He was inept.* In this terrible national crisis of the famine, Israel would find no help from their king! He did not propose any course of action which would save the nation. His grass hunting expedition was the best he could do. How pathetic.

But is this not like many governments today, even our own? When crises come, the efforts and programs they put forth to solve the problems of the land are about as helpful in stopping the problems as the grass hunting was in stoping the famine. The slaughter on the highway is a good example of the inept administration of our government. Alcohol slays thousands every year on the highway. What does our government do? They pass laws about air bags, seat belts, infant child seats, etc. while they conspicuously and adamantly refuse to take decisive action against the real problem—alcohol. If they would get rid of alcohol, they would drastically reduce the bloodletting on the highway. And getting rid of alcohol would minimize a host of other problems in society, too. But the government seems to prefer the grass expeditions instead.

Ahab's behavior in the critical hour of the famine reveals his poor administration. He was a very poor king. His administration only hurt the people; it did not help them.

## 2. The Accusation by Ahab

When Ahab and Elijah first met, Ahab greeted Elijah with a cutting accusation. He said, "Art thou he who troubleth Israel?" (v. 17). It was a bit of scornful, slanderous talk which would endeavor to make out that Elijah was the cause of all Israel's troubles.

In every age the ungodly hurl these slanderous and scurrilous, charges against the godly. "It is a common charge against the prophets and people of God. The saints are always in the wrong. It is always they who 'turn the world upside down' (Acts 17:6,8); always they who 'do exceedingly trouble our city' (Acts 16:20). Our Lord was accused of sedition. The first Christians were called 'enemies of the human race.' All manner of evil is said against them falsely" (J. Hammond).

This unjust accusation shows up even in the secular world. The police are castigated more than the criminal. Hitler blamed the Jews for Germany's problem when he, himself, was the number one problem. The United States was accused of being the aggressor and the troubler in Vietnam while the communists were pictured as only defending justice. And in the sixties the National Guard was blamed for the ugly confrontations on college campuses, not the leftist rabble rousers who would come to the campus and stir up the student body to riotous behavior.

This slanderous accusation is often seen in the church, too. Many churches have their Achans who cause all sorts of problems and scandals, but it is generally Pastor Joshua who is blamed for all the troubles. And instead of getting rid of the troubling Achans, the churches only add to their troubles by getting rid of their Joshua pastors.

It may hurt the faithful deeply when the ungodly accuse them of being troublemakers, but to be thusly accused by the ungodly is more of a compliment than a curse. F. B. Meyer said, "There is no higher testimony to the consistency of our life than the hearty hatred of the Ahabs around us." On the other hand, if Ahabs compliment instead of criticize you, it may mean you are not doing well at all in your Christian walk. Such is the condemnation of Obadiah. He was not rebuked by Ahab, but Elijah was. If, like Obadiah, you can get along well with the world, you are not getting along well with God. The praise of the world indicts a person more than it compliments. When an unholy community throws accolades at a church, it will not be a good church. A good church will be despised by such a community.

### 3. The Arraignment of Ahab

Ahab's diabolical accusation of Elijah was met by a stern denunciation of Ahab by Elijah. Elijah said, "I have not troubled Israel; but thou, and thy father's house, in that ye have forsaken the commandments of the LORD, and thou hast followed Baalim" (v. 18). Vance Havner said, "Ahab was the troublemaker, but Elijah was the troubleshooter." Elijah knew where the problem was, but Ahab did not. Ahab accused the wrong person, but Elijah put the finger on the sore spot and arraigned the right person. The arraignment was both intrepid and instructive.

# The Wanderers

*It was intrepid.* Elijah demonstrated tremendous courage in his indicting the king as the troubler of the land. Here is a prophet who has been the subject of a vigorous manhunt by the king. Now he is in the presence of this very ruler who so hated him and sought him. To stand before him and call him the troubler of the land takes tremendous boldness! "But the righteous are bold as a lion" (Proverbs 28:1).

A good many preachers could learn from Elijah's fearless expostulating. They are too often intimidated by their church members, especially the ones who have money and influence; and they fear to preach the whole counsel of God lest they upset these folk and jeopardize their (the preacher's) esteem and employment by the church. But Pink said, "Let not the ministers of Christ hesitate to boldly deliver their message, nor be afraid of the displeasure of the most influential in their congregations." If preachers do hesitate and fear to denounce sin and point out the troublemaker, they will never do much good. Vance Havner said, "Preachers used to point the finger at the individual and say, like Nathan to David, 'Thou art the man!' But today too many wave a hand at the audience in general and no one knows just who is being addressed." So no one gets the message, no one repents, and the trouble in the land continues.

*It was instructive.* Elijah did more than just call Ahab a troubler. He told Ahab why he was a troubler, and that is very important. He said Ahab had troubled the land because "Ye have forsaken the commandments of the LORD, and thou hast followed Baalim" (v. 18). Note the order here, first the Word is forsaken then Baal is followed. That which primarily constitutes a troubler is forsaking the Word of God. It is not the pursuing of Baalim that is the primary reason for being a troubler. Pursuing Baalim was simply a troubling result of forsaking the Word. But the basic, fundamental reason why one becomes a troubler is because he forsakes God's Word.

We wonder why we have so much trouble in our churches. The answer is that many of the church members have forsaken the Word of the Lord. They are not abiding by Divine principles in governing their lives. They, therefore, become troublemakers. Much trouble is brought into the churches because of apostate preachers, too. They will not preach the Word of God faithfully but forsake it in a wholesale way. Their unscriptural message troubles many souls in this life and will condemn many souls to eternal trouble in the next life.

We, like Israel of old, are troubled as a nation because both the citizens and the government leaders have forsaken the Word of God. Not only do we forsake it, but we outlaw it in schools and government places. All that this does is bring trouble. Our school officials, courts, and government leaders think they are helping to keep the peace in the land when they rule against the Bible; but how mistaken they are! They are only bringing trouble in the land, for forsaking God's Word invites great troubles.

Individually we need to take this fact to heart. Are we tempted to pursue a course of action that is disapproved by the Scriptures? Can we be so foolish as to think any gain will offset the trouble incurred by forsaking the Word? Is your proposed marriage Scriptural? Is your employment Scriptural? Is your lifestyle Scriptural? Others around you may put much pressure upon you to conform to the world and thus reject the Word, but that invites untold troubles to your life.

### 4. The Assignment for Ahab

Elijah did not stop with an arraignment of Ahab, he also gave Ahab an assignment. Ahab was indeed experiencing an unusual day. He was not used to being told he is the troubler of the land, and neither was he used to being given orders (unless it was from Jezebel who obviously ordered him around as she pleased). But here was fearless Elijah denouncing Ahab's sin and then giving him, the king, orders!

Elijah's orders for Ahab were to "Send, and gather to me [Elijah] all Israel unto mount Carmel, and the prophets of Baal four hundred and fifty, and the prophets of the groves [the prophets of Ashtoreth, the female god of Baalism] four hundred, which eat at Jezebel's table" (v. 19). Elijah is getting things ready for the contest on Mount Carmel. He wants the prophets of Baal there, and he wants the people of Israel there, too, so they can see who is God—Jehovah or Baal. So he orders Ahab to see to it that these people are assembled on Mount Carmel. This assignment for Ahab was fitting, and it was also fulfilled.

*It was fitting.* Elijah was wise to give the king this order, for "The king had the means for effecting the invitations. He would not have to visit all personally, as would Elijah, but by means of official posts would contact everyone efficiently and quickly" (Leon Wood). Ahab, as king, not only had the means to do the task; but he also had the advantage of government power to command the task be done and to order the people to assemble. And Ahab's close connection with the foul religion of Baalism gave him great advantage in seeing to it that the prophets of Baal were assembled at Mount Carmel, too. These prophets may have needed the pressure and persuasion of government orders to show up at Carmel. They had nothing to gain by this confrontation, but everything to lose. So it was very fitting that Ahab be given the assignment of assembling the people

*It was fulfilled.* Ahab's performance in regards to this assignment is amazing. Ahab obeyed Elijah! "So Ahab sent unto all the children of Israel, and gathered the prophets together unto mount Carmel" (v. 20). We are surprised that Ahab did not make some derisive remarks, and then scornfully ask Elijah who he thought he was to be ordering the king around. But Ahab did not do that. Ahab acquiesced to Elijah's assignment and plan for the Mount Carmel confrontation. Why? Matthew Pole gives four reasons why Ahab obeyed. He said, "He complied with Elijah's motion; [1] partly because it was so fair and reasonable that he could not refuse it with honor, nor without the discontent of all his people, this being proposed in order to their deliverance from this terrible famine; [2] partly, because the urgency of the present distress made him willing to try all means to remove it; [3] partly, from a curiosity of seeing some extraordinary events; and [4] principally, because God inclined his heart to close [agree] with it."

Indeed, principally, Ahab's compliance was a result of the power of God. F. C. Cook said, "There is no passage of Scripture which exhibits more forcibly the ascendancy that a Prophet of the Lord, armed with His spiritual powers, could, if he were firm and brave, exercise even over the most powerful and most unscrupulous of monarchs." Ahab obeying Elijah was nothing short of a miracle. But when we are doing God's work, we can expect God to work mightily on our behalf. It may not be a great sensational scene (it wasn't here), but the work accomplished will be astounding.

Churches have programs, schemes, gimmicks, pubic relations men, news conferences—but no power. We study psychology, psychiatry, examine the sales techniques of automobile salesmen, try Madison Avenue ways and means in order to do the work of God. But can we not learn from Elijah? His program was to walk uprightly with God, embrace the truth regardless and be acquainted with fervent prayer and with the Word of God. This gave him power, great power from God.

Seldom do we see much in church these days that can only be explained by the power of God. Vance Havner said that if what goes on at church can be explained, it is not of God. He said that if the Holy Spirit left the church the average church member would not miss Him and 95% of the church program would go on without a hitch. Unfortunately, Havner is right. The church needs to refocus its emphasis, pitch out its worldly programs that they are so enchanted with, and take up God's program. Then the church, though it would not be nearly as popular, would be much more powerful; and it could do something about stemming the tide of evil—something it definitely is not doing today.

# VI.

# THE WAVERING

## I KINGS 18:21–40

THE TIME HAS come for the great confrontation of Elijah with Baalism. The confrontation will take the form of a contest on Mount Carmel between Elijah and the prophets of Baal. The drought has conditioned the people, Ahab included, to be more receptive to the ministry of Elijah. So they have accepted his invitation to meet at Mount Carmel for the contest.

Regarding Mount Carmel, Edersheim said, "No spot in Palestine is more beautiful, more bracing, or healthful than Carmel . . . Up in the northwest, it juts as a promontory into the Mediterranean, rising to a height of five hundred feet. Thence it stretches about twelve miles to the S.S.E., rising into two other peaks. The first of these, about four miles from the promontory, is not less than 1740 feet high. Still further to the southeast is a third peak 1687 feet high which to this day bears the name of El-Mahrakah, or 'place of burning' (sacrifice). This, there can scarcely be a doubt, was the place of Elijah's sacrifice."

The location and topography of Mount Carmel made it a most suitable place for the contest. The plateaus made it possible for a great crowd to assemble to view the proceedings. Also the height at which the contest took place would make it possible for people some miles away to see the fire come down from heaven to consume Elijah's sacrifice. Jezebel, who was in Jezreel at the time, could have seen the fire come down if she had been looking that way.

The crowd which gathered at Carmel for the contest was considerable. It had to be in order to subdue and slay the 450 prophets of Baal. We estimate ten to twenty thousand at least. Many estimate only 1,500 to 2,000; but considering the slaughter of the prophets, the royal invitation (I Kings 18:20), the stress of the times which would greatly increase the interest in the meeting, and that Christ had crowds of 5,000 "besides women and children" (Matthew 14:21) in the same land, we think the crowd was easily in the five digit category.

The outstanding feature of the crowd, which Elijah deals with at the very outset, is that they were wavering. "The assemblage on Carmel was, for the most part, wavering between the claims of Jehovah and Baal" (D. Merson). The contest on Mount Carmel was to stop this wavering and to lead the people to follow Jehovah.

In this study of the contest between Elijah and the prophets of Baal, we will look at the preliminaries, the proclamations, and the persuasions of the contest.

## A. THE PRELIMINARIES OF THE CONTEST

Before Elijah began the contest, he first addressed the crowd. In this address he indicted the crowd and introduced the contest.

### 1. The Indicting of the Crowd

Elijah indicted the wavering practice of the people with a question. He asked, "How long halt ye between two opinions?" (v. 21). We will note the character, condemnation, and consequences of this practice.

*The character of the practice.* The wavering practice of the people is revealed in the word "halt." This word does not mean to stop and think something over, as some may believe. Wilson, in his *Old Testament Word Studies,* says the word means "to waver between two opinions [positions, attitudes, convictions, thoughts]." That is, a person never makes up his mind as to what position, action, or attitude he is going to take. One day a person leans this way, and the next day he leans the opposite way. In the case of the Jehovah-Baal issue, the people were try-

## The Wavering

ing to play both sides of the street. F. C. Cook said, "They wished to unite the worship of Jehovah with that of Baal—to avoid breaking with the past and completely rejecting the old national worship, yet at the same time to have the enjoyment of the new rites, which were certainly sensuous." This question of Elijah reveals where the people stood. They were not completely sold out to Baal, but neither were they loyal to Jehovah. The prophets of Baal were, of course, completely committed to Baal. But the people were vacillating.

*The condemnation of the practice.* The wavering of the Israelites was intolerable to Elijah. He said, "If the LORD be God, follow him; but if Baal, then follow him" (v. 21). This exhortation urged the people to make up their minds; to get in or get out; and to stop their politicking and talking out of both sides of the mouth. With Elijah it was either yes or no, true or false, good or evil, for or against, Jehovah or Baal. There was no middle ground with Elijah. It is the same with God. As I. M. Haldeman says of God, "He demands decision. You must be for Him or against Him. He will permit no compromise. A half way attitude before Him is impossible. You must declare yourself." God had no use for the Laodicean attitude. "Because thou art lukewarm, and neither cold nor hot, I will spew thee out of my mouth" (Revelation 3:16). Other Scripture also condemns this position. Deuteronomy 22:10 says, "Thou shalt not plow with an ox and an ass together." Matthew 6:24 says, "No man can serve two masters." Hosea 7:8 condemns it when describing the people as "a cake not turned."

That which added to the condemnation of Israel in practicing this halting position was that they had practiced it a long time. Elijah said, "How long" are you going to halt between two positions? Year after year they continued this wavering. And even after the drought came, they still continued to practice this vacillating habit.

This halting has been practiced a long time by all mankind. It is not unique to the Israelites of Elijah's day, but it also condemns our day. Krummacher says, "O that the generation of those halting ones did not constitute the majority among us! But, alas! is it not so?" Many want the smile of God but also the favor of the world. This attitude is seen in the advice Norman Vincent Peale gave a girl who asked if she should still work in burlesque now that she was a Christian. Incredibly, he encouraged her to keep working in burlesque. This attitude is seen in the practice of entertainers, such as Pat Boone, who hit the night clubs on Saturday night but sing in church on Sunday morning. It is Tennessee Ernie Ford singing the songs of the world in his program but at the end singing a hymn. This fools a lot of people, but not an Elijah who would see in it the double standard—the wavering between Baal and Jehovah.

It has always seemed clever and smart to man to have two faces and to show one or the other at advantageous times. The politician likes folks in the Bible Belt to think he is a Bible believer; but he wants the folk in a gambling community to think he is for gambling legislation, too. So he has different speeches, each suited to his crowd; and he thinks he is so clever to get both sides to vote for him. But this halting attitude is severely condemned in Scripture. It is a great breakdown of character. Clever, yes, but corrupt. And no cleverness will compensate for corruption.

*The consequences of the practice.* Israel was paying a big price for their vacillating habit. A drought had come and devastated the land. Fields were parched, water was becoming a real problem, food was scarce, people were dying, and a nation was threatened with its very existence. What a price for wavering, for trying to please both the world and God, for not taking the right stand. Taking a stand for God will extract a cost—there is no question about that. But what we need to realize is that failure to take a stand costs so much more. The halting and wavering practice looks like the easy road; it looks appealing to just keep quiet and say neither good nor bad. But the attraction of wavering is most deceitful.

## The Wavering

After Elijah spoke to them about halting, "The people answered him not a word" (v. 21). We should not be surprised at their silence for that is exactly what a waverer would do. It is a consequence of wavering. They would not "amen" Elijah for fear of offending the prophets of Baal, but they would not "boo" Elijah either lest they incur more of his wrath. Such silence is the mark of a coward.

Sometimes church business meetings exhibit this problem. Many of the members think by keeping quiet and not voicing themselves for or against an issue they will keep the peace. But their silence only opens the door for evil to monopolize the floor. Many a recommendation from the pastor and church leadership has been defeated because God's people would not take a stand either way. They were neither for nor against, and in so doing they think they will be friends with all concerned. But it will not work. They will not be friends with anyone. No one will trust them. Furthermore, the damage they do to the church will be immense. They will stifle the work of God, hinder its forward progress, dampen the enthusiasm and zeal of the faithful, and permit evil to gain great inroads into the church. Yes, the consequences of the double standard, of the wavering spirit are severe.

### 2. The Introducing of the Contest

After indicting the people, Elijah presented the plan for the contest between him and the prophets of Baal. He said, "Let them therefore give us two bullocks; and let them choose one bullock for themselves, and cut it in pieces, and lay it on wood, and put no fire under [it]; and I will dress [prepare] the other bullock, and lay it on wood, and put no fire under [it]. And call ye on the name of your gods, and I will call on the name of the LORD [Jehovah]; and the God that answereth by fire, let him be God" (vv. 23, 24). We will consider the essentialness, equitableness, expediency, and endorsement of this contest.

*The essentialness of the contest.* The proposed contest to

examine the claims of two religions was a very necessary thing. It was not just for mere entertainment. Good reasons supported having this contest.

First, the contest was needed because of the *precepts of God*. God ordered it. All that Elijah did was done "at thy word" (v. 36). Having this contest was following a principle which God has given all ages; namely, we are to examine religious claims to check on their validity. In the Old Testament, God gave ample guidelines to Israel on how to prove if a prophet was true or false. In the New Testament, we are told to "Try the spirits whether they are of God" (I John 4:1) and "prove all things" (I Thessalonians 5:21). Let us not fail to heed God's command to examine religious claims.

Second, the contest was needed because the *peril of error*. Israel had paid a terrible price because of Baal worship. The drought had nearly destroyed the land and the people. Failure to duly examine religious claims had brought untold harm to Israel. Examining religious claims is so necessary if one wishes to avoid the devastating consequences of being deceived by false religions. But, unfortunately, when it comes to religion, many are like Jacob was in regards to the report about Joseph's death. He did not examine things carefully. If Jacob had examined Joseph's coat, he would not have been in hopeless misery; for he would have seen that his boys' story was full of holes because the coat was not full of holes. A converted Jehovah Witness said that intellectual laziness was the reason so many folk are taken in by the cults. That is, they fail to test religious doctrine to see if it is true or not. So today a multitude of people gullibly take in the many bogus religious programs on radio and TV; and, as a result, they are oftentimes fleeced of their faith and fortunes because they did not take the time to examine the programs by the Word of God.

Third, the contest was needed because it would give *praise to truth*. While the contest would expose error for all its evil, it would on the other hand give great honor to truth. In Israel truth was being dishonored, rejected, and despised. It was time to reverse that practice. No land prospers when truth is not honored. Error needs to be examined to show it is fraud. Truth needs to be examined to show it is fact. And truth invites examination because it will be honored by the testing. So it was Elijah, not the prophets of Baal, who proposed the test. Error shuns examination. That is why the Roman Catholic Church, as an example, is so reluctant to allow examination of its relics to see if they are real or bogus. It is also why religious healers and other cults and isms shun honest examination.

*The equitableness of the contest.* This contest was a fair contest. Each religion was given the same test. It was one bullock and one altar for each. And each was to call upon their god, and the one that answered by fire would be the true God.

Giving the same test is vital. Error would not give the same test. It would look at error through rose-tinted glasses, but it would look at truth with a dirty microscope and magnify dislikes as evil facts. Sometimes church dissidents are this way with themselves and their pastor. They do not want to judge their pastor in the same way they judge themselves. To use runners' language, they would use a slow watch and a short and easy course to examine their performance but require the pastor to run a long and hard course with a fast watch. Of course, the people will have a better performance this way than the pastor because the test was not fair. But error is always this way in examining claims.

Another thing Elijah did to show his fairness was to let the prophets of Baal go first. This would show that Elijah was not staging a contest that would favor him and give him advantage over the prophets of Baal. Truth does not need special privilege to prove it is valid. Just give it a fair test, the same test as given to error; and truth will come out a winner. You do not need to cheat, lie, or manipulate in order to prove the claims of truth. Error needs unfairness in order to excel but not truth.

*The expediency of the contest.* This is expediency in a good sense. The contest was suited to the circumstances and to the belief of both the followers of Baal and Jehovah. Elijah said, "The God that answereth by fire, let him be God" (v. 24). This was a wise proposal because it was fire, and because it spoke of judgment.

First, it was *fire*. "The contest for fire was well-chosen. Both heathen mythology and Israel's own history made supernatural fire to be the highest way that divine approval could be shown for a sacrifice" (Leon Wood). Furthermore, fire was prominent in many other ways in both the religion of Baal and of Jehovah. In Baal religion, Baal was considered the fire-god. Baal was considered the fire or body of the sun, rather than the light. Fire would be just fine with the prophets of Baal, for it fit their god. (Interestingly, according to J. A. MacDonald in *Pulpit Commentary,* our word "bonfire" probably came from the Saxon word "Bael-fyr" which is all related to Baal and fire.)

Jehovah religion not only focused on fire on the altar; but fire was prominent in other significant experiences such as the burning bush which Moses saw and the pillar of fire which led the Israelites at night in the wilderness. Hence, no Jehovah follower would oppose fire as a test, either.

Second, it spoke of *judgment*. With the drought so severe, we might have expected the sign would have been rain instead of fire. We would have expected Elijah to have said the God Who answereth by rain, let him be God. The land needed water, but rain was not the sign—though it would seem to be the logical sign of Who was God. Instead, fire was the sign. Why? Because fire spoke of judgment, and judgment must first come before blessing. Though circumstances did call for rain, they first called for judgment upon Israel's sin. Before God's blessings come upon mankind, the principle is that judgment must fall upon the sin of man. As an example, the cross, where judgment came upon man's sin, must first occur before man can experience the blessing of salvation. So there is great wisdom in having fire, the symbol of judgment, be the test in this contest instead of rain.

## The Wavering

*The endorsement of the contest.* After Elijah proposed the contest plan, "All the people answered and said, It is well spoken" (v. 24). The people finally took a stand. They endorsed the plan unanimously.

There was great wisdom in Elijah presenting the plan to the people and not just to the prophets of Baal. For "When the appeal of Elijah to the people had gained their applause, he had the prophets of Baal at his command . . . The voice of the people rendered it impossible for them to evade the trial" (J. A. MacDonald). Had Elijah talked first with the prophets of Baal, they could have become very difficult regarding the plan. They might have wanted to change some of the details to benefit them. The people, wavering as they were, would not be inclined to give much support, if any, to Elijah. The contest then would have fallen flat. But by giving the plan to the people and having them approve it so enthusiastically, the prophets of Baal had no recourse but to go along with it.

## B. THE PROCLAMATIONS OF THE CONTEST

The primary proclamation of the contest was that Jehovah was God. But in proclaiming Who was God, the contest also proclaimed a number of distinctives of both the Baal and Jehovah religions. We want to look at some of those distinctives in this study. In doing so, we will see how great the contrast was between these religions and also how great the contrast is between true and false religions in any day.

### 1. The Distinctives of Baal Worship

A number of things were proclaimed about Baal worship during this contest. We will look at the representation, dissimulation, dedication, laceration, and mortification of Baal worship.

*Representation.* The constituents of Baal represented quite an impressive group in both numbers and worldly status. They had many more prophets than Jehovah. On Mount Carmel they outnumbered the prophets of Jehovah 450 to 1 (v. 22). They had more followers than Jehovah, too. Scripture says there were only 7,000 "which have not bowed unto Baal" (I Kings 19:18), which meant those who bowed to Baal numbered in the millions.

Baalism also had much worldly status because of its governmental representation. In fact, as we noted earlier, it was the government (particularly Jezebel) which promoted Baalism. But the worship of Jehovah had little representation in high places. Those who embraced it were not in the status positions of life. They were of the despised and rejected group. Oh yes, there was Obadiah, who had a very high position in government. But he was no champion for Jehovah. Baalism had silenced him and caused him to compromise. Generally that is the case with those in high positions who claim to be Christian. They do not honor their faith by their prestigious office, rather the office weakens their faith and corrupts their manners.

False religions usually do much better than true religions in their worldly representation. They generally have more followers than true religion and more earthly rank and respect. But truth is not verified by popularity nor by the celebrity status of its members. It is not who is the loudest and longest or who is the first and foremost that establishes which is right. But too often we judge things by popularity and prestige anyway. If it is popular, we think it is right; if it is in an important position, we think it must be proper. The church with the biggest offerings and the most impressive statistics is judged the best church. But on Mount Carmel it would be the fire, not any of these other things, which would establish Who was God.

*Dissimulation.* Fraud abounds in false religions. Deceit is one of their most common trademarks. They are ever feigning, dissimulating, pretending, and misleading. So twice Elijah told the prophets of Baal to "put no fire under" the sacrifice on the altar (vv. 23,25). Why? Because that was the practice of Baalism. They secretly added fire to their altars to make it look like Baal was answering them with supernatural fire. Some of the altars of paganism had little dugouts under the altar where a priest could hide and covertly set the sacrifice on fire. But here on Mount Carmel it would be different. "For the first time in their history, these false priests were unable to inset the secret spark of fire among the faggots which lay on the altar" (Pink).

Much false fire is evident in many religious movements. From the "strange fire" of Nadab and Abihu (Leviticus 10:1) in Moses' day to the fleshly fires of the tongues and healing movements of our day, we can witness this false fire. Many want to stir up the people; but lacking true spirituality, they substitute their own fleshly fire which only destroys.

Satan is a liar and the father of lies (John 8:44); and we must not be so naïve as to think that just because something is religious it is honest. Check for the truth. Where it is lacking, validity is lacking.

*Dedication.* False religious movements certainly do not lack for zeal. In fact, they often put the followers of truth to shame by their earnestness. The prophets of Baal put on quite a show on Mount Carmel. For some six hours they were loud and long in crying for Baal to answer them. And in their earnestness "they leaped upon [or around] the altar" (v. 26) and "cut themselves . . . with knives and lancets, till the blood gushed out upon them" (v. 28). What zeal! What dedication! Also what excitement and entertainment for the people who witnessed all of the actions of the Baal prophets. As one said, "Of one thing I am assured—the devil-dancer never shams excitement" (Caldwell, as quoted by J. A. MacDonald in *Pulpit Commentary*).

But earnestness is not the test of validity. Sincerity does not guarantee truth. We must not be like Charlie Brown who lamented after losing a baseball game, "One hundred and eighty four to nothing. I don't understand it. How can we lose when we're so sincere?" Dedication is great, but only when it is on the right track. Apostle Paul said Israel had a "zeal of God, but not according to knowledge" (Romans 10:2). Many are in that category. But such zeal only makes the results very frustrating. As Joseph Parker so aptly said of the enthusiasm of the prophets of Baal and its results, "Prodigious exertions finish in prodigious emptiness."

*Laceration.* As we noted above, the prophets of Baal "cut themselves . . . with knives and lancets, till the blood gushed out upon them" (v. 28). Cruelty is a common distinctive of false religions. Pagan gods are supposed to be appeased and pleased with the blood of humans. So the prophets of Baal lacerated themselves till the blood flowed around the altar on which they were sacrificing to Baal. It had to be a gory sight. "The whole appalling performance was a bestial blood bath. Even the toughest onlookers in the crowd must have blanched at the bedlam" (Phillip Keller). Paganism is basically cruel. But what would you expect of religion that has the devil behind it, for he is a murderer (John 8:44). The worshippers of Jehovah were expressly forbidden to "cut yourselves" (Deuteronomy 14:1). But when God is left out, men become cruel. And this is true of governments, such as communism as well as religion. Governments which reject God's way and prohibit worshipping of Him are cruel, barbaric, and unmerciful.

*Mortification.* The future of truth is honor; but the future of error, like the idolatry of Baalism, is shame, great shame. Isaiah said, "They shall be ashamed, and also confounded, all of them; they shall go to confusion together that are makers [and worshippers] of idols" (Isaiah 45:16). The time had come for Baalism to be brought low. And what mortification it was for the prophets of Baal. They received no response from their god, they gained no respect from Elijah, and they experienced no regard from the people.

First, they received *no response* from Baal. Of course not. Baal is no living creature. Call upon him forever if you will, but you still will get no response. They "called on the name of Baal from morning even until noon . . . But there was no voice, nor any that answered" (v. 26). It was an embarrassing experience. But with the true God, it is a different story. He says, "Call unto me, and I will answer thee, and show thee great and mighty things, which thou knowest not" (Jeremiah 33:3).

Second, they gained *no respect* from Elijah. "And it came to pass at noon, that Elijah mocked them, and said, Cry aloud; for he is a god, either he is talking, or he is pursuing, or he is in a journey, or peradventure he sleepeth, and must be awaked" (v. 27). Some have criticized this mocking by Elijah. But Matthew Henry says, "The worship of idols is a most ridiculous thing, and it is but justice to represent it so and expose it to scorn." We agree. Those who do not like Elijah's words are the same ones who do not like preachers to call sin by its real names. They do not want sin to be put in its proper place. They would salvage some honor for sin. They are compromisers who only reveal the corruption of their own heart by their criticism. Such folk will be of little help in stopping evil.

It is interesting that the prophets of Baal did not seem to be offended by the sanctified sarcasm of Elijah. Pink says, "So infatuated and stupid were those devotees of Baal that they do not appear to have discerned the drift of his words, but rather to have regarded them as containing good advice." Oh, the blindness of those in false religion. Error always blinds; and the longer you embrace it, the more blind you become. It is the curse of God for rejecting truth. "As they did not like to retain God in their knowledge, God gave them over to a reprobate mind" (Romans 1:28).

Third, they experienced *no regard* from the people After the prophets of Baal had gone on from morning till the time of the "evening sacrifice [which was the middle of the afternoon, for the time of the evening sacrifice was about 3 P.M.] . . . there was neither voice, nor any to answer, nor any that regarded" (v. 29). Matthew Poole said that "nor any regarded" means "there was no attention." This, he added, not only can refer to their god who did not answer them, but also to "the people, who were now tired out with so long attention and expectation; and therefore more readily deserted them and approached to Elijah and his altar, at his call." These false prophets gave the people nothing to cheer about, nothing to rejoice in, nothing to encourage their hopes. So the people finally left them and turned towards Elijah. How mortifying it must have been for Baal's prophets to be so rejected by the people. For false religion, unlike true religion, lives and dies on the praise of men.

## 2. The Distinctives of Jehovah Worship

The great distinctives of Jehovah worship, revealed at the contest on Mount Carmel, can be seen in the invitation Elijah gave to the people, the restoration of the altar, the saturation of the altar with water, the supplication by Elijah to God, and the conflagration of the altar by the fire from above.

*Invitation.* When it became Elijah's turn to offer a sacrifice, he said "unto all the people, Come near unto me" (v. 30). This invitation spoke of the honesty of Jehovah worship, and it spoke of the grace of Jehovah.

First, the invitation spoke of the *honesty of Jehovah worship.* In contrast to Baal worship, Jehovah worship was not filled with dishonesty. True religion has nothing to conceal, nothing to hide. It can invite people to come near to examine closely the facts. Truth begs to be examined, investigated, and scrutinized; for when it is, it will shine forth in its glory. Hence, Jesus said, "Search the scriptures" (John 5:39). Examine them; study them closely; look at them in detail. You will not come away in disbelief when you do that. The Bible is not so poorly put together and so weak in its claims that we dare not search it for fear of being disappointed. Truth says, "Come near."

Second, the invitation spoke of the *grace of Jehovah.* How wicked Israel had been and for a long time. God would have been justified had He destroyed them all. But God's grace would save the vilest sinner; and so grace gives the Israelites an invitation to come back to God. Whenever God says, "Come," it is grace. God could say, "Get" or "Beat it" or as He did to Satan, "Get thee behind me" (Luke 4:8). Someday God will say to those who refuse Him, "Depart from me, ye cursed, into everlasting fire" (Matthew 25:41). What a terrible day when grace is no longer offered to man. But it will be man's fault, not God's.

Grace is not a characteristic of false religions. Their gods are cruel, vindictive, heartless, and unloving. We only learn of grace through true religion.

*Restoration.* "And he repaired the altar of the LORD [Jehovah] that was broken down" (v. 30). Elijah needed an altar on which to put his sacrifice. So he restored the one on Mount Carmel which had been broken down. We note the communion, condition, construction, and contents of the altar of Jehovah.

First, the *communion* of the altar. The altar speaks of communion with God. One's communion with God can be easily discerned by whether or not he has an altar in his life. As an example, when Abraham was in good communion with God, he had an altar. But when he went astray, he left the altar.

True religion promotes communion with God. It brings fellowship with God. It does not drive us from God as false religion does (it drives multitudes from communion with God). We need this communion with God. It is absolutely essential to the well-being of our life. Do you have an altar in your life? We often call it a devotional time. But whatever we call it, we need to have it.

Second, the *condition* of the altar. The altar of Jehovah on Mount Carmel had been broken down. Baal worship had so influenced the people that they had broken down the altars to Jehovah. Elijah mentioned this to God later when he was at Horeb. He said, "For the children of Israel have . . . thrown down thine altars" (I Kings 19:10).

False religion is very destructive. It destroys so many good things, and it especially destroys us spiritually. But true religion is in the business of repairing, restoring, and healing. If your life has been made a shambles by false religions, by false philosophies of the world, come back to the Lord and let Him put your life together again.

Third, the *construction* of the altar. Elijah built the altar with "twelve stones" (v. 31). This spoke of the twelve tribes of Israel and was a rebuke of the division of the nation—a division which had its root cause in idolatry. It started with Solomon because of his many wives, and it ruined him and divided the nation. False religions divide, they put a great division between God and man, and they also break up sanctified relationships of man with man. But true religion unites. It brings people together through the common bond of the Lord.

Note here that Elijah built the altar "in the name of the LORD" (v. 32). It was not constructed in the name of Elijah or in some denomination. Elijah has his place and so do denominations; but we need to build our churches, our schools, and our ministries in the name of the Lord, not in our own names. Religions and religious leaders which emphasize themselves and not God expose themselves as fraudulent.

Fourth, the *contents* of the altar. Two items especially attract our attention on the altar. One was the sacrifice. It was a bullock. A bullock was a sin offering. It recognized the sinfulness of man and the need for the mercy of God. How appropriate this was in the case of Israel. Sin was the problem in the land of Israel, and God's mercy was desperately needed to forgive the people and heal the land. A bullock was also on Baal's altar, but it was Elijah who directed that the bullocks should be on both altars. True religion knows what the real problem is and also what the right answer to the problem is.

The other item on the altar was the wood. "He put the wood in order" (v. 33). This reminds us that true religion will put things in order in our life. Sin brings disorder and confusion. False religion only adds to it. But true religion takes us to the Lord Who straightens things out in our life.

Putting the wood in order also tells us Elijah would do things "decently and in order" (I Corinthians 14:40) in the Lord's work. God's work demands we do things right. But so many churches leave the "wood" scattered around haphazardly. Neatness, tidiness, efficiency, and orderliness are often lacking in the care of facilities and in the administration of the business of the church. It is disgusting to see how messy things get in the Lord's work. Oftentimes the reason the wood is not put in order is that people simply do not care. They only want to do just enough to get by. They are not respectful of God's work.

*Saturation.* After putting the wood in order and cutting the bullock in pieces, Elijah said, "Fill four barrels with water, and pour it on the burnt sacrifice, and on the wood" (v. 33). After this was done, he had it repeated two more times. This saturated the altar with water. The water demonstrated the practice of integrity, the power of God, and the priority of the Word.

First, it demonstrated the *practice of integrity.* As we noted earlier, one of the contrasts in distinctives of Baalism and Jehovah religion was in the matter of integrity. Baal worship was notorious for deceit, as are all false religions. Jehovah worship had integrity as a hallmark. Pouring water on the sacrifice emphasized that the fire would be supernatural—not started clandestinely by man.

Oh, for more integrity in God's people. The followers of the One Who said He was the Truth should be characterized by truthfulness. But, alas, this is often not the case. Church statistics are often padded, lied about, and dishonestly reported. Church members are often dishonest when they file their income tax reports. Christian salesmen and business men are often no different than the world in lying about their products.

One would think that people would have rejected Baalism a long time ago because of its obvious dishonesty and would have followed a man like Elijah whose honesty was so evident. But the fact is people often prefer dishonesty to honesty. The unholy prefer the unholy. Isaiah said the rebellious Israelites tell their prophets to, "Prophesy not unto us right things; speak unto us smooth things, prophesy deceits" (Isaiah 30:10).

An honest ministry will offend many. Let a church get an honest pastor and the church may lose a number of members. Many leave the church because they are corrupt and cannot stand to be in the presence of a man of God who walks in truth.

We hear little about this fact today, but we ought to hear more.

Second, it demonstrated the *power of God*. False religion could not get a fire started in the middle of the day when the sun was the hottest and when everything was tinder dry. But true religion can start a fire when the sacrifice, wood, etc. are thoroughly saturated with water.

How this demonstrates the power of God in the gospel. The Gospel will remedy man's problems unlike any of the world's exalted programs. The gospel will solve more problems in five minutes than all the boasted programs of the world will solve in five millenniums.

This also demonstrates the power of God in working on our behalf in our daily life. God delights to work when conditions are the worst, and He often lets our circumstances get drenched with impossibilities before He works. This assures that He will be given the glory. So it was on Mount Carmel. It was obvious in this contest that the circumstances were being arranged so Baal would have every advantage compared to Jehovah. They offered their sacrifice first, they had the advantage of the heat of the day to kindle fire on the altar, they greatly outnumbered Jehovah's prophets, and their opponent's altar was drenched with water. But all of this simply made the triumph of Jehovah greater. It emphasized the superiority of Jehovah over Baal. Truth does not need earthly advantages to come out ahead. Error does but not truth.

Third, the water demonstrated the *priority of the Word*. Elijah had the water poured on the altar because God commanded it (v. 36). It did not look like the smart thing to do; in fact, it looked like it would hinder the desired result. But the Word commanded, and Elijah obeyed, for true religion puts great priority on the Word.

This reminds us of Peter who was instructed by Christ to "Launch out into the deep, and let down your nets for a draught" (Luke 5:4). It was not the time to fish, and Peter's recent fishing experience indicated it was not the place to fish either. But his response was, "Nevertheless, *at thy word* I will let down the net" (Luke 5:5). The Word was given the priority in his life, and, as a result, he received much blessing; for he caught many fish.

Are we willing to put the Word in such a prominent place in our lives? Will we obey the Word of God even though its commands look impractical and impossible? Are we willing to obey the Word even though it seems to oppose what we are doing rather than support it?

Several questions—one concerning the obtaining of the water and one concerning the trench—need to be answered here.

First, where did Elijah get the water since the land was parched dry by the drought? The answer is he could have gotten it easily from the Mediterranean Sea or from a nearby spring (which tradition says ran even in the driest of times) or from the brook Kishon (which some say also ran even in the driest of times). The spring and brook would be supported at their source by the Mediterranean Sea, thus helping them to continue even in times of drought. Earlier, we noted this effect of the Mediterranean Sea in regards to the water supply at Zarephath.

Second, why did Elijah dig the trench around the altar? One reason was to catch the water; so when the water was poured on the altar, it would stay near the altar and would not run all over the ground where the people were. The people were gathered around Elijah; and without the trench, the people would have scattered when all the water ran over the dry ground making instant mud. Another reason was that the trenches filled with water served to increase the display of the power of God when the fire "licked up the water that was in the trench" (v. 38).

*Supplication.* Elijah, as did the prophets of Baal, prayed before the altar. But his praying was unlike the praying of the prophets of Baal. It did not include loud shouting, was not long (it was just a bit over sixty words), and was not accompanied by the lacerating of the body. But length and loudness and lacerations are not proofs of nobility in prayer. The nobility of Elijah's supplication is in seen in the four requests he made to God.

First, he prayed for the *glory of God*. "Let it be known this day that thou art God in Israel" (v. 36). It was not rain first, but God's glory first. The reason for their problems was that God was not first. In our praying we must correct the lack of honor for God before we get to the lack of rain. True religion makes the primary petition and desire of any prayer to be the glory of God. Many do not do this, however. Some, as an example, pray for the conversion of a girlfriend or boyfriend primarily so they can marry them, not primarily for the glory of God. If they were interested in the glory of God, they would not be going with the unsaved person in the first place.

Second, he prayed for his own *testimony*. He said, "Let it be known . . . that I am thy servant" (v. 36). This is not bragging. This is a wise prayer which says he wants everyone to know Whom he lives for and Whom he serves. It is a prayer that his testimony might ring true regardless. That is not an easy prayer to pray when you are outnumbered 450 to 1 as Elijah was. It is not an easy prayer to pray when the crowd is not on your side. Too often in such situations folk hope no one will find out they are a Christian. But Elijah wanted all the world to know where he stood. True religion is not ashamed.

Are you willing to be this kind of a testimony for Christ in the midst of heathendom? Are you willing to pray that there will be no doubt in other people's minds where you stand regarding Jesus Christ? Your answer reveals the genuineness of your faith.

Third, he prayed for the *exalting of God's Word*. He said, "Let it be known . . . that I have done all these things at thy word" (v. 36). As we noted earlier, true religion will put great emphasis on the Word of God. It will desire the Word to be front and center, and will want the Word to be the authority. False religions talk about other books and writings. And carnal churches give themselves away by their lack of emphasis on the Word. Many churches which claim to be in the fundamentalist camp do not give much place to the Word in their program. Such churches, though they have a fundamental name and reputation, are not good churches. Get in a church which gives much attention to the Word of God. Remember that where the Word is not emphasized, you have evidence of spiritual corruption. Avoid that at all costs.

Fourth, he prayed for *revival* amongst the people. He said, "Hear me, O LORD hear me, that this people may know that thou art the LORD God, and that thou hast turned their heart back again" (v. 37). He still has not prayed for rain yet! He is wise; they needed revival before they needed rain. Mankind's primary need is spiritual, not material; and true religion puts the emphasis on spiritual programs, not on social programs. Keep first things first. It is revival then rain, not rain then revival.

That which reveals much decay in fundamental circles today is an increase emphasis on the social, physical, and material in the church program. Recreation is getting more attention than consecration. More emphasis is being placed on suppers than sermons. We have fewer Bible classes and preaching times at our church camps so we can have more time for socializing and playing games. It has been a subtle change over the last couple of decades, but it has been a bad one.

*Conflagration.* "Then the fire of the LORD fell, and consumed the burnt sacrifice, and the wood, and the stones, and the dust, and licked up the water that was in the trench" (v. 38). The fire fell in abundance and it fell on the altar.

First, it fell in *abundance*. It consumed everything, not just the sacrifice and the wood; but it also consumed the stones, the dust, and the water. "Where moments before an altar and sacrifice had stood shining in the sun, there now remained only a burned, fire-blackened depression in the scorched soil" (Phillip Keller). What great evidence that Jehovah is God! What a great demonstration of the power of Jehovah God!

A distinctive principle of true religion is that proof is abundant for its claims as it was here. Who was God? He was Jehovah! Was there any doubt? Absolutely not! The evidence was overwhelming. Yet, today, in spite of overwhelming evidence, men still reject the proof for truth and cling tenaciously to error.

Like Pharaoh of old, they have so hardened their hearts that they simply cannot believe even though the evidence is super abundant. Woe be to the soul that rejects such evidence!

Second, it fell on the *altar*. It did not fall on the people. The great Gospel message of substitution is seen here in where the fire fell. Sin demands judgment, and fire speaks of this judgment. But the sacrifice took the judgment so sinners did not have to suffer for it. Christ is the great substitute for our sins. He died on the cross, and the fiery judgment of God fell on Him instead of on us. When Christ said, "I thirst" (John 19:28) it was more than just a physical problem—it spoke of the fire of the judgment of God which came upon Him for our sins. The rich man in hell cried for water because he was experiencing the fiery judgment of God upon him for his sins. Christ was not his Savior; so he suffered for his own sins and is still suffering in the fire. But we do not have to have the fire fall on us. We can come to Christ and be saved through Him from the just judgment due for our sins. That is the great message of true religion. it does not focus on works, on our own merits, on our own blood shedding (such as the blood shedding of Baal's prophets); but it focuses on the work of Christ on the cross for us.

## C. THE PERSUASIONS OF THE CONTEST

The result of the contest was indeed persuasive. It persuaded the people to do two things. They were persuaded to exalt Jehovah and to execute evildoers.

### 1. The Exaltation of Jehovah

"When all the people saw it [the consuming fire], they fell on their faces, and they said, The LORD, he is God; the LORD, he is God" (v. 39). We want to note the declaration of this praise and the delinquency of this praise.

*The declaration of this praise.* This praise of Jehovah declared that He was God and that Baal was not God. It was a great declaration. It was a healing declaration. In New Testament terminology, it declared the Deity of Jesus Christ. The Jehovah of the Old Testament is the Jesus of the New Testament, and the only right way to praise Jehovah/Jesus is to praise Him as God. The Deity of Christ is a great truth which true religion will declare. But false religions—be it modernism or the cults—will oppose it vigorously. As an example, some years ago Harry Emerson Fosdick, a leader among modernists in our country, wrote a book, *The Hope of the World,* in which he had a sermon entitled, "The Peril of Worshiping Jesus." What a farce! There is no hope for a world that thinks in terms of peril regarding the worshipping of Jesus. But false religion strongly opposes the Deity of Christ. They prefer their Baals to Jehovah.

*The delinquency of this praise.* It was right that the crowd on Mount Carmel should fall on their faces and shout out that Jehovah was God. But oh, if they had only done it sooner. What catastrophe could have been avoided if they had not been delinquent in the praise of Jehovah. The delay in praising Jehovah as God cost them just about everything they had. When you put off obedience to God, when you procrastinate honoring God, you add to your judgment and to your loss of blessings. So many will tell us that they have things in their lives that are not right, but they never do anything about them. How perilous, how tragic.

## 2. The Execution of Evildoers

After the crowd had prostrated themselves in praise of Jehovah, Elijah said to them, "Take the prophets of Baal; let not one of them escape. And they took them. And Elijah brought them down to the brook Kishon, and slew them there" (v. 40). This execution of the evil prophets was proof, proper, and partial.

*Proof.* It is one thing to talk, but it is another thing to walk. The talk which praised Jehovah sounded good, but the people would have to prove their profession by their deeds. Their confession would be tested by Elijah's command. And to their credit they did obey Elijah and helped him execute the prophets of Baal. Thus they gave evidence that their praise of Jehovah was something more than just words.

*Proper.* Many criticize the slaying of the 450 prophets of Baal. Some are very severe in their criticism. Others say it was allowed in Elijah's day, but it should not be practiced in our day because our New Testament age is of a different spirit than that of Elijah. All such talk and philosophy are the same attitudes which are behind opposing capital punishment. It is not good reasoning at all. The slaying of the prophets of Baal was proper. It was proper for two important reasons: it was Scriptural and it was beneficial.

First, it was proper because it was Scriptural. The Word of God commands false prophets to be slain. (Deuteronomy 13:5). You criticize this destruction of Baal's prophets and you criticize the Word of God! If Jehovah is God you must obey His commands.

Second, the slaying of the prophets was proper because it was beneficial. These false prophets had brought untold harm to Israel. "These prophets had been the cause of the grievous famine, the death of . . . human beings not a few. They had also sacrificed thousands of dear children to Baal. The rites of Baal were frequently celebrated with human victims . . . These men suffered nothing but the due reward of their deeds" (J. H. Cadoux).

The greatest harm done to society by these prophets of Baal was spiritual. Through their teaching they damned the souls of multitudes. This is the worst harm of all. No crime is greater than leading souls to a Christless grave. Slaying the prophets of Baal would not only benefit society physically and materially; but, most importantly, it would also spare souls from eternal damnation.

To not deal with these evil prophets would further curse the land. Either slay the cruel criminal or many innocent will be slain. Whom you want to survive reveals your heart!

## The Wavering

*Partial.* The judgment of the false prophets was partial, that is, it was not complete Not all the prophets connected with Baal worship were slain. All 450 prophets of Baal were slain, true; but the 400 prophets of Ashtoreth (female counterpart of Baal worship) were not slain. They did not come to Mount Carmel as ordered by Elijah. They were the ones who ate at Jezebel's table. She may have suspected trouble when Elijah ordered them (through Ahab) to come to Mount Carmel, and so she got Ahab to leave them home. But Ahab's failure to bring these 400 prophets to Mount Carmel cost him dearly. He may have thought he and Jezebel were pulling a fast one on Elijah and God, but he only pulled a bad one on himself. This is discovered in I Kings 22. There is the record of Ahab seeking advice from the prophets about going to battle at Ramoth-gilead. Micaiah, God's faithful prophet, advised him not to go. But the 400 prophets that did not show up at Mount Carmel advised Ahab to go to battle. Ahab listened to those 400 false prophets and as a result was killed in battle.

No one mocks God and gets away with it. About the time you think you have pulled a fast one on God, you will discover you only pulled a bad one on yourself. The 400 escaped judgment that day but to Ahab's future tragedy. What a lesson on the peril of not obeying completely!

# VII.

# THE WATER

I KINGS 18:41–46

ELIJAH WITNESSED A great and thrilling victory for Jehovah on Mount Carmel. Jehovah was proclaimed as God and the 450 prophets of Baal were slain. God can now bless the land. Rain is on the way. The dried and parched ground will once again be watered by rain after three and a half years of drought. Water will again flow in the rivers and streams. The wells will again be filled with water. The grievous famine is about to end because Israel has dealt firmly with the cause of the famine. It is always this way. Once we deal with the sin that is causing our problems, we will remove the hindrance to blessing. But how slow we are to deal with the hindering sins in our lives and churches and communities. We try a multitude of ways to obtain the blessing without removing the hindrances, but all to no avail. For we cannot tolerate the virus and still enjoy good health.

That triumphant day on Mount Carmel was a most momentous day for Israel as well as for Elijah. Few days in the history of God's chosen people will stand out like this one. God answered by fire and gave tremendous proof of the validity of Jehovah and of the falsity of Baal. The people responded by giving earnest praise to Jehovah; and in an act no one would have predicted in the preceding years when Baal worship was so popular and powerful in the land, the people helped Elijah slay the prophets of Baal. What conversations the people would have on their way home. What deep thoughts would penetrate their hearts. And before many of them reached home, they would be deluged with a most welcomed rain. No one likes to be caught out in a rain storm, but this day would prove an exception for many in Israel. After the terrible drought, the people would be anything but upset when drenched with rain. The joy of seeing water flowing everywhere would more than compensate for any discomfort from getting caught in the rain.

While we can only speculate on what much of the multitude at Carmel did after the events of the day, we can, however, know with certainty what Elijah and Ahab did. Their actions, which are consistent with their contrasting characters, are detailed for us. In them we see the passions of the flesh, the persistency of the faithful, and the pace of the feet.

## A. THE PASSIONS OF THE FLESH

Ahab's weakness was very evident in the events on Mount Carmel. Elijah was in control of the situation, not Ahab, though Ahab was the king. And Elijah was in such great control of things that he could order the execution of 450 prophets of Baal, the very prophets to whom Ahab as king had given much favor and support. But Ahab could do nothing and did nothing to prevent their slaughter. The prophets of Baal doubtless looked to Ahab to save them, but they looked in vain. Ahab was nothing but a bystander and probably a terrified bystander at that. For if the people could slay all those prophets, how could he escape if Elijah told the people to turn on the king?

What rendered Ahab so helplessly weak in this crisis? The answer is that he was a man given to the passions of the flesh. Fleshly appetites and interests greatly controlled him. And anyone so given to the appetites and interests of the flesh will be stripped of strength and made weak. Yes, the drinker, the gambler, the adulterer, and other like scum of society act big, talk scornfully out of the side of their mouths, and try to give forth a macho appearance; but in truth they are not strong but weak, very weak. The strong man is the one who rules, not is ruled, by his passions.

This domination of Ahab by the passions of the flesh is emphasized in the command Elijah gave Ahab right after the slaughter of the 450 prophets of Baal. Elijah told Ahab, "Get thee up, eat and drink; for there is a sound of abundance of rain" (v. 41). The command to eat and drink both revealed and rejected Ahab. It revealed that Ahab was indeed dominated by fleshly passions, and it rejected Ahab for the spiritual service of prayer with Elijah because he, Ahab, was dominated by fleshly passions.

**1. The Revealing of Ahab**

Elijah's command fit the interest, lifestyle, and character of Ahab. Elijah told Ahab to do the only thing Ahab would be interested in doing at the time. Pink said, "How well Elijah knew the man he was dealing with." Controlled by the flesh, Ahab's primary interests were in such things as eating and drinking. He rose no higher. The day's events on Carmel did not move him. He could sit through a soul stirring meeting without emotion. But mention fleshly pleasures, and he is all attentive. "So Ahab went up to eat and to drink" (v. 42).

Ahab's quick compliance to the command really revealed how greatly the passions of the flesh controlled him. F. B. Meyer said of Ahab's eager willingness to eat and drink, "It is no more than we might have expected of the king. When his people were suffering the extremities of drought, he cared only to find grass enough to save his stud; and now, though his faithful priests had died by hundreds, he thought only of the banquet that awaited him in his pavilion."

We reveal how prominent the flesh is in us by how we pursue fleshly appetites after a moving spiritual event. If the flesh had not controlled Ahab, he would have remonstrated with Elijah and said something like, "It is not time to eat and drink. This has been a very sobering and convicting day. It is time to pray and confess sin." Or he might have said, "I do not feel like eating, I have no appetite to eat, my soul is so troubled and trembling before Jehovah that I have lost all interest in the pursuit of fleshly appetites at this time." But that is not Ahab. "Eating and drinking was all this Satan-blinded sot cared about" (Pink).

## The Water

Some try to justify Ahab's pursuit by the fact he had probably gone all day without eating and drinking. But Elijah had not eaten or drank, either; yet he still went to prayer instead of the banquet table. Elijah was like Christ in John 4. When the disciples came back from town after buying food and found Him speaking with the woman at the well about her soul, they "prayed him, saying, Master, eat" (John 4:31). Their main concern was the attending to the appetite of the flesh, for it was meal time. His response, a rebuke to them, was, "I have meat to eat that ye know not of" (John 4:32). Sometimes men get so involved in their work they hardly pay any attention to eating and drinking. But how many people do you know who get so excited in spiritual things that eating and drinking and other fleshly pursuits take a back seat as it did with Elijah and Christ?

Listen to folk talk after a church service, and you can tell where their interests are. With most men it seems sports is the predominate talk before and after church. Some of them cannot wait to get out of church in order to get home and watch some ball game on TV. A moving sermon and service does not penetrate well those who are dominated by fleshy passions. As soon as it is over, these folk, like Ahab, turn immediately to pursue other things. But how different it is when we go to some secular event such as a sporting event. If the event has been especially exciting, we talk about it all the way home and for some time after we have gotten home. But few do that about spiritual things. Few, if any, come away from a moving church service talking enthusiastically about it and spiritual things all the way home and even after they get home. Ah, the passions of the flesh dominates us more that we realize. "Eat and drink" appeals too quickly to us. The spiritual has not sunk in. We have in us more of the spirit of Ahab than of Elijah.

The condition of the people of our churches is also quickly revealed by what meetings they get most enthused about. Schedule an extra prayer meeting after a church service and few will stay. But schedule a pot-luck dinner, and people will come out of the woodwork to crowd the church fellowship hall. Feed their stomach and they will gladly show up at church, but feed only their soul and their attendance will be spasmodic at best. The flesh prefers to eat and drink rather than climb the summit to pray with Elijah.

## 2. The Rejecting of Ahab

Elijah's command indirectly told Ahab he was not wanted for the time of prayer which Elijah had planned to have up on one of the peaks of Carmel. Krummacher said, "In these words [Elijah's command] we cannot help discerning . . . a cutting reproof, as implying that the king's presence was not wanted; especially while Elijah was about to converse with God."

Those dominated by the passions of the flesh are of no help in spiritual pursuits. All they can do is cool off the spiritual temperature of such an endeavor. They must be rejected by our churches if the churches want to be on fire spiritually. Yet our churches often foolishly appoint or vote into prominent church positions those who are dominated by fleshly appetites. Then we stupidly wonder why the spiritual temperature of the church has so declined.

Nothing cuts us off so quickly from blessing and privilege as letting the flesh rule in our life. Belshazzar was given to the appetites of the flesh and it cost him a kingdom and his life (Daniel 5). Ben-hadad, king of Syria, "was drinking himself drunk" (I Kings 20:16) when he should have been preparing for battle. As a result he was defeated in battle and lost much territory. In World War II many danced and drank in bomb shelters while their cities were being destroyed by bombs. One would have thought they would have been praying. Some did, of course, but most caroused in a pursuit of fleshly passions instead and perished in their folly.

The problem of letting fleshly passions dominate is summed up well in the book of Isaiah when it says, "Woe unto them that rise up early in the morning, that they may follow strong drink; who continue until night, till wine inflame them! And the harp, and the viol, the tabret, and pipe, and wine, are in their feasts;

but they regard not [are not interested in] the work of the LORD, neither consider the operation of his hands" (Isaiah 5:11,12). Those given to fleshly passions cut themselves off from the best and most needful things in life.

## B. THE PERSISTENCY OF THE FAITHFUL

Elijah's performance on Mount Carmel was so excellent. Everything he did spoke of high spiritual character. Not only was his public performance superb, but so also was his private performance. For when the people left and he was alone with his servant, his dedication to spiritual excellence continued. He was very persistent in his performance. Here we note particularly his persistency in interests, faith, reverence, and prayer.

### 1. Persistency in Interests

A short attention span is a mark of a babe or a very young child. The same is true spiritually. Your attention span in spiritual matters reveals where you are spiritually. It tells us if you have or have not grown much in the Lord. Obviously most church members are still babes in Christ, for their attention span in spiritual matters is extremely short.

Elijah, however, was not like the run-of-the-mill. His attention span, his interests in spiritual things were very persistent. After the showdown with the prophets of Baal and their slaying, Elijah did not stop his pursuit of spiritual things. He went to prayer. He was still interested in spiritual exercise.

Not many folk would stay after an all day service to spend extra time in prayer. But that is exactly what Elijah did. His interest in spiritual matters was not a passing thing, but it was his life. Would that we saw more of this in professing Christians. But most seem only too glad to get to the benediction of a service so they can rush out and pursue the things of the flesh where their attention span is far, far greater.

One conspicuous evidence that a good many church members have a short attention span spiritually is in their complaint of the length of sermons. Sometimes sermons are too long, especially when they are bad sermons as many of them are. But the reason most people complain about sermon length is that their spiritual attention span is so short; their interest in spiritual matters is so very poor. Their complaint does not indict their pastor but themselves. I have heard some church members say, "If the pastor can't say it in twenty minutes, it is not worth saying." That means the pastor is not to preach longer than twenty minutes. The "twenty minutes" statement appeals to many. But we would make a different statement, one which presents the picture much more accurately. Our statement is as follows: If your interest in spiritual things only lasts twenty minutes, then you are in deep trouble with God.

Those who complain the most about long sermons will often be found engrossed by the hour in ball games, quiz shows, talk shows, afternoon soaps, and the late night movies on TV without one word of complaint. They have persistency in their interests, but their interests are not spiritual.

Persistency in spiritual interests is vital if we are to reap the spiritual seeds we have sown. If our interest in the Lord's work is not persistent, we will fail to complete our tasks. Elijah had more work to do after the fire had come down and after the prophets of Baal had been slain. He still must pray for rain. So his interests in spiritual things must not abate. It must be persistent or he ends up with incomplete victory.

Often we start out well, seem on our way to great victory; but we fail to keep going and thus do not realize the full blessing or victory. Many go to church and sit in a good service and hear a good sermon. But they never do any personal follow up after the service. Thus they lose it all. Like the birds in the parable in the Gospels who pluck the seed of the trodden soil, these people never see the seed enter their lives and produce fruit because they do not have enough persistency in their spiritual interest to pursue any spiritual endeavor to the finish. These folk are casualties in church work, casualtics in pursuing Christian training (as an example, they drop out of school after a year or so to get married and never go back to school), and casualties as

## The Water

missionaries. They are easily distracted by carnal pursuits. They come up barren spiritually when they looked so promising.

Preachers can learn something here, too, about persistency in interests. When the public service is over, we need to continue pursuit of our work. We not only need to pray before the service; but we also need to pray after the service. Preparation before the service is very important, but what we do after the service can be just as important.

### 2. Persistency in Faith

Elijah's faith was very persistent even though the rain had not come yet after the showdown at Mount Carmel. He demonstrated this persistency of faith both before he prayed and after he prayed.

*Before he prayed.* Though the skies were still barren of any clouds, Elijah said to Ahab, "There is a sound of abundance of rain" (v. 41). Leon Wood, referring to the Hebrew text, said, "He used the word *geshem,* meaning a more heavy rain, rather than *matar,* and this yet qualified by the word *hamon,* meaning abundance" And in a footnote, Wood adds that "*Geshem* and *matar* are used about an equal number of times in the Old Testament, but when a heavy rain is in mind, as with the flood (Genesis 7:12; 8:2), *geshem* is used." So Elijah made a bold statement in predicting the coming of rain. It was not just a normal rain he predicted by faith, but it was a heavy rain and an abundance of that no less! It was a statement of great faith. It revealed the persistency of his faith. He had not given up hope. He still believed God would bring rain and that it would be a big rain.

It is instructive that Elijah said there was the "sound" of rain. We would have expected him to simply say that rain was on the way. But no, he speaks of the "sound" of rain. That says something about faith, too. Faith has better hearing than the flesh. Pink said, "Elijah hears that which shall be . . . If the Divine Word dwelt in us more richly and faith was exercised more upon it, we would hear that which is inaudible to the dull comprehension of the carnal mind."

Faith is discerning. It detects things, such as the "sound" of rain here, when the flesh does not. And not only is this true in regards to coming blessings, as in Elijah's case; but it is also true in regards to detecting evil. The flesh cannot detect evil in anything it seems. But faith can. It not only sees evil, but it hears the "sound" of evil when the flesh cannot. Hearing the "sound" of evil is something many professing Christians have trouble with today, especially in music. What rot passes off as Christian music, but the carnal say they do not hear anything wrong. Their deafness is not Christian tolerance but a revelation of their lack of faith!

*After he prayed.* Elijah's faith continued to show after he prayed even though he only had "a little cloud" (v. 44). With only that small cloud in the sky, he sent an urgent message to Ahab which told him to "Prepare thy chariot, and get thee down, that the rain stop thee not" (Ibid.). Like the woman in the New Testament who only had "crumbs" of privilege (Matthew 15:27,28), he honored small evidence and saw great blessing deluge him. Persistent faith will always honor the smallest tokens of blessings.

### 3. Persistency in Reverence

When Elijah went to prayer, "he cast himself down upon the earth, and put his face between his knees" (v. 42). Elijah bowed down on the ground to the extent that his forehead touched the ground and his face looked back toward his knees. This position is the Oriental position of great prostration. It is considered to be the humblest of all positions a person can take. It says volumes about Elijah's reverence for God.

Mackintosh said, "Mark the difference between Elijah's bearing in the presence of man and in the presence of God. He met Obadiah, a saint in wrong circumstances, with an air of dignity and elevation; he met Ahab in righteous sternness; he stood amid the thousands of his deluded and erring brethren with the firmness and grace of a true reformer; and lastly, he met the prophets of Baal with mocking, and then with the sword of vengeance. Thus had he carried himself in the presence of man. But how did he meet God? 'He cast himself down upon the earth and put his face between his knees.'" Elijah had not lost his reverence for God through his own elevation from his triumphant victory on Mount Carmel. Yet, in contrast, how quickly we lose our reverence for God. In humble circumstances we bow low to God; but let us get promoted, have some public successes, and then we become self-sufficient, think we are somebody, get away from God and our dependency upon Him, and destroy ourselves.

Elijah's persistent reverence for God through all his different experiences says much about his character. Though great before men, he saw himself lowly before God and cast himself down in humble prostration before Him. That's a good way to get your prayers answered. It is a good way to get along with God. And it is the only way to be before God.

**4. Persistency in Prayer**

It is not expressly stated in our text that Elijah prayed when on Mount Carmel after he told Ahab to eat and drink. However, in comparing Scripture with Scripture, we have no doubt about his praying. James 5:17 and 18 says Elijah "prayed earnestly that it might not rain; and it rained not on the earth by the space of three years and six months. And he prayed again, and the heaven gave rain, and the earth brought forth her fruit." He "prayed again, and the heaven gave rain" obviously refers to Elijah's activity on Carmel in our text.

Much is said in Scripture about Elijah praying. We tend to miss that as we read about him. But his praying is a prominent feature of his life. J. Hammond says, "It is pre-eminently in the matter of prayer that Elijah is proposed to us as an example in the New Testament." Thus far in his story, he has prayed for the drought, for the life of the widow's boy, before the altar on Mount Carmel, and here for rain.

## Elijah

The important feature of his prayer before us is the persistency of it. Elijah continued to pray even though the assurance of rain had already been given and even though the answer to his prayer was delayed. We have trouble demonstrating persistency in prayer in both cases.

*The assurance was given.* Why pray when God has already promised to send rain? Many in the world ask that question. Even some Christians ask the same question. God had told Elijah, "I will send rain upon the earth" (18:1). So these folk ask why was it necessary for Elijah to pray so earnestly for rain.

Elijah's praying, even though the answer had already been promised, teaches us that promises are not given to stop praying but to inspire praying. F. B. Meyer said, "God's promises are given not to restrain, but to incite to prayer. They show the direction in which we may ask, and the extent to which we may expect an answer." A promise is like a check given us from God. It will do us little good, however, if we do not take it to the bank and cash it. When God told Elijah it would rain, it was an open invitation for Elijah to pray for rain. Let us always remember this about promises. The idea that God's promises should cause us to cease spiritual exercise is preposterous. Instead of stopping prayer, promises should greatly encourage it.

*The answer was delayed.* Eight times Elijah sent his servant to see if any clouds could be seen over the Mediterranean Sea (v. 43). Only on the eighth time (the seventh time the servant was told to "go again") was the answer affirmative and then it was only "a little cloud" (v. 44). Elijah experienced what we all have and will experience, namely, a delay in receiving many of the answers to our prayers. Of course, no one likes the delays. We are generally like the Psalmist who said, "When I call answer me speedily" (Psalm 102:2).

Elijah's experience tells us that delay is not necessarily denial. It also says that when delay comes, "It is not that God is hard to persuade; it is that He will have us mean what we say"

## The Water

(J. Hammond). So delay checks our sincerity. Krummacher said, "The reason why we generally so easily grow weary, and so soon cease from praying, is because we are not sufficiently in earnest for the blessing we implore." And F. B. Meyer said, "God keeps it [the answer] back, that we may be led on to a point of intensity, which shall bless our spirits forever, and from which we shall never recede."

Few things will kill the effectiveness of our praying as a lack of persistency in our praying. Sometimes answers do come quickly. When Elijah prayed for fire to fall, it did indeed fall on the altar immediately. But circumstances dictated that a quick answer was needed there. When our circumstances dictate a quick answer, we can expect God to respond promptly. But many times, if not most of the time, answers do not come the moment we pray. If they always did, it would not be good for our character. Patience in praying improves our character. As Krummacher said, "During the process of persevering prayer, our corrupt nature receives the most painful and deadly blows." One who wants to gain blessing through prayer must practice perseverance in prayer.

### C. THE PACE OF THE FEET

"The heaven was black with clouds and wind" (v. 45). The small cloud had turned quickly into a whole sky of clouds, and soon a "great rain" (Ibid.) came upon the land. When Elijah was told by his servant that a "little cloud" had been spotted, Elijah sent an urgent message to Ahab to hurry for home lest the rain hinder him (v. 44). With the land dry and dusty from the long drought, it would not take long for rain to make everything a sea of mud. This would bring Ahab's chariot to a stand still. The iron wheels of a chariot, unlike our air-filled rubber tires today, would sink quickly in mud. So Ahab got in his chariot and hurried to Jezreel.

Elijah made haste for Jezreel, too. He did not go by chariot, however. He ran. And he beat Ahab to Jezreel! The pace of his feet was a great feat of the feet to say the least. When we examine his running, we will note that he was forced into running, enabled for running, and wise in running.

### 1. Forced Into Running

Elijah had no choice but to travel by feet. Ahab did not offer him a ride. He was, therefore, forced to run. Matthew Henry said, "If Ahab had paid the respect to Elijah that he deserved he would have taken him into his chariot, as the eunuch did Philip [Acts 8:31], that he might honor him before the elders of Israel, and confer with him further about the reformation of the kingdom." But Ahab's heart was as hard as stone. Though he had witnessed unprecedented experiences that day which completely discredited Baal and Baal's prophets and greatly honored Jehovah and His prophet Elijah, and though he had been spared by Elijah from death, yet Ahab still despises Elijah and will later call him "mine enemy" (21:20).

Ahab is like many governments in the world in that they will give little or no assistance to fundamentalists. Even though the work of Bible-believing movements have proven to be the most honest and most beneficial to the land, yet the governments will seldom help them. They prefer to help organizations whose value is nil and whose operation is suspect. Like Ahab, they prefer to support and aid the corrupt movements (Baal) rather than help character ministries (Jehovah). So Christian schools are harassed and often pressured out of existence while taverns are licensed to sell alcohol which destroys and curses society. And churches are given a bad time by the government while gambling is legalized, and all sorts of shady practices in the gambling business are overlooked. Elijah can walk as far as Ahab and most governments are concerned.

### 2. Enabled for Running

The pace of Elijah's feet was supernatural. He ran from fifteen to twenty miles or more (depending on the exact distance to Jezreel) faster than Ahab's chariot traveled. He "ran before Ahab to the entrance of Jezreel" (v. 46).

## The Water

With running being so popular today, it is not difficult for us to perceive the greatness and the incredibleness of his feat. First of all, he ran nearly a marathon (26.2 miles); and he did it in sandals! To add to the achievement, we need to remember he was not running on a smooth, asphalt road but on a dusty, dirty road. Furthermore, he had eaten little or nothing all day and had to be physically very weary from the experiences of the day. And he was not in training either. He had not gone out every day and run ten to fifteen miles to get in shape for the Mount Carmel to Jezreel run. True, he was not a "couch potato"; for he had done a lot of walking in going from place to place in the previous years of the drought. But, as any runner knows, that will not put one in shape for the kind of performance he exhibited in running to Jezreel. So how did he do it? The Scripture gives us the answer. "The hand of the LORD was on Elijah" (v. 46). He was supernaturally enabled to run. He had to be. No way could he have run like he did without Divine enabling.

The lesson here in Elijah's feat is that God can enable His servants to do the impossible. In fact, we cannot do the Lord's work at all unless "the hand of the LORD" is upon us. God's assignments may look impossible; but when "the hand of the LORD" is upon us, we can do the impossible. Our problem today is that we discredit the influence and importance of "the hand of the LORD." We glory in our own strength and savvy and think we can do it alone. But we will never make it to Jezreel before Ahab unless God is enabling us.

### 3. Wise in Running

Elijah exercised some wisdom in his running that is instructive. Both in his clothes and in his caution we see some wise action on Elijah's part. God may enable us greatly, but we must be wise in the use of the help God gives us.

*His clothes.* Elijah was helped by God to run to Jezreel or he would never have made it. But notice that right after the Bible says, "the hand of the LORD was on Elijah," it then says, "he [Elijah] girded up his loins" (v. 46). His loose flowing garment would have greatly impeded his running to Jezreel. God does not enable us to the place where we do not have to assume any responsibilities. He does not perform a miracle which is not necessary. Elijah must tie up his robes, or he will be slowed down and perhaps even trip over them—which could have resulted in his being injured or even in his being run over by Ahab's horses and chariot.

Elijah's girding up his loins reminds us of Hebrews 12:1 which says to "lay aside every weight" so we can run the race unencumbered. So many Christians are so loaded down and entangled with obligations, interests, and pursuits that they cannot even walk for God let alone run for Him. These things may not be evil in themselves, but they need to be put in their proper place in life, or they will affect us evilly. Unfortunately, many Christians have never learned their priorities. They have never put their life in order so they can be free to serve God as they ought. But as Elijah tied his garment together so it would not hinder his running, so let us put things in order in our lives so they do not hinder our service for the Lord.

*His caution.* It is interesting and instructive to note that when Elijah finished his run—his great feat of the feet—and arrived at Jezreel, he did not go into Jezreel. The Scripture says he "ran before Ahab to the entrance of Jezreel" (v. 46). He stopped at the entrance of Jezreel. F. C. Cook said, "Elijah's caution in accompanying Ahab only to 'the entrance' is like that of the modern Arabs, who can seldom be induced to trust themselves within walls. He rested on the outskirts of the town, waiting to learn what Jezebel would say or do, knowing that it was she, and not Ahab, who really governed the country."

Sometimes in our excitement we fail to take due caution. Elijah, however, gives us a good example to follow. Be careful. Do not run clear off the reservation in your enthusiasm. If the devil cannot stop you from getting excited about the Lord's work, he will then try to over excite you to the place where you

## The Water

become extreme and careless. One hesitates to tell folk to be careful here, for so few get excited, and you do not want to dampen their spirits. The problem in our churches is seldom over-excitement but generally under-excitement. But just the same the peril is there, and Elijah's caution gives us a good example to follow. It is part of the responsibility we need to exercise in serving God. It is as important as girding up the loins to run.

# VIII.

# THE WARRANT

## I KINGS 19:1–8

THE TRIUMPH FOR Jehovah on Mount Carmel was a great defeat for Satan. But Satan does not give up easily or quickly; and he does not take long to retaliate, either. Hence, soon after Elijah arrived in Jezreel, he received a warrant from that wretched Jezebel decreeing his death within twenty-four hours.

The battle is not over yet. Mount Carmel was a great victory for truth and righteousness, but it was not the end of the war. That will only come when Jesus Christ comes to earth and ushers in His kingdom. Until then the battle will rage, and we must never lay down our armor until it is over.

In our study of Elijah and the warrant, we will consider the persecution, pessimism, and preservation of Elijah.

### A. THE PERSECUTION OF ELIJAH

It is the nature of evil to be very aggressive. Its zeal often puts to shame those of us who profess allegiance to the truth. We seldom get as excited and as earnest about the truth as evil does about the lie.

The aggressiveness of evil is repeatedly seen in Ahab and Jezebel. In our text they show it in how they reacted to the devastating blow Baal worship was given on Mount Carmel. They did not sit down and quit. They aggressively renewed their efforts to try and undo the work of Mount Carmel. And they directed their attack against the prophet Elijah, the key person in the discrediting of Baal worship.

In this persecution of Elijah after his Mount Carmel victory,

## The Warrant

we will note the instigator, the inflicter, and the incentive of the persecution.

### 1. The Instigator of the Persecution

As soon as Ahab reached his palace in Jezreel, he "told Jezebel all that Elijah had done, and withal how he had slain all the prophets with the sword" (v. 1). This was a most distorted report of the day's events. The emphasis was on Elijah's slaying of the prophets. It was not on the fact that Jehovah was proven to be God, that Baalism was proven to be a bogus religion, and that it was now raining again after Elijah had prayed for rain. No, Ahab put the emphasis elsewhere. He had not been converted on Carmel; and he did not like the results which gave Jehovah overwhelming victory and which exalted Elijah, his hated enemy. So his report to Jezebel was given in such a way that it would stir up her evil nature to go after Elijah. Ahab was too spineless to take action himself; but he knew that if he stirred up Jezebel enough, she would let nothing stop her from taking action.

We've known a number of people in church who were like Ahab in his reporting to Jezebel. They appeared to go along with the spirit of a public meting; but after the meeting, they would go out and give a distorted report. Their report was always slanted, always negative. They especially complained about how evil had been treated. No matter how you treat evil, these folk will insist the action was unkind, unjust, and unnecessary. And they will give a great show of charity for disciplined church members and for any whose evil has been preached against rather forcefully by the pastor. Though blessings may abound and Christ be greatly honored by the ministry, they will see to it that a negative report is given and in such a way that it will create an outcry against the Lord's work and especially against His faithful workers.

Ahab's report not only instigated Jezebel to attack Elijah, but it also revealed his own wicked condition. It revealed his hardness of heart and his hatred of the godly.

*His hardness.* Ahab witnessed a tremendous demonstration on Mount Carmel which gave overwhelming proof that Jehovah was God and that Baalism was a stupid, fraudulent religion. But it never dented his hard heart. He never caught on. What hardness of heart! What blindness! You would think he would have been affected better than that by the events at Mount Carmel, but he wasn't.

In spite of the fact that Ahab's attitude was so unreasonable and inexcusable, such adamant unbelief is not uncommon. Men in every age callous their hearts to the truth until it cannot be felt even though it deals a mighty sledgehammer blow against unbelief. No evidence will convince them. No argument, no matter how logical and sensible, will persuade them.

It is well to remind ourselves here that when we harden our hearts to the truth, God will in judgment often harden our hearts, too. Romans 1:28 says, "As they did not like to retain God in their knowledge, God gave them over to a reprobate mind." When Pharaoh hardened his heart (Exodus 8:15), God hardened Pharaoh's heart (9:12). So it was with Ahab. He kept rejecting truth when it was given him, and finally he could not believe even though the evidence was so overwhelming.

One of the worst forms of judgment is to have God help harden your heart. But it is a fitting judgment for insistent unbelief. And it tells us, as an example, why conversions decline with increase in age. The longer one rejects Christ the less likely he will be saved because his heart gets so hard from his own hardening of it and from God's hardening of it. If you are fighting the will of God today, stop it before your rebellion gets an iron grip on you; and God, in an act of judgment, confirms you to persistent rebellion with its attendant curse.

*His hatred.* Ahab's report not only revealed his hard heart, but it also revealed that he still hated God's man. This hatred should not surprise us, however. First, it should not surprise us because it was Ahab's nature to hate God's servants. Later on he plainly said of the prophet Micaiah, "I hate him" (I Kings 22:8).

Second, it should not surprise us because a hard heart will always have trouble having affection for God's man. One who rejects God and His ways will not be receptive to God's ministers—you can be sure of that.

It will profit our churches much if they will be more cognizant of this fact. Too often, however, most church members are too ignorant spiritually to recognize that those who are always criticizing and opposing godly pastors are a most unsavory bunch. They represent a more serious problem than most church members realize. Their dissident ways reveal that they have a hard heart of unbelief and rebellion towards God and a heart that is filled with hatred for God's man. These impostors need to be exposed for what they really are and voted out of the church membership. Failure to do so will impede any church's ministry, cost the church many valuable pastors, and ruin the church's testimony.

### 2. The Inflicter of the Persecution

Ahab's tactic worked. The report Ahab gave to Jezebel infuriated her to action. Emphasizing the slaying of the prophets of Baal touched Jezebel to the quick and made her want Elijah's life to be "as the life of one of them" (v. 2). One's imagination can readily see her face redden with anger as Ahab reports the slaying of the prophets, and then after the report see her furiously stomping around in the palace shouting out anathemas, and then finally calling for a messenger and ordering him to hasten and tell Elijah he will be a dead man within twenty-four hours!

Many Bible students believe that Jezebel's message to Elijah was nothing more than an intended bluff. They believe that if she had really been serious about killing Elijah, she would have sent an executioner instead of a messenger. This view says that Jezebel would feel it most unwise and even dangerous to kill Elijah at this time, for she would fear that the killing of Elijah would only rally the worshippers of Jehovah to inspired efforts in opposing Baal worship and in opposing Jezebel herself. Therefore, she will only threaten Elijah but in such a way that it will cause him to flee the country. Being out of the country will keep him from further opposing Baal worship but will not upset Jehovah worshippers to the inspired opposition that his martyrdom would have done.

Though many believe Jezebel was bluffing, we definitely do not. We do not believe that the context of Scripture, the character of Jezebel, the courageousness of Elijah, or the conclusions of Jehovah's followers justifies the bluffing view. Let us look in more detail at these reasons which oppose the bluffing view.

First, the *context of Scripture*. The Scripture does not give any hint at all that Jezebel was only bluffing. "So let the gods do to me, and more also, if I make not thy life as the life of one of them by tomorrow about this time" (v. 2) does not suggest bluffing. Rather, it was the boasting of a murderous rage about its bloody intentions.

Second, the *character of Jezebel*. Bluffing is not characteristic of Jezebel She had never demonstrated she would be satisfied at such lenient treatment of those who oppose her. Jezebel had already slain many of Jehovah's prophets. And she will later on order the slaying of righteous Naboth so Ahab could have his vineyard (I Kings 21). Jezebel is a butcherer, not a bluffer.

Third, the *courageousness of Elijah*. Jezebel had no reason to think Elijah would run when he received her message. Elijah did indeed run, but that surprised everybody. His past performances, however, would not give Jezebel or anyone any reason to think she could so easily get rid of him. He was known for boldness. He had marched into the kings' presence and boldly announced he was Jehovah's man and that a drought was coming. He had boldly come back to the land even though his life was wanted. He had boldly withstood all the prophets of Baal on Mount Carmel, and had boldly ordered the slaying of the prophets of Baal even though King Ahab stood by. To think such a man would be easily bluffed does not make sense. The fact that all are surprised he ran negates the idea that Jezebel thought she could bluff him.

## The Warrant

Fourth, the *conclusions of Jehovah's followers*. The idea that killing Elijah would inspire Jehovah worshippers is not valid either. Sometimes martyrdom does greatly inspire followers, but here the circumstances dictate it would only put great fear into the hearts of the followers. If Elijah was slain, the attitude of the followers of Jehovah, especially of those who helped to kill the prophets, would be one of great fear for their own life. They would conclude that if Jezebel could kill the mighty Elijah then what chance did they have of opposing her and surviving.

So if Jezebel was not bluffing, then why did she send a messenger to Elijah rather than an executioner? The answer is Jezebel blundered. She was not bluffing at all but simply made a big blunder. She really wanted the blood of Elijah and was in a rage to get it. But she blundered away her opportunity. Krummacher said, "'He [who] taketh the wise in their own craftiness [Job 5:13] . . . has only to leave Jezebel to the madness of her own evil passions, and lo she so imprudently forgets herself, as to send and apprise the prophet of her murderous intention against him. This was, of course, the very way to defeat it." Joseph Parker says, "Why does Jezebel send warning? Why does she delay for a whole day? . . . It is thus that God puts his hook into the leviathan, and turns to confusion the counsel of the ungodly." Jezebel in her murderous rage failed to cover all the bases. She had blundered not bluffed. Wickedness often betrays itself. Evil, by its very nature, often foils its own schemes by stupid strategy. A hot head will always have trouble acting with coolness.

### 3. The Incentive of the Persecution

Why should Elijah be so vehemently attacked? Was he a curse upon the nation? Was he a peril to the prosperity of the country? The way Jezebel and Ahab reacted, you would have thought he was the greatest problem Israel had. But not so. He was instead Israel's greatest asset, their greatest blessing. Yet, in spite of that fact, he is viciously persecuted. His life is sought.

To logical thinking it does not make sense. Elijah should be honored, not harassed. Matthew Henry says, "One would have expected, after such a public and sensible manifestation of the glory of God and such a clear decision of the controversy . . . between him and Baal, to the honor of Elijah . . . that now they would all, as one man, return to the worship of the God of Israel and take Elijah for their guide and oracle, that he would thenceforward be prime minister of state, and his directions would be as laws both to king and kingdom. But it is quite otherwise; he is neglected whom God honored; as no respect is paid to him, no care taken of him, nor any use made of him, but on the contrary, the land of Israel, to which he had been, and might have been, so great a blessing, is now made too hot for him."

So what is the answer to this perplexity? What is the incentive for persecuting the best person in the land? The answer is that evil ever persecutes good. And the greater the good, the greater the attack upon it by evil. Elijah had given evil a devastating blow on Mount Carmel, and so he is going to be a special object of attack by evil.

We should not be ignorant of this battle between good and evil. Many are, however. Phillip Keller said, "It is surprising how few, even within the church, are acutely aware of this battle that is fought unceasingly." But the Bible duly warns of the fight. As an example, Paul said, "All that will live godly in Christ Jesus shall suffer persecution" (II Timothy 3:12). And history is a continuous record that "He that is upright in the way is an abomination to the wicked" (Proverbs 29:27). Wickedness ever opposes righteousness and will ridicule it, harass it, legislate against it, and do whatever else it can to eliminate it. If we live godly and promote godliness, opposition will show its ugly head in pronounced ways. The godly can expect a fight!

This fact of evil ever opposing righteousness explains many things. It explains why Christianity is attacked even though its lifestyle and creeds are so noble and beneficial. It explains why true spiritual awakenings result in a stirring up of great animosity and antagonism to God's workers and His work even though it has made a number of bad people good. It explains attacks upon good morals and upright living. It explains why in church business and board meetings some habitually oppose and scorn good programs advocated by a godly pastor for improving the church's ministry. And it explains why godly pastors are sometimes forced out of their churches.

Let us learn well this fact that evil ever opposes right. Learning this fact well will help us to better oppose evil, to deal more wisely with church problems, and to more ardently long for Christ's return.

## B. THE PESSIMISM OF ELIJAH

Jezebel's warrant had a profound effect upon Elijah. It put him in the throes of despair. He became very despondent, extremely pessimistic. He gave up hope and ended up under the juniper tree, which has made it a symbol of despondency for ages. We are surprised to read of Elijah's pessimism and for two reasons.

First, we are surprised to read of Elijah's pessimism because Elijah was a man of faith who was not easily discouraged. It is hard to imagine a person with his character suddenly going into great despair. Elijah had demonstrated his undaunted faith again and again in the past. He boldly told Ahab it would not rain, he boldly walked across Israel in the famine when he was a hunted man to a town in very dangerous territory for him, he had faced the circumstance of a dead child without despairing, and though he was the only one against 450 prophets of Baal, he never let the overwhelming numerical advantage of those pagan prophets dampen his spirits in the least. Also, he had prayed for rain and heard repeated reports from his servant that not a cloud was in the sky, but he never gave a hint of giving up.

Second, we are surprised to read of Elijah's pessimism because the events of that day were so victorious for Elijah. What a victory on Carmel! Fire came down from heaven in tremendous proof that Jehovah was God, the people fell on their faces and praised Jehovah as God, the prophets of Baal were slaughtered, and rain came and in abundance. Surely this should make his hope stronger than ever. But instead of increased optimism, he was overwhelmed with pessimism.

However, though we are surprised at his fall, we probably shouldn't be; for sieges of despair are common. Elijah is not the only one to have this experience. We all have times under the juniper tree (actually it is not a tree, but a bush which provides good protection from sun and wind in the desert). Even the best of men have had times of great despondency. Not only did Elijah get discouraged, but so did such great saints as Jonah, Peter, and John the Baptist. John the Baptist became so discouraged in prison that he sent a message to Christ asking, "Art thou he that should come, or do we look for another?" (Matthew 11:3). John Wesley was also no stranger to this experience. "Wesley's new life began in glorious experiences in Aldersgate Street, yet within a year of these glowing feelings we find that he suffered a sad relapse into darkness and doubt; he even wrote, 'I am not a Christian'" (W. L. Watkinson). The juniper experience is so common that some years ago in England, in the city of Edinburg, there was an organization which called themselves "The Order of the Juniper Tree."

The fact that pessimism is not an uncommon problem and that even great men like Elijah have had trouble with pessimism inspires us to look earnestly into Elijah's experience so we can learn important lessons from it to help us better deal with the problem. In studying this pessimism of Elijah, we will consider the cause, conduct, and consequences of it.

## 1. The Cause of His Pessimism

After we get over our initial shock of Elijah's lapse of faith, we then start asking why he failed. As we have just noted, here is a man who has a record of great faith. Previously he had met danger, adamant unbelief, opposition to God's work, personal rejection, and other problems without despair. But now he goes to pieces and nearly drowns in the slough of despond. Why? What were the factors that contributed to his utter despair and to his great pessimism here?

In looking at Elijah's situation at the time of the warrant and at his behavior after he got the warrant, one will discover some significant reasons why he lost hope, gave up, left the country, and wanted to die. We will look at four of these reasons. They are the problems of physical fatigue, expended emotions, fleshly pride, and misdirected vision.

*The problem of physical fatigue.* When arriving at Jezreel, Elijah had to be exhausted. Elijah had just gone through a grueling day. The contest with the prophets of Baal had to be extremely taxing physically. To add to this fatigue was his little or no intake of food that day. And to cap off his weariness was the run of some fifteen to twenty miles or more to Jezreel. Yes, God helped him run; but physically it still had to extract a toll from him. So Elijah was really exhausted. Doubtless he was more exhausted than he realized. Sometimes in the excitement of the moment, the adrenaline really flows; and that covers up the fact we are running out of fuel physically.

One of the problems of physical exhaustion is its effect on our mental outlook. "A sick body tends towards melancholy and depression" (Leon Wood). When we are weak and fatigued from activities or sickness, our outlook is seldom upbeat; but in such times we tend to be downcast. Elijah's physical condition made him ripe for an attack of severe pessimism.

Spiritual men have a habit of completely ignoring the physical as a cause of melancholy while the worldly man has a habit of completely ignoring the spiritual as a cause of melancholy. Both are wrong. Here the warning is to the spiritual men to not unduly neglect the physical body lest they bring upon themselves unnecessary and misleading despair. Spurgeon, in speaking on the minister's fainting fits in his book, *Lectures to My Students,* said, "To sit long in one posture, pouring over a book, or driving a quill [today it would be such things as a pen, typewriter, or computer], is in itself a taxing of nature; but add to this a badly ventilated chamber, a body which has long been without muscular exercise, and a heart burdened with many cares, and we have all the elements for preparing a seething caldron of despair." Ministers need to beware of such things as long hours with inadequate rest, lack of exercise, overeating, and improper diet; for these things can make one susceptible to attacks of melancholy. When run down physically, it does not even take a serious attack by a Jezebel to send us into the slough of despond. Just a little irritant can do it at such times.

*The problem of expended emotions.* The day's events which Elijah experienced would drain anyone of their emotions. We have an emotional reservoir which, like any reservoir, when drained does not immediately fill up. When we experience an emotional "high" there will be the inevitable let down. Spurgeon said, "We cannot have great exhilaration without having some measure of depression afterwards." And Maclaren says, "the height of the crest of one wave measures the depth of the trough of the next." If we will remember these facts, we will be prepared to handle our down times better and especially when we face some difficulty or problem during an emotional low.

Surely there is a lesson here about taking care of our emotions, about being careful when and where and on what we expend them. We cannot criticize Elijah for expending his emotions on Carmel. But we can denounce many Christians for where they dispense their emotions. Many foolishly drain their emotional reservoir dry over some ball game on Saturday or on a Sunday afternoon; and does that ever affect their performance at church—and especially if their team has lost! The same can be said about those who watch the TV soaps.

*The problem of fleshly pride.* Under the juniper Elijah lamented, "I am not better than my fathers" (v. 4). J. Hammond said, "What do these words reveal, but that he *had* thought himself better than they." Pride gave Elijah some serious trouble. But it is not difficult to understand why Elijah had trouble with pride at this time. The danger of pride is very great after we have had a most successful performance. Elijah had performed very magnificently that day, so the temptation of pride would be very great. We have trouble with pride and its attendant boasting even when we do some little deed that is most insignificant compared to Elijah's great performance. Therefore, it is not surprising that pride was present in Elijah's situation.

There are many perils in pride. We usually think of such problems as boasting, haughtiness, and overconfidence; but we need also to remember that pride can foster a lot of pessimism, too. "A man's pride shall bring him low" (Proverbs 29:23), and sometimes that "low" is the low of despair. Pride has made us think we are something we are not; and when the truth is discovered, it throws us into the pit of despair with very ungentle hands. You can avoid much pessimism if you keep yourself humbled before the Lord.

*The problem of misdirected vision.* "And when he saw that, he arose, and went for his life" (v. 3). Elijah was looking in the wrong direction and at the wrong thing. We can have much victory when we keep our eyes upon the Lord and His Word. But when we look elsewhere, such as upon negative circumstances, we will suffer much defeat. Peter walked on a stormy sea until he took his eyes off the Lord and focused instead upon the storm. Elijah had been walking on a stormy sea, too, and for a long time. Ahab had a warrant out on Elijah's life for the past several years, but during that time Elijah kept his eyes on the Lord and so walked on water the whole time. Now, however, he sinks because he looks at the storm instead of the Sovereign. He took his eyes off what God had done and looked only at what man was doing. He did not consider the promises of God but only the promise of Jezebel. No wonder he had trouble with pessimism.

We, too, will have considerable trouble with pessimism if we insist on focusing on everything but the Lord. The circumstances around us in this old world today are anything but hopeful. Focusing on them will drive a man to abject despair. Keep your eyes on God, or despair will overwhelm you.

## 2. The Conduct of His Pessimism

Humanity does not act well when in the grip of pessimism. Despondency will disable us from behaving well. Elijah was no exception. This attack of the spirit of pessimism upon him affected his conduct most adversely. We see it in his location, evaluation, and supplication.

*His location.* "And when he saw that, he arose, and went for his life, and came to Beer-sheba, which belongeth to Judah, and left his servant there. But he himself went a day's journey into the wilderness, and came and sat down under a juniper tree" (vv. 3,4). His location went from Jezreel to Beer-sheba to a day's journey into the wilderness before he stopped. His location says he greatly overreacted to Jezebel's warrant. Leaving Jezreel does not condemn Elijah, but going as far away as he did does indeed condemn him.

Some folk criticize Elijah for leaving Jezreel because he did not receive orders from God to leave. But neither do we have any record that he received orders from God to leave Mount Carmel—yet, "the hand of the LORD" was upon him to run to Jezreel. What we need to remember here is that we do not need a special word from God for every action in our life. God has given us enough precepts and principles in the Scripture to guide our life without special revelation every time we do something. Elijah needed special orders to go to Cherith, to Zarephath, and to guide the proceedings on Mount Carmel. But when his life was threatened, he did not need a special revelation from God to take sensible precautions to protect himself. Neither do we. As an example, if a drunk veers into your lane on the highway, you do not need a special communique from God to take evasive action. Where a special word from God would be necessary in this situation is to stop you from taking evasive action. Elijah needed special orders to stay in Jezreel, not to leave Jezreel. Paul is not condemned for fleeing murderous plots on his life (Acts 14:4,5), and neither should Elijah be condemned for fleeing the same. Elijah's failure was his great overreacting to the situation. He went a hundred miles south to Beer-sheba, then left his servant there and went another day's journey into the wilderness. That was totally unnecessary and out of order.

Overreacting, however, is one of the effects of despondency. Despondency has a tendency to drive us to extremism. We make decisions and do deeds that lack common sense and maturity. We may start out in the right direction, but we become so extreme that we make a right a wrong. When despair grips us, we must take extra caution in all that we do lest we add to our troubles by overreacting to our situation.

*His evaluation.* In his prayer under the juniper, Elijah said, "I am not better than my fathers" (v. 4). This betrayed his pride, as we noted earlier; but it also indicated a very poor evaluation of his performance. History will definitely not agree that Elijah was not better than all those who went before him. His performance stands out higher than almost all men. His accomplishments for God were many and mighty. But when pessimism gets an iron grip on us, we tend to evaluate things in the worst way. We play down any success and magnify every defeat. We have difficulty giving a true appraisal of anything. Elijah had experienced great victory. Thousands had come back to Jehovah. One, Jezebel had not. His spirit of hopelessness lets that one rejection of Jehovah color the evaluation of the whole situation.

*His supplication.* Elijah's prayer under the juniper "requested for himself that he might die, and said, It is enough!" (v. 4). Elijah wanted to quit. His "It is enough!" is like our "I've had it!" statement. And we've all said "I've had it!" and much more time than Elijah; that's for sure. Elijah's request to die was a request of pessimism. It was not a request of faith or of hope or of dedication to the Lord. It was a shameful request. It says he can't take it. It denies the power and will of God.

When we start throwing in the towel be sure it is not the flesh acting in a fit of despair. Despair is a quitter. Satan may not be able to pollute you with immorality; but if he can get you into a spirit of pessimism, he has rendered you about as useless as one who has committed immorality. Neither will do anything for God.

Elijah's request to die shows how strange and illogical we pray when we are depressed. If he had wanted to die, he could have stayed in Jezreel and let Jezebel take his life as she wanted to do. His request is a strange contradiction, He flees death on one hand and, yet, seeks it on the other. One of the two men who would not die (Enoch was the other) requests to die. Pessimism certainly does not help us pray well.

### 3. The Consequences of His Pessimism

Here we are looking at the influence of his pessimism on others. We do not live unto ourselves (Romans 14:7), and when we get down in the dumps, it will have an adverse effect on many around us. Elijah's pessimism deflated the momentum of the movement back to Jehovah, it discouraged the converts of Jehovah, and it delighted the opposition to Jehovah.

*It deflated the momentum of the movement back to Jehovah.* Elijah was the leader of the Jehovah movement. But when the leader is gone, a movement loses much momentum and often even dies. Experience abundantly verifies this fact. Elijah was gone for eight weeks at least. So for several months there was no follow up; there was no capitalizing on the victory on Carmel. The return to Jehovah did not stop, but the momentum did; and while the movement was charged again by his return, it certainly had to suffer by his untimely absence.

*It discouraged the converts of Jehovah.* Can anyone imagine any convert being anything but discouraged when they heard that Elijah had "hit the road" and fled the country? He who had stood so tall on Carmel was not acting tall at all any more. If he had simply hidden for a time to escape the murderous attempts of Israel's government, he would have been esteemed for his continued ability to survive great opposition. But fleeing far, far away was not impressive. It would do nothing to encourage new converts.

Discouraging others in their devotion and service to Jehovah can also be seen in what Elijah did with his servant when he fled Jezebel. After taking his servant many miles from home, he "left his servant there [Beer-sheba]" (v. 3) to fend for himself while he, Elijah, went further on his journey. Tradition says the servant was the widow's son who was raised from the dead in Zarephath. If that was so, it must have been very bewildering and discouraging to the servant to see Elijah in such a state of mind and to see him suddenly dump this one whom he had raised from the dead. But whether the servant was the widow's son or someone else, it certainly was a disheartening experience. He had been faithful to Elijah (such as going eight times to look for clouds when Elijah was praying on Carmel, and in following him to Beer-sheba), but Elijah was not being faithful to him. Being left alone at Beer-sheba, a long ways from home, certainly did not encourage service for Jehovah.

*It delighted the opposition to Jehovah.* Jezebel would probably fume that she failed to shed Elijah's blood, but his leaving the country would not totally upset her. With him gone she could operate more freely. She would not have to worry about any more showdowns and embarrassing defeats for her paganism. She would be very glad for his riddance. When we sit down under the juniper, we are only helping the enemy. We do not gladden God, but we delight the devil.

## C. THE PRESERVATION OF ELIJAH

Elijah needed help if he was going to survive this attack of despondency. Both his body and spirit were in bad shape. But God stepped in and rescued His discouraged servant. This is typical of God. "God is faithful" (I Corinthians 1:9, 10:13) and will never forsake His own. Man, however, is often unfaithful; but God never is.

# Elijah

There were three significant factors in Elijah's preservation. They were the miracle of God, the messenger of God, and the mercy of God.

## 1. The Miracle of God

Elijah's preservation involved a Divine miracle regarding his food. In both the supplying of the food and in the strengthening by the food the miraculous occurred.

*The supplying of the food.* For the third time in the past three and a half years, Elijah was fed by a miracle. After Elijah finished his "devotions" under the juniper, he laid down and slept (vv. 4,5). After he had slept awhile, an angel came and awoke him and said, "Arise and eat" (v. 5). Elijah "looked, and, behold, there was a cake baken on the coals, and a cruse of water at his head" (v. 6). Food and water were miraculously supplied by the angel. Elijah's caterers are improving! First, it was ravens, then it was a widow, and now it is an angel that provides the food. That ought to do something to lift his spirits.

The food provided for Elijah was not second rate. Keil says of this food, "a bread cake baked over red-hot stones, [is] a savory article of food which is still a great favorite with the Bedouins." And the cruse of water provided must have been just as welcomed in the hot desert where he was located.

*The strengthening by the food.* The providing of the food was not the only miracle regarding the food. The strength the food gave was also a miracle. Scripture says Elijah "went in the strength of that meat forty days and forty nights" (v. 8). Health food stores would really like to get a hold of some food like that!

The lesson in the miracle nourishing of the food is that God supplies our need when we need it. Elijah was going to make a long forty day journey to Horeb. God knew and supplied for it. Mackintosh said, "The Lord knows better than we do the demands that may be made on us, and He graciously strengthens us according to His estimate of those demands." Therefore, let us view our blessings as that which God has given us to enable us to do His will and then use them accordingly.

## 2. The Messenger of God

God sent an angel (the Hebrew word means messenger and is often translated messenger) to help in the preservation of Elijah's life at this critical juncture of his experience. We note the identity of the messenger and the instructions of the messenger.

*The identity of the messenger.* The angel that visited Elijah was none other than the "angel of the LORD" (v. 7). This angel is distinguished from other angels in Scripture. The angel was a theophany, a visible manifestation of God. This was an Old Testament manifestation of the Son of God. The angel was Jehovah, the very One Whom Elijah had been so zealous for and Who was proven on Mount Carmel to be God.

Those who have served their Master will not be forsaken by Him in the dark times. Elijah had greatly honored Jehovah before the people and now Jehovah comes to take care of him. If you want God to honor you by His care, you had better care about honoring God in your service as Elijah had done. Some complain that God never seems to be near, He never seems to be around in time of trouble. But those who have served Him well will find that God manifests His presence in real ways when discouragement, trials, and troubles come upon them.

*The instructions of the messenger.* The angel had two important instructions to communicate to Elijah. One concerned eating, the other concerned traveling.

First, the *eating*. The angel told Elijah to "Arise and eat" (vv. 5,7). How instructive those three words are. Food may be provided by a miracle, but we are still instructed to put forth the effort to eat it. God will not work a miracle when it is not needed. A miracle was required to provide the food, but it was not required to partake of it. God does not make lazy saints with

His miracles. He is not running a welfare program like that of our government.

Second, the *traveling*. The angel told Elijah that "the journey is too great for thee" (v. 7). Indeed, Elijah had a forty day trip to Horeb through the desert. Human strength could not do it alone, He needed Divine strength and must avail himself of Divine provisions.

How well Elijah's provisions speak of the Word of God, the bread for our soul. We cannot make it through life victoriously on our own strength. We need the Divine nourishment of the Word of God which gives us supernatural strength. The world does not respect the Word of God and ridicules our need of it. But that does not diminish one bit the fact that it is God's miracle food for the soul and without it we cannot make it through life victoriously.

### 3. The Mercy of God

We are dependent on God's mercy for every blessing we get. And God's mercy was certainly evident in the preservation of Elijah. The mercy of God was evidenced in the refusing by God to grant Elijah's prayer request, in the touching of Elijah by the angel, and in the repeated visiting of Elijah by the angel.

*The refusing.* God did not answer Elijah's prayer in which he requested to die. What a mercy that God does not answer all our prayer requests the way we want Him to. Do not fuss and complain to God about those requests you did not get answered which, like Elijah's request, were prayed outside the will of God. His mercy refused you. If He would have answered many of your prayers as you had desired, you would be miserable. God is not mean, but merciful; and so He refuses many of our requests.

*The touching.* Twice we are told the angel "touched him" (vv. 5,7). God could have had the angel hit him, for Elijah deserved it. But God in mercy only touched him; for when God endeavors to bring us back to Him, back onto the right path, He does not first hit us but gently touches us. God says, "As many as I love, I rebuke and chasten" (Revelation 3:19). It is rebuke before chasten. It is reasoning before the rod. Oh, that we would heed the merciful gentle touch so God does not have to hit us harder. Our losses would be so much less.

*The visiting.* The angel not only visited Elijah once, but He "came again the second time" (v. 7). That is mercy. Once ought to be enough, but how few of us ever respond to just one call. God must come a second time, yea time and time again before we pay attention. But His repeated visits are all a reflection of His mercy. Let us not despise this grace but honor it by responding more quickly to God's calls. Do not reject God's calls again and again until they cease to come—then you will be left helpless forever.

# IX.

# THE WILDERNESS

## I KINGS 19:8–18

IN FLEEING JEZEBEL, Elijah spent forty days traveling in the same wilderness that Israel traveled in for forty years. And as Israel was sustained by miracle food for their forty years journey, so Elijah was strengthened by miracle food for his journey (I Kings 19:7,8). But Elijah's trip in the wilderness was in the opposite direction of Israel's journey. Israel left Mount Horeb (also known as Mount Sinai) to go to Canaan. Elijah left Canaan to go to Mount Horeb.

Horeb was called "the mount of God" (v. 8, cp. Exodus 3:1, 4:27). Here was holy ground indeed. Here Moses saw the burning bush (Exodus 3). Here God first gave Israel water from a rock (Exodus 17). Here Moses twice spent forty days and forty nights on the mount (Exodus 24:18, 34:28) during which time he received the law on the two tables of stone and was given the instructions for the Tabernacle. And here, in this most significant, sacred, solemn spot deep in the wilderness, Elijah had a most dramatic and instructive experience which put him back into his Master's service.

To examine Elijah's experience at Horeb, we will consider the probing of the question God asked Elijah, the pedagogy of the Divine demonstration for Elijah, and the predictions of the future given to Elijah.

### A. THE PROBING OF THE QUESTION

The "word of the LORD" asked Elijah a very pertinent question twice. It was asked before the supernatural demonstration and

## The Wilderness

after the demonstration. The question was, "What doest thou here, Elijah?" (vv. 9,13). The question, though short and simple, went to the heart of the problem. It was a very skillful probing. We see this in both the analysis and the answer of the question.

**1. The Analysis of the Question**

The question was twofold. It concerned Elijah's occupation ("doest") and his location ("here").

*Occupation.* The question first addressed the matter of what Elijah was doing. "What *doest* thou?" What Elijah was doing was not complimentary. He was needlessly and shamefully brooding. He was deserting his post of duty. Just the first three words of the simple question and Elijah is condemned. How quickly the probe of God touches the sore spot.

How quickly such a question, if duly pondered, can also touch us where we need to be touched. But how often we have failed to ponder the question as we ought. We all could have avoided many problems if we had pondered this question more. Like Elijah, many have wasted much time and effort because they did not give much thought to what they were doing. Like the prodigal son, many have blown ("spent all" Luke 15:14) their heritage, their endowments, their health, and their character and have ended up in a pigsty coveting the "husks that the swine did eat" (Luke 15:16) because they did not duly ponder this question. This question which the Lord asked Elijah needs to be posted prominently in our hearts and perhaps also on our bulletin boards, desks, walls, doors, and other conspicuous places so we can see it constantly and, therefore, check our deeds to see that they are what God would have us to be doing.

*Location.* The second thing the question addressed was Elijah's location. "What doest thou *here*?" Elijah was a long ways from where he ought to have been. Oftentimes it is the craving for worldly pleasures that leads many into places where they should not be. But Elijah got in the wrong place by a bad case of melancholy; for it, too, can put one in the wrong place.

We need to consider our location, as well as our occupation, more frequently than we do; for it is so easy to become located far from where we ought to be, as was the case with Elijah. Some need to ask this question on Sunday when they are in places other than church. As an example, many sports fans and athletes need to ask this question on Sundays; for football stadiums, gyms, baseball parks, golf courses, and race tracks are where they are located on Sunday instead at church. Also some travelers need to ask this question when they travel on the highways on Sunday instead of worshipping. They seem to think they can make better time getting to some location by skipping church. But that is not smart thinking at all. Such folk will someday discover that they will have to do a lot of back tracking as Elijah did. Still others need to consider this question in regards to what church they are located in; for they are attending a modernistic, apostate church which does not preach the Word of God faithfully. And many professing Christians need to ask themselves this question when they are found in cinemas, drive-in movies, dancing saloons, night clubs, and other dens of iniquity. It is said of Charles Spurgeon that once when passing a place of ill repute and seeing a professing Christian man there, he went into the man and put his hand on his shoulder and asked this question, "What doest thou here?" A good question for the man then and a good question for us at all times.

## 2. The Answer of the Question

Elijah's response to the question both times it was asked was, "I have been very jealous for the LORD God of hosts; for the children of Israel have forsaken thy covenant, thrown down thine altars, and slain thy prophets with the sword; and I, even I only, am left; and they seek my life, to take it away" (vv. 10,14). Elijah's answer not only revealed his own condition, but it also revealed the condition of Israel.

*Elijah's condition is revealed.* Elijah's answer revealed he

## The Wilderness

was a "has been" ("have been"). Elijah missed the present tense character of the question. His answer was all about the past. But God said, "What doest thou?" not "What have you done?"

Elijah did have a tremendous past. He had indeed been "very jealous" for God. Not many in the history of man can equal Elijah for his great zeal for God. Our zeal is very poor in comparison. Though situations become so rotten with sin that they reek to high heaven in gross dishonor of God, we have so little concern for God's honor that we go right on our way hardly noticing the great dishonor being done to God. But not so Elijah, he had indeed been "very jealous" for God. But his great past will not cover for the present. Past performances, no matter how great they are, will not answer for the present.

In focusing on the past instead of the present, Elijah sang the same tune Obadiah sang. Obadiah, as we noted in a previous chapter, was quite concerned that Elijah knew of the great work of Obadiah—his past work that is. But Obadiah was not very interested in present service.

This reminds us of many members in our churches. They love to strut around the church and point out what they did in building the church facilities, how they used to teach a class, lead the young people, sing in the choir, etc. But we notice that their service is all in the past tense. The present tense sees them doing nothing but sitting and boasting of their past. They, as well as all of us, need to see that the emphasis in the question is on present tense performance. We may have been zealous in the past, but are we zealous *now* to serve the Lord?

*Israel's condition is revealed.* Elijah's answer summed up Israel's spiritual condition about as well as it could be stated. It was a threefold indictment upon Israel. First, they had "forsaken thy covenant" (which had been given to Israel right there at Mount Horeb where Elijah was); second, they had "thrown down thine altars" (Elijah had rebuilt one on Carmel); and third, they had "slain thy prophets," until Elijah (in his thinking) seemed to be the only one left (and Jezebel was seeking to kill him, too, just as she had the other prophets). To put this threefold indictment in another way, Israel had forsaken the Word of God ("covenant"), the worship of God ("altars"), and the workers of God ("prophets").

The first indictment, forsaking the Word of God, is the cause of the second and third indictments—the forsaking of the worship and workers of God. This is always so in every age. As an example, when people forsake the Word of God today, it will soon be followed by their slacking off and then eventually quitting attendance at a church where the Word is faithfully proclaimed; and it will also lead to rejecting, criticizing, and opposing their godly pastor.

If we remembered this truth, we would understand better why some people leave a church. Oftentimes when folk leave a sound Bible-believing church, the people in the church act puzzled and perplexed as to why "so and so" left. Many reasons are advanced for their leaving, but seldom does anyone have wit enough to realize that they left primarily because they have forsaken the Word as the rule in some area or areas of their life. Where the Word is faithfully preached, it will be most uncomfortable for these folks; and so they will someday leave that church. And when you ask them why they have forsaken the worship of God at the church they used to attend, they will eventually get around to the third indictment—forsaking (evidenced by criticizing, slandering, opposing) the worker of God, namely, the pastor. So do not be so naïve about people leaving a good church. When folk forsake the Word of God they will forsake the worship of God and the workers of God.

This threefold indictment of Israel by Elijah is referred to by the Apostle Paul in Romans 11:2,3. He said it was Elijah's "intercession to God against Israel." In referring to Paul's reference to Elijah's prayer, Matthew Henry said, "Those are truly miserable that have the testimony and prayers of God's prophets against them." True indeed. It will not be well for anyone who is in the prayers of the godly pastors and Christian workers because they have been burdensome troublemakers.

## B. THE PEDAGOGY OF THE DEMONSTRATION

After Elijah had answered God's question the first time, God commanded Elijah to "Go forth, and stand upon the mount before the LORD" (v. 11). God was going to give Elijah a unique demonstration. But before He did so, He first ordered Elijah to stand before Him on the mount. As we noted in a previous chapter, the term, "stand before the LORD," meant to be in the service of God. Here the fact that Elijah had to be told to stand before the Lord indicates that Elijah's recent conduct had gotten him out of God's service. He was no longer standing before the Lord in service. So God orders him back into that position with the command.

After the command, God gave Elijah a fourfold demonstration. First, "a great and strong wind rent the mountains, and brake in pieces the rocks" (v. 11). Second, an "earthquake" shook the area (Ibid.). Third, a "fire" (v. 12), which according to the meaning of the Hebrew word can include lightning, swept through the mount. And fourth, a "still small voice" (Ibid.), which was a great contrast to the first three events of the demonstration, was heard. Scripture says "the LORD was not in" the wind, earthquake, or fire (vv. 11,12). But the "still small voice" was a different story. The "still small voice" so moved Elijah that he "wrapped his face in his mantle" (v. 13). God was speaking to him.

This demonstration was intended to teach Elijah several important lessons which would help to counter his pessimistic thinking that had paralyzed his service for God for some six weeks. The pedagogy of the demonstration was twofold. First, it taught that just because something is big and spectacular, it does not guarantee that God is in it. Second, it taught that just because something is small and quiet, it does not rule out God from being in it.

**1. Bigness Does Not Guarantee God's Presence**

The fact that God was not in the wind, earthquake, and fire would be a great surprise to Elijah. Elijah had witnessed a great drought in the land, and God was in that. And he had witnessed the dramatic event of the fire coming down from heaven at Mount Carmel, and God was definitely in that. But here on Horeb, God was not in the great display of power. It was a new and unexpected experience for him.

But Elijah is not the only one surprised. We, who live in the twentieth century where the dramatic and sensational are practically worshipped, will be even more surprised that God was not in the wind, earthquake, and fire. We tend to measure everything by the velocity of the wind or by the Richter scale or by how spectacular it is. If a preacher is bombastic, pounds the pulpit, tells tear-jerking stories, or breaks up the crowd in laughter with his humor, we think he is really something even though he may, in fact, be saying very little from a spiritual standpoint. If a church has a very large attendance, weekly offerings in the thousands, many spacious and expensive looking buildings, and a network TV program, we conclude it must really be a great work of God even though it may be doctrinally shaky and lacking high moral standards. If an evangelist can boast of filling stadiums and coliseums, and if he travels to foreign countries and has great crowds there, we dare not suggest, to hear some talk, that God is not in the work even though his message deviates frequently from the Bible. So this lesson on Horeb is needed not only by Elijah but by all of us, too. Bigness does not guarantee God's presence. It is not the criteria by which we are to judge a work as to whether it is of God or not.

Of course, this de-emphasis on the big and dramatic does not say that all large works are invalid. Mount Carmel was certainly a work of God, and some large churches and movements are also great works of God. But the way to measure the work is not by the wind, earthquake, and fire but by the Word of God.

The fact God was not in the wind, earthquake, and fire says God is not primarily in the business of turning heads but of moving hearts. Oh, how we need this truth emphasized more in our churches. So many church programs are geared to turn heads rather than move hearts. Special Sundays are a dime a dozen. Celebrities, such as famous athletes, politicians, karate experts, war heroes, and the like, are brought in to attract people with the unusual and the spectacular. And some pastors, from their message titles to the announcements, continually emphasize the sensational. Everything has to be fantastic, super-duper, outstanding, and tremendous. Many big name evangelists are no different; for their messages, books, radio, and TV programs are one constant emphasis on the wind, earthquake, and fire. It is a head turning ministry, and God is not in it.

One of the great perils of having a continuous wind, earthquake, and fire program is that it makes people carnal with all the emphasis on that which excites the flesh. Hence the people become disinterested in the spiritual, and they will get to the place where they will not come to church unless you have a show for them. They are not interested in the regular preaching and teaching of the Word of God, but they are addicted to the "special" attraction program. Many a pastor who has followed a wind-earthquake-and-fire-emphasis pastor has discovered rather quickly how addicted the church is to that type of a ministry. To bring the church back to a more solid ministry is very difficult, if not impossible. In fact, the poor pastor who tries to steer a church from a program of sensationalism to a more spiritual program will often be voted out in short order by the church congregation.

## 2. Smallness Does Not Rule Out God's Presence

We despise the small, the common and the ordinary. When planning church programs, we simply cannot believe a program without the unusual, extraordinary, big, and impressive could do much at all. But such a conclusion is very, very wrong. Elijah learned that fact on Horeb. He learned that other things beside a Mount Carmel show would move souls. And he learned it by his own personal reaction to the demonstration. The wind, earthquake, and fire did not move him. But when the "still small voice" was heard, he wrapped his face in his mantle; for Elijah was moved to the depths of his heart. God did not speak to him in the wind, earthquake, and fire; but He did speak to him in the "still small voice."

This truth should really encourage us. It says we do not have to "wow" the people with some unusual, special program in order to do God's work well. We may not have a big crowd, a large choir, super talented musicians, important citizens of the community dotting our church membership, or a host of special meetings and occasions; but we can still have a work that God is in. We can still have services in which the Holy Spirit will work mightily, and a service that will move hearts to the Lord. We must not feel helpless and despondent if we lack the big and impressive and if the big and impressive has not moved some people. This was Elijah's problem. Mount Carmel did not move everyone and so the conclusion is that if a Mount Carmel show does not move them then there is no hope. But that is not so. Both we and Elijah must learn that God works through the "still, small voice" method, too.

And not only does God work through the "still small voice" method, but it is also His usual method by which He works. It is the common, the ordinary, not the unusual and dramatic that is God's regular way of doing things. Israel had but one Mount Carmel experience. Christ had but one Mount of Transfiguration experience. Furthermore, Christ did not spend most of His time working miracles which awed the onlookers. Rather, He spent most of His time in a less spectacular ministry of teaching and preaching. So do not despise the "still small voice" ministry. Those who do despise it are filled with much unbelief, for it was this kind of person that kept asking Christ for additional signs.

Experience will also teach us that it is the common and the ordinary which comprises most of life and which is the most valuable to us. As an example, a newspaper is not made up entirely of headlines, but mostly it is made up of small print. Headlines are often in the sensational category, and they do turn heads (so people will buy the paper at the newsstand). But if you want to learn anything, you had better spend most of your time reading the small print. It is the small print that gives real value to the newspaper. The same principle is seen in contrasting the spectacular display of fireworks with the fire in the furnace of your home. The fireworks are a head turner and draw many "ohs" and "ahs" from a fascinated crowd. But its value is nothing compared to the small, inconspicuous, quiet fire in the furnace of a house or building. So do not despise the common, the small, and the ordinary. You need it more than all that is big and impressive put together.

We would add here a word of caution regarding the emphasis on the "still small voice." Some will use this emphasis to deplore strong, earnest, crying out against sin; and they will exhort all ministers to use a quiet, soft voice in preaching. The "still small voice" approach sanctions none of that thinking. We are instructed plainly in the Word to cry out vigorously against sin. Though God does most of His work through the "still small voice" method, we must not make the mistake of thinking He does all of it that way.

## C. THE PREDICTIONS OF THE FUTURE

After the demonstration and question were over, God said to Elijah, "Go, return on thy way" (v. 15). This was God's command to Elijah to get back into his harness and start serving the Lord again. And to guide and encourage Elijah's service, God gave Elijah five very significant predictions—five important revelations about the future.

Some, however, do not believe Elijah was reinstated to the position he held before his failure. After all, they argue, his ministry after his failure was not as prominent and dramatic as before. But such folk ignore many facts.

First, they ignore the *demonstrations for Elijah*. The lessons of the demonstration on Mount Horeb said the ordinary was God's work, too, and the dramatic was not necessary for God to be in the work. Second, they ignore the *predictions for Elijah*. God gave Elijah these five great predictions (which we are about to study). No demoted prophet is given such significant revelation from God. Third, they ignore the *ministry for Elijah*.

God gave Elijah quite a ministry after Horeb. While it was mostly in the "still small voice" category, it still included some very dramatic scenes, It included a confrontation with Ahab in Naboth's vineyard, the calling down of fire from heaven to consume several companies of soldiers, and the anointing (or directing of it) of two kings and one of the greatest prophets in Israel's history—none of which is the work of a demoted prophet. Fourth, they ignore the *exit for Elijah*. God provided a grand and glorious exit from the world for Elijah. This is hardly the kind of exit a demoted prophet experiences!

It is true that some are disqualified and removed from their post because of their failures. But those failures will be found to be extremely serious, such as a moral failure. Elijah's problem was discouragement. And God is not in the business of kicking out of employment those who have a bout of discouragement now and then. If He did, there would be no one left to serve Him! Elijah's lapse is not excused, however. It hurt, and it is no justification for our lapses. And if he had not submitted to God's call to return to duty, he could have indeed been shelved. But he did respond to God's call, he was reinstated to his post, and he served God extremely well the rest of his life.

The five predictions given Elijah, to help him get back into service, climaxed Elijah's great experience on Mount Horeb. These revelations from God concern the potentate of Syria, the prince of Israel, the prophet of God, the punishment of evil, and the people of faith.

## 1. The Potentate of Syria

The first prediction revealed who would be Syria's king in about twenty years. Elijah was instructed to "return on thy way to the wilderness of Damascus; and when thou comest, anoint Hazael to be king over Syria" (v. 15). Scripture does not record Elijah as anointing Hazael but rather that Elisha fulfilled this task in his stead (which was sometimes the case with prophets). We learn this from a record of a conversation between Hazael and Elisha, Elijah's successor, in which Elisha says, "The LORD hath showed me that thou shalt be king over Syria" (II Kings 8:13). That revelation doubtless came from Elijah.

Hazael was one of God's main chastening rods to punish Israel for their evil which came from following Baalism. The punishment was severe, for Hazael was a brutal butcherer. But though severe, it was fitting for Israel's vile deeds which were inspired by Baalism. Elisha detailed the brutal, bloody character of Hazael when he said to him, "I know the evil that thou wilt do unto the children of Israel: their strong holds wilt thou set on fire, and their young men wilt thou slay with the sword, and wilt dash [a gruesome, violent smashing of bodies and heads against stones or other hard surfaces] their children, and rip up their women with child" (II Kings 8:12). Hazael brought to Israel wars "more desolating than any that had preceded" (Edersheim). But it all served as the rod of Divine justice.

## 2. The Prince of Israel

The second prediction concerned Jehu (he was the one who drove "furiously," [II Kings 9:20]) and revealed he would one day be king of Israel. God said to Elijah, "And Jehu the son of Nimshi shalt thou anoint to be king over Israel" (v. 16). As the predicting of Hazael to be king of Syria promised punishment for the nation of Israel for their sins, so the predicting of Jehu to be king of Israel promised destruction for the house of Ahab for their evil. When Jehu was anointed (like Hazael, he was not anointed directly by Elijah, either; in his case he was anointed by one of the sons of the prophets under the direction of Elijah's successor Elisha), the message to him was, "Thou shall smite the house of Ahab thy master, that I may avenge the blood of my servants the prophets, and the blood of all the servants of the LORD, at the hand of Jezebel" (II Kings 9:7). As we will note later, Elijah predicted to Ahab in Naboth's vineyard some of the details of this bloody, humiliating destruction of Ahab's house (I Kings 21:21–24).

Jehu certainly fulfilled his calling! First he killed King Jehoram, Ahab's son, by shooting an arrow through Jehoram's heart when Jehoram tried to flee in his chariot from Jehu (II Kings 9:24). Then he ordered Jezebel thrown down from an upper palace window and "trode her under foot" (II Kings 9:33) with his chariot and horses—a fitting end for the killer of prophets. Following this he had the city leaders of Samaria behead the seventy sons of Ahab that were in Samaria, and he had their heads laid in two heaps (II Kings 10:1–8). Then the Scripture says, "Jehu slew all who remained of the house of Ahab in Jezreel, and all his great men, and his kinfolks, and his priests, until he left him none remaining" (II Kings 10:11). Ahab's family was destroyed as predicted. Righteousness was vindicated.

### 3. The Prophet of God

The third prediction revealed to Elijah that his successor would be Elisha. God said, "Elisha the son of Shaphat of Abelmeholah shalt thou anoint to be prophet in thy room" (v. 16). This did not mean Elisha was going to take Elijah's place right then because Elijah was being benched by God, but it meant Elisha would become Elijah's successor when Elijah passed from the earth.

It is significant that the first thing Elijah did when he got back to the land was look up Elisha and extend to him God's call (I Kings 19:19–21). Joseph Parker said, "The anointing of these kings [Hazael and Jehu] was a comparatively insignificant circumstance, the great point of the [Elijah's] commission we find in the conclusion of the sixteenth verse [which is to anoint Elisha]." Rulers have their place, but what the land needs more than kings and presidents and politicians is God's prophets! So the first thing Elijah did when he left Horeb was to head for Abel-meholah to anoint Elisha (for a study on the life of Elisha, see the author's book on Elisha).

### 4. The Punishment of Evil

The fourth prediction amplified the first three predictions, It said, "And it shall come to pass, that him that escapeth the sword of Hazael shall Jehu slay; and him that escapeth from the sword of Jehu shall Elisha slay" (v. 17). The message of this prediction emphasizes the truth that God does indeed punish evil. This had to be a great encouragement to Elijah, not because he was bloodthirsty, but because it vindicated the holiness of God, something he fervently championed.

One of the great trials of the faithful followers of God is seeing wickedness continue on without apparent punishment while the righteous, often victims of the evil of wickedness, seem to suffer more and more. But the mills of God's justice, while often appearing to grind very slowly do grind relentlessly. They also grind exceedingly fine which means that eventually they will pulverize the wicked. The work of Hazael, Jehu, and Elisha was some twenty years or so down the road from the time Elijah was on Horeb. But the time was coming when Ahab's house and the land of Israel would pay very dearly for their wickedness. Then the righteous, such as Elijah, would be greatly vindicated. Ahab and much of Israel had ignored the chastisement of the devastating drought. Hence, they will experience even worse judgment.

Considering the awful flood of evil in our country, this prediction does not encourage us to see a bright future for our land, either. With all the promoting and legalizing of abortion, homosexuality, gambling, alcohol, and other evils, and the ever increasing anti-God sentiment in our land, we would say as Krummacher said, "Who knows what . . . [we] have still to experience?" Judgment is coming; we can be sure of that.

This fourth prediction frequently raises a question concerning Elisha. We read clearly of Hazael and Jehu slaying with the sword, but how can it be said that Elisha also slew with the sword? The answer is that Elisha's sword was his words. "It was by the breath of his lips he slew the wicked" (J. Hammond). Such Scripture as "I have slain them by the words of my mouth" (Hosea 6:5) and "the Lord shall consume with the spirit [breath] of his mouth" (II Thessalonians 2:8) conveys this idea well. An example of this in Elisha's life is found in his early ministry when a gang of teenage rowdies came out of the city of Bethel to mock him. The Bible said Elisha "turned back, and looked on them, and cursed [condemned] them in the name of the LORD. And there came forth two she bears out the wood, and tare forty and two children of them" (II Kings 2:24).

**5. The People of Faith**

The fifth prediction revealed that not everyone was a Baal follower. God said, "I have left me seven thousand in Israel, all the knees which have not bowed unto Baal, and every mouth which hath not kissed him" (v. 18).

There is a question about this statement of the seven thousand as to whether it is a prediction of the future or a revelation of the present. The KJV makes the statement a revelation of the present. But the Hebrew, according to most scholars, favors the future tense. And most translations, going back as far as the Septuagint, also make it a prediction of the future. The context also favors a prediction of the future, for everything else God told Elijah here concerned the future. If the seven thousand was a present condition, however, we have to say as F. B. Meyer said, "It has often been a subject of wonder to me how these seven thousand secret disciples could keep so close as to be unknown by their great leader . . . It is to be feared, therefore, that the godliness of these hidden ones was very vague and colorless, needing the eye of omniscience to detect it."

Whether the statement is a prediction of the future or a revelation of the present, it would be a great encouragement to Elijah. Elijah had complained about being the only prophet, and the implication was that he felt he was also the only one of all Israel who took a strong stand for Jehovah. It can be very disheartening to be the only one standing for the truth. But God revealed to Elijah that not only was there an Elisha who would stand true, but there were also seven thousand who would stand true. This was indeed good news not only for Elijah but also for us. God always has His remnant. Even in the worst of days there will always be some who will be true. It seldom is a large crowd, for what were seven thousand compared to the many

## The Wilderness

millions in Israel. However, it is God's crowd.

These five great predictions given Elijah on Mount Horeb, along with the great demonstration he witnessed there, certainly did much to get Elijah back into service. Thus, Elijah left Mount Horeb, that spiritual oasis in the wilderness, in much better shape than when he first arrived. His spirits were lifted, his vision was cleared, and his commission was renewed. God had spoken to him and he had listened. And when we listen to God's Word, we, too, will be encouraged, edified, and enabled to serve the Lord well.

# X.

# THE WICKED

## I KINGS 21

AFTER ELIJAH RETURNED to the land from his sojourn in the wilderness, some time passed before he again came into the spotlight. At least two, maybe three or more years went by. We deduce this from several situations in Scripture. First, in our chapter a vineyard is thriving in Jezreel which means the effects of the three and a half year drought have been overcome. This would take at least a year or two to occur. Second, after Elijah's return to the land, Israel had several wars with Syria which occurred before the events of this chapter. These wars lasted over a period of at least two different years (I Kings 20).

That which brings Elijah on the scene again was the criminal conduct of Ahab, the most wicked king Israel had experienced up to that time, and of Jezebel his extremely wicked wife. Ahab and Jezebel had committed a dastardly deed against a godly citizen of Israel. Evil still emanates in abundance from the throne of Israel, and Elijah is sent by the Lord to confront wicked Ahab concerning this crime.

In this study of Elijah and the wicked, we will consider the proposition of Ahab, the plot of Jezebel, and the proclamation of Elijah.

### A. THE PROPOSITION OF AHAB

A bit of tranquility has come to the land of Israel. There has been a lull in the conflicts with Syria, and the land has recovered from the severe three and a half year drought. King Ahab now has some time to sit around in his palace in Jezreel and

## THE WICKED

think about such things as the palace's decor and environs and how they could be improved. The palace in Jezreel was not the royal couple's main home. That was in Samaria, the capital of the Northern Kingdom. The Jezreel dwelling would correspond to a Camp David or a similar place which our presidents have to reside in other than the White House. Such residences are generally located in places of natural beauty and are often the favorite dwelling places of the heads of government.

Scripture often records Ahab and Jezebel as being in Jezreel. The comfort and beauty of the location doubtless would encourage them to live there as much as they could. And Ahab was interested in improving the grounds and landscape. Especially did he want a vineyard which was right next to the palace grounds. This vineyard belonged to a man by the name of Naboth. Naboth had obviously taken good care of his vineyard and this would arrest the eye of his royal neighbor, Ahab.

One day Ahab went to Naboth and made an offer to buy the vineyard. We want to look at the offer and note that it was a reasonable offer but also a rejected offer.

### 1. A Reasonable Offer

"And Ahab spake unto Naboth, saying, Give me thy vineyard, that I may have it for a garden of herbs, because it is near unto my house; and I will give thee for it a better vineyard than it; or, if it seem good to thee, I will give thee the worth of it in money" (v. 2). On the surface this offer looks fair and square. And it was very generous, too; for it offered Naboth a "better" vineyard in return if he did not want to take money for it. The terms were certainly reasonable. In fact, we are surprised that wicked Ahab would offer such an equitable deal. But when Jezebel was not influencing him, it seems Ahab could act rather decent at times.

One can readily understand why Ahab would like to purchase Naboth's property. It would make a handsome addition to the palace grounds. Kings are wont to make their palaces and palace grounds attractive and desirable not only for practical reasons but also to impress others. Naboth's vineyard would offer both advantages. Therefore, Ahab made his offer, an offer which indicated that Ahab saw the great value of the land and was very earnest about purchasing the land.

**2. A Rejected Offer**

Naboth's response to Ahab's offer is not what most folk would expect. The worldling would grab at the offer from the king and think himself privileged to be so favorably courted by royalty. But not so Naboth, for "Naboth said to Ahab, The LORD forbid it me, that I should give the inheritance of my fathers unto thee" (v. 3). He flatly rejected Ahab's offer. And he did it with a finality that stopped Ahab from further negotiation.

We want to consider three things about this rejection of Ahab's offer. We will consider the cause of the rejection, the conquering in the rejection, and the crestfallen by the rejection.

*The cause of the rejection.* Naboth would not sell his vineyard, for God's Word forbade it. "The LORD forbid me," (v. 3) he said. God's law given to Moses centuries before said, "So shall not the inheritance of the children of Israel remove from tribe to tribe; for everyone of the children of Israel shall keep himself to the inheritance of the tribe of his fathers" (Numbers 36:7). If Naboth was to obey God, he could not sell his vineyard to Ahab. And Naboth determined to obey God.

Naboth was one of those seven thousand of whom God spoke to Elijah about at Mount Horeb. He may have lived in the midst of pagan idolatry and had land which bordered the palace grounds of the wicked ruler of the nation, but he had not bowed to Baal! It was the Word of Jehovah which guided his conduct, not the word of Baal or his adherents.

We see very few people as faithful to the Word as Naboth was. Some look quite loyal in church on Sunday, but come Monday, and it is business as the world does it, not as the Word decrees it. Folk bow before God on Sunday, but like to deal with Ahab the rest of the week. It is a double standard that is practiced nearly universally. Naboth, however, gives us a great example of letting the Word be our guide in every matter of our life, of letting it be the basis of all our behavior.

*The conquering in the rejection.* Ahab's proposal to Naboth was very tempting. In rejecting it, Naboth conquered a strong temptation. This offer and its rejection give us some good lessons about temptation. We will note the dignity, dividends, and defeat of temptation here.

First, the *dignity of temptation*. The offer was made by a king! Not everyone has a king come knocking on his door. And when a king knocks on the doors, it takes real character to keep one's moral equilibrium during such an occasion. Human nature has a tendency to get giddy and unreserved when favored by royal attention. But when temptation comes in the apparel of a tramp, it has little power, if any, to persuade, to seduce, or to break down our reserves. Coming in the robes of royalty, however, gives authority, officialdom, and acceptance to temptation. This makes it very attractive, respectable, and hard to turn down—just what the devil wants it to be. Therefore, the devil loves to put temptation in dignified apparel. So TV, magazines, and newspaper ads, as an example, often feature famous and important folk in costly array advocating some sinful pursuit, some unholy practice.

Second, the *dividends of temptation*. As we noted above, Ahab's offer was very generous to the extent that if Naboth wanted another vineyard for the one he had by Ahab's palace, Ahab would give Naboth a better vineyard. What a tempting offer. This was profit. This was gain. This was improvement. But be careful, for it was profit and gain only in the material—not the spiritual. Sin cannot give spiritual gain. It may give material gain in abundance, but it only depletes spiritually. Therefore, if we are going to avoid serious blunders, we must put our spiritual welfare above material profits.

Third, the *defeat of temptation*. Naboth won the victory because he knew the Word and obeyed the Word. Every temptation can be overcome by knowing the Word and obeying the Word. Away with the idea that temptations are too strong, too impractical, or too unpopular to oppose; and, therefore, one has to yield. With the Word of God, every temptation can be defeated. Christ demonstrated that truth in His battle with the devil recorded in the Gospels. He, like Naboth, knew the Word and obeyed the Word. If we, however, are ignorant of the Word or disobey the Word, we will be quickly overcome by temptation. There will be no triumph over temptation.

*The crestfallen by the rejection.* Ahab did not react well to Naboth's rejection. He was despicably crestfallen. "Ahab came into his house heavy [sullen] and displeased because of the word which Naboth the Jezreelite had spoken to him . . . And he laid down upon his bed, and turned away his face, and would eat no bread" (v. 4). How pathetic was Ahab's behavior. It manifested immaturity, revealed that his affections were in the wrong place, and prepared him for doing greater evil.

First, his *response was immature*. Edersheim said of Ahab's response, "It was utter and childish petulance." There was no manhood in such pouting, in refusing to eat, in turning his face to the wall, and in not communicating with those around him. This is the behavior of a small child who makes no attempt to control his actions or passions. Ahab, like many politicians, wanted to rule a nation; but he could not even rule himself.

Second, his *response was revealing*. The response revealed that Ahab had his affections in the wrong place. Here is a man who had several palaces, the position of a king, wealth, prestige, and power; and yet he was pouting because he could not buy a vineyard. When one has his affections so out of perspective with true value, he will act very poorly even though he is favored with many advantages in life. Matthew Henry said, "Inordinate desires expose men to continual vexations." And Henry pointed out the great contrast between Ahab and the Apostle Paul. Paul had contentment in prison, but Ahab did not have contentment in a palace. Well for us to heed, then, the admonition of Paul which says, "Set your affection on things above, and not on things on the earth" (Colossians 3:2). Contentment and a host of other valuable things depend on where our affections are located.

Third, the *response was preparatory*. Ahab was preparing his heart for greater evil by the way he responded to Naboth's rejection of the offer. Ahab's pouting does tell us, however, that Ahab did not initiate the plotting against Naboth. That was Jezebel's idea. But his pouting conditioned his heart to be most susceptible to going along with Jezebel's evil ways. Being "heavy [sullen] and displeased" about God's ways ever conditions the heart to be an easy prey of the tempter to do greater evil. Farmers condition the ground before they plant the seed. Satan does likewise. He encourages us to hold our grudges and persist in our sour moods. He knows the longer we stay in such a state of mind, the more the heart will be conditioned to listen to him and his evil propositions.

## B. THE PLOT OF JEZEBEL

Ahab turned to the wall and pouting is a bad enough scene, but it gets far worse when Jezebel strides into the picture. When she saw Ahab in his childish pout, she inquired as to what the trouble was. "Jezebel his wife came to him, and said unto him, Why is thy spirit so sad, that thou eatest no bread?" (v. 5). In response to her question, Ahab, like a spoiled child, related his problem concerning Naboth's refusal to sell his vineyard. Jezebel should have given Ahab a scolding and told him to act better, especially in front of the royal servants who must have had plenty of secret disdain for such disgusting behavior. But instead of trying to help Ahab, Jezebel panders to his peevish ways and sets out to get whatever toy it is that Ahab wants.

To obtain the vineyard for Ahab, Jezebel devised an extensive plot. She ordered a phony trial which would accuse and condemn Naboth of blaspheming God and the king. Then Naboth was to be stoned which would pave the way for Ahab to take the vineyard (vv. 8–10).

We will consider the contempt in the plot, the craftiness of the plot, the compliance with the plot, and the cruelty of the plot.

## 1. The Contempt in the Plot

Jezebel's contempt was twofold. She had contempt for godliness and for government. She did not care for the rules of righteousness nor for the responsibilities of royalty.

*Contempt for godliness.* Naboth's refusal to sell his vineyard was an act of godliness. As we noted above, his reason for refusing to part with his property was based on the law of God. But such noble action and character are held in contempt by Satan and his workers, such as Jezebel. "He that is upright in the way is abomination to the wicked" (Proverbs 29:27). And so all Naboths will be the target of evil.

We badly mistake things if we think righteous living is the key to acceptance and honors in this world. Just the opposite is generally the situation. Naboth would not have suffered such cruel treatment by the world had he not been so pious. But his being pious hastened his end. This is a truth taught repeatedly throughout Scripture. And it explains a lot of inequities in life—from pastors being fired to the ACLU opposing the Bible and prayer being in our public schools.

*Contempt for government.* Jezebel saw government position only for personal gain., She looked with disdain on the idea that government authority was given primarily to help benefit the nation. So she told Ahab, "Dost thou now govern the kingdom of Israel? Arise, and eat bread, and let thine heart be merry. I will give thee the vineyard of Naboth the Jezreelite" (v. 7). She exhorts him to use his power (in this case delegate it to her to carry out her plot) to get what he wants. What a misuse of government power! Instead of using it to help the people, it was used to hurt the people.

Jezebel is not alone in this attitude about government. Many are the rulers in every age whose use of office reveals their contempt for true government. The laws they devise and pass are for personal reasons, such as vendettas against their enemies and the obtaining of personal profit. Such abuse of government power is contempt for true government as God ordained it.

**2. The Craftiness of the Plot**

Jezebel was a wicked wizard. Her plot, though terribly evil, would be craftily disguised so it would appear she was honoring both Jehovah and justice, both the Lord and the law, both the religion of the people and the rules of the nation. Such a scheme did indeed have a stroke of genius to it, but that only made the guile of the plot even worse. God does not give us genius for guile, but for good. Cursed are those who use their cleverness criminally.

*Jehovah appeared to be honored.* Jezebel "wrote letters in Ahab's name, and sealed them with his seal, and sent the letters unto the elders and to the nobles that were in his city, dwelling with Naboth. And she wrote in the letters, saying, Proclaim a fast . . . and set two men . . . before him [Naboth], to bear witness against him, saying, Thou didst blaspheme God and the king" (vv. 8–10). Jezebel was following a practice, taught in the law of Moses, which laid upon the city fathers grave responsibility for serious misdeeds within the city and its environs. Edersheim says, "When blood had been shed and the doer of the crime remained unknown, the elders of the district had by a solemn act to clear themselves of the guilt (Leviticus 4:13, etc.; Deuteronomy 21:1–9), and that, as here, when a great crime was supposed to have been committed, all would humble themselves in fasting before they put away the evildoer from among them."

Though Jezebel was the great Baal advocate, she makes it seem here in some ways that she is following the tenants of Jehovah worship. After the Mount Carmel episode and a turning back to Jehovah of some, she did some crafty politicking to curry the people's favor and support. She will have a religious "fast" to commence her evil designs. It will be a very solemn occasion causing people to think some terrible deed has been done and that the evil one must be ferreted out and duly punished. She wants the people to think the leaders of the land are really out to oppose impiety, and especially impiety in regards to Jehovah (the "God" supposedly being blasphemed here obviously refers to Jehovah, not Baal), when all the while they are practicing and encouraging it.

Thus Jezebel endeavored to disguise her evil under the cloak of religion, the religion of Jehovah. But she was not the first and will not be the last to use religion as a cloak for doing evil, for using religion as a cloak of evil is a common practice. Matthew Henry said, "There is no wickedness so vile, so horrid, but religion has sometimes been made a cloak and cover for it." Let us, therefore, not be so gullible to think that just because something is "churchy" or has the appearance of religion that it is a work worthy of trust and support. Many are the radio, TV, and mail appeals, as an example, which given an appearance of religious charity though they are, in fact, nothing but slick con operations out to take people for all they can get.

*Justice appeared to be honored.* Her plot called for a public trial. This certainly would make it appear that justice was being honored. It was not to be a private lynching, but all the people would be able to observe the trial and thus approve of the condemnation. Also, Jezebel insisted on two witnesses (which also would honor Jehovah, for He decreed the two witnesses as a minimum in His law [Deuteronomy 19:15]). This would confirm the accusation and give appearance of integrity. And integrity is absolutely necessary if justice is to occur.

Yes, Jezebel was really clever in her plot. In the name of religion, she was being grossly irreligious; and in the name of justice, she was perpetrating a great injustice. Unfortunately, our day has seen constant repetition of this hypocrisy. In the name of liberation, communism has enslaved many nations. In the name of welfare, many people's welfare has been hurt by government welfare programs. In the name of education, we have made many fools. In the name of fairness, the Federal Communication Commission's "fairness doctrine" stopped some Gospel broadcasts in past years. On and on it goes. The devil comes as an angel of light many times, and in that he is exceedingly effective. Hence, let us be more diligent in learning the Word so we are not deceived by this clever technique of evil.

### 3. The Compliance With the Plot

Jezebel obtained ready compliance with her murderous plot. "The men of his [Naboth's] city, even the elders and the nobles who were the inhabitants in his city, did as Jezebel had sent unto them, and as it was written in the letters which she had sent unto them" (v. 11). What degraded men to have as city leaders! Their readiness to do as Jezebel said demonstrated great deficiency of character in these men.

Governments in every age are filled with these kind of people. They look out for themselves and care not a whit about their fellow men. They will do anything to get and keep a prestigious position. They have no loyalties except for self, as was the case here; for the ready compliance of Jezreel's elders and nobles with Jezebel's murderous wishes did not mean they were loyal to Ahab's administration; but only that at the time, it was best for their selfish interests to go along with this wicked rule. For a few years later when Jehu came to the town, he told the elders of this city to deliver up Ahab's seventy sons; and they obliged and beheaded seventy of Ahab's sons (II Kings 10). Wicked people are not loyal people but only act out of self-interest.

Not only did wicked men go along with Jezebel, but what bothers many is that it appears God went along with Jezebel, too. God did not stop her murderous plot. This causes some to cry out, "Where is God?" And, frankly, on the surface it seems like a valid cry. Here is Naboth, a godly man, who bucks the times and faithfully stands for God; but God allows evil to take his life. It indeed can be very difficult at times to understand. Krummacher, however, helps us here when he says, "Why, when the Almighty saw the impious deed devising, did he not interpose to prevent it? Why did he not rescue innocent Naboth, who was his servant and his child, and brought into peril by his faith and obedience? For replies to such questions as these, the Scripture refers us to the world to come. Till that arrives, we must silently and resignedly submit to the many mysterious disposals which occur in God's government of the world."

While, as Krummacher states, we may not know all the answers until eternity, there are, however, some basic truths which the Word teaches repeatedly and which we can indeed know in this life which will encourage us regarding cases like this. We list three of these important truths which we can know now. They involve the sovereignty of God, the wisdom of God, and the compensation by God. First, the *sovereignty of God*. God is never a helpless victim—no Naboth dies unless God permits it. Second, the *wisdom of God*. God always acts with wisdom—when He allows a Naboth to die, He has infinite wise reasons for allowing it. Third, the *compensation by God*. God is never a debtor to any man—whenever His children are permitted to suffer for righteousness sake, He will duly reward them, and so much so that they will be more than compensated for every pain and privation they have experienced. These are not always easy truths to perceive, especially when you may be a Naboth yourself going through some very unjust treatment. But time and eternity will verify them abundantly.

### 4. The Cruelty of the Plot

Though Jezebel's plot appeared to honor the Lord and the law, yet it was a very, very, cruel plot. The cruelty of Jezebel's plot was threefold. The plot involved slandering, stoning, and stealing.

*The slandering.* Jezebel instructed the elders of the city to get two "sons of Beliah" (an Old Testament figure of speech for a person with a debased character) to testify against Naboth that "Thou didst blaspheme God and the king" (v. 10). Such an accusation was a blatant lie. Naboth, instead of blaspheming God, gave God great honor by refusing to part with his vineyard. And his actions before King Ahab cannot be faulted, either. But evil does not need facts to accuse. It will invent lies of the worst kind and tell them as publicly as possible.

In spite of the fact that the witnesses were of extremely poor character, their testimony was not challenged. How typical this is of society. Let a righteous Naboth be viciously slandered by men of vile character, and society and the news media will readily accept and report as fact this slanderous testimony. But when the ungodly are spoken against, though it be uncontestable fact and though the witnesses are the most trustworthy of people, such testimony will be scorned, ridiculed, thoroughly scrutinized, and finally rejected.

This certainly reminds us of what often goes on in church. A member who is backslidden, living in sin, unfaithful, etc. will make some snide and grossly untrue remark about a godly pastor; but regardless of the unsavory character of the slanderer, people will often give ready assent to the remark without question. Good men can prove the slanderous remark as a terrible lie and show abundant proof of the pastor's character, but people will often be slow to believe their report. However, the people's slowness to believe the truth and their quickness to go along with the testimony of the "sons of Beliah" does not negate the character of the godly who are slanderously accused. Rather, it exposes the bad character of the ones who are so ready to accept the testimony of evil men.

*The stoning.* Jezebel's plot decreed that Naboth should be stoned (v. 10). Stoning was the legal punishment for blasphemy (Leviticus 24:15,16). But Naboth had not blasphemed. That was simply a slanderous charge to cover up the real reasons behind the stoning. He was stoned to get him out of the way so Ahab could have his vineyard. Therefore, what beastly, barbaric cruelty it was to stone him.

How cruel a godless world is. The more godless a society,

the less life will be respected. Communism, Nazism, and Fascism have all demonstrated this truth pronouncedly. And so does the crime situation in our land. The alarming increase in bloody crimes manifest an alarming increase in ungodliness.

The stoning did not stop with Naboth. We discover in another text that his sons were also included in the stoning. II Kings 9:26 says, "Surely I have seen yesterday the blood of Naboth, and the blood of his sons, saith the LORD." J. Hammond says, "This was the rule of the East (Daniel 6:24). The principle of visiting the sins of the parents upon the children seems to have been carried to an excess [however], as we find Joash (II Kings 14:6) instituting a more merciful rule." Stoning Naboth's sons would be done under the cover of visiting the sins of the parents upon the children. But the main reason for stoning them was to take away any claim for the vineyard by near relatives and thus make it easier for Ahab to take the vineyard, which we will note next.

*The stealing.* "And it came to pass, when Jezebel heard that Naboth was stoned, and was dead, that Jezebel said to Ahab, Arise, take possession of the vineyard of Naboth the Jezreelite, which he refused to give thee for money; for Naboth is not alive, but dead" (v. 15).

Stealing would not bother Ahab and Jezebel. They killed people whenever they felt like it; hence, stealing certainly would not bother them. But Jezebel did not want the citizenry to think it was stealing. Thus her crafty but cruel plot manipulated things so it looked like Ahab's possession of the vineyard was all very legal and proper. Keil said that in those days "the king was able to confiscate his property; not, indeed, on any rule laid down in the Mosaic law, but according to a principle involved in the very idea of high treason. Since, for example, in the case of blasphemy the property of the criminal was forfeited to the Lord (Deut. 13:16), the property of traitors was regarded as forfeited to the king." And as we have just noted, this confiscation of property would be without any contesting by near relatives as

Naboth's sons had been killed, too.

Yes, it was a very, very cruel plot Jezebel executed against Naboth. In cruelty Naboth was deprived of his reputation, his life, and his possessions (which included his sons). But because he lost these things as a result of being faithful to God, God has seen to it that he has more than recovered from his loss. Naboth's reputation has been restored abundantly through God's Word these past 3,000 years. His soul lives on in delight with God, and his eternal inheritance makes any earthly loss nil in comparison. God takes care of His own!

Naboth's ordeal with Ahab and Jezebel has made him an excellent type of Jesus Christ. Pink cites ten ways in which Naboth was a type of Christ. "First, he possessed a vineyard: so also did Christ (Matthew 21:33). Second, as Naboth's vineyard was desired by one who had no respect for God's Law so was Christ's (Matthew 21:38). Third, each was tempted to disobey God and part with his inheritance (Matthew 4:9). Fourth, each refused to heed the voice of the Tempter. Fifth, each was falsely accused by those who sought his death. Sixth, each was charged with 'blaspheming God and the king' (Matthew 26:65; Luke 23:1,2). Seventh, each was put to death by violent hands. Eighth, each was slain 'outside' the city (Hebrews 13:12–14). Ninth, the murders of each were charged with their crime (I Kings 21:19; Acts 2:22,23). Tenth, the murderers of each were destroyed by Divine judgment (I Kings 21:19–23; Matthew 21:41; 22:7).

## C. THE PROCLAMATION OF ELIJAH

"And the word of the LORD came to Elijah the Tishbite, saying, Arise, go down to meet Ahab . . . in the vineyard of Naboth . . . And thou shalt speak unto him" (vv. 17–19). The evil proceedings in Jezreel, though orchestrated with clever deceptive precision, did not escape the omniscient eye of the Almighty! He will now enter the scene and in a most discomforting way so that the fruits of sin will be impossible to enjoy. No matter how promising sin appears, it will not be without the Divine intrusion which will end its pleasures and replace the pleasures with judgment.

The way in which God comes into the picture is through Elijah. Elijah is summoned to take a message to Ahab that will announce extremely unpleasant news for the royal family. Elijah's commission to go to Ahab is not an enviable task. He must walk into great personal danger in going to Jezreel. And he was not given an honorable welcome either. In fact, upon meeting Ahab, he was greeted with a scornful, "Hast thou found me, O mine enemy?" (v. 20). Elijah who was Israel's most valuable citizen, was treated as an arch enemy. Poor Ahab was so blinded by his sin that he mistakes his friends for foes and his foes for friends. He thought Elijah was his enemy and Jezebel was his friend. But as F. B. Meyer says, "Sin distorts everything."

The mistreatment given Elijah by Ahab's greeting will be the experience of anyone who dares to stand against the evils of the day. It is not a pleasant task to speak out against evil. "Those who are engaged in evil doing are annoyed at him who detects them, whether he be a minister of Christ or a policeman" (Pink). The prophet Amos said, "They hate him that rebuketh in the gate" (Amos 5:10). And Krummacher said, "How commonly, my brethren, is it the lot of your ministers to be treated like Elijah, when they succeed in finding out sinners in the church; or rather, when by their instrumentality, sinners are found of God! Yes, when our arrows hit the mark—when one and another of our hearers is compelled, against his will, to see his moral deformities in the mirror we place before his eyes—then it is immediately said of us, in the hearts of those that are thus smitten, 'Hast thou found me, O my enemy?' We are then regarded as disturbers of men's peace, and as taking a malicious pleasure in distressing their minds. As for charity, we are accused as strangers to it . . . Our sermons are considered unsound and extravagant."

Elijah's message to Ahab was a proclamation of the wrath of God. It was a most fitting message for Ahab; for when men have embraced and honored sin, it is time to preach judgment, not some other theme which does not stir the conscience. We

## THE WICKED

have too many today, however, who want to major on the love of God when they ought to be majoring on the law of God and how it has been broken and what judgment is coming as a result.

In studying Elijah's proclamation of the wrath of God, we will consider the details of the proclamation, the effect of the proclamation, and the witnesses of the proclamation.

### 1. The Details of the Proclamation

Elijah's message on God's wrath concerned six things. It concerned the discovering, the deeds, the death, the deal, the dynasty, and the dame (wife) of Ahab.

*The discovering of Ahab.* "I have found thee" (v. 20). It was surely an unpleasant shock for Ahab to look up and suddenly see and hear Elijah and know that his evil had been found out. But "Be sure your sin will find you out" (Numbers 32:23). No matter how clever and crafty has been the evil deed, it will sooner or later be discovered and exposed. Ahab may have been a king, but all the power and prestige of a king cannot keep sin from finding out a man.

Many famous folk have been found out in our day, too. As an example, some of our presidents, who endeavored to carefully create for themselves a most honorable reputation, have been discovered to be most decadent in their morals and their political practices. They have been found out and often to the great distress of their family and followers who would like to keep the lid on such revelations of truth. Others, who have been famous crusaders of various causes, such as equal treatment of races, have been exposed as having barnyard morals. And some preachers, especially the famous TV hucksters, have had their evil found out, too. No one can sin without being discovered sooner or later.

*The deeds of Ahab.* The terrible crime against Naboth was attributed to Ahab by God when He said, "Hast thou killed, and also taken possession?" (v. 19). Most folk can readily accept the idea that Ahab took "possession" of Naboth's vineyard. But some folk will argue that Ahab should not be charged with the murder of Naboth. Ahab did not plot Naboth's death; he did not throw any stones at Naboth. But God says he is guilty of Naboth's death anyway. So we learn here a very important truth about guilt; namely, you do not have to do the actual deed in order to be guilty of the deed. There are other ways of being guilty of the evil.

Ahab was guilty of the deed of murdering Naboth in at least four ways even though he actually did not throw any stones. These four ways have to do with promoting evil, prohibiting evil, profiting from evil, and punishing evil. First, *promoting evil*. Ahab was guilty because he encouraged the deed. He promoted it by his sullen, pouting behavior; for that behavior is what prompted Jezebel to take action. And he also encouraged it by allowing Jezebel to use his seal to give authority to her dastardly plot. Aiding and abetting an evil deed makes you guilty of the deed. Second, *prohibiting evil*. Ahab was guilty because he did not stop the deed though he was the one man who could have stopped it. When you have within your power the ability to stop evil, and you do not, you will be assessed much guilt in the evil. Third, *profiting from evil*. Ahab was guilty because he gladly and willingly seized the profit of the evil deed of others. He did not hesitate to take the vineyard of Naboth. Fourth, *punishing evil*. he was guilty because as the chief executive of the nation, he did not punish the evil doers. That was his responsibility; but he ignored it and for obvious reasons—he would not do anything to Jezebel, and he wanted the vineyard.

These truths about establishing guilt ought to be very sobering to us. What evils are we guilty of even though we have not actually done them? Are we encouraging evil by our poor conduct? Are we failing to stop evil when we indeed could stop it? Do we frown on evil but gladly take the profits of it? And do we fail to bring due punishment upon evil when it is our responsibility to do so? An honest examination of these questions will cause many of us to confess that we are guilty of a lot more evil than we care to admit.

These truths about guilt also tell us how very guilty are the makers, sellers, and advertisers of booze, tobacco, evil magazines, films, etc. They encourage and inspire many evil deeds, and they ought to be punished just as much as the one who has done the evil. But such thinking, though it be straight from heaven, goes over like a lead balloon in the courtrooms of our land.

*The death of Ahab.* The third thing Elijah's message spoke about was Ahab's death which was part of Ahab's judgment for his evil in Naboth's injustice. It was a gruesome prediction. Elijah said, "In the place where dogs licked the blood of Naboth shall dogs lick thy blood" (v. 19). Ahab is going to reap what he has sown. His death will be a bloody affair. Ahab was cruel, and his death will be cruel. He will not die in old age greatly honored and revered of men. But he will die a violent death. It was a terse announcement which would take all the joy out of possessing the vineyard. But he deserved the judgment.

*The deal of Ahab.* Elijah also spoke of Ahab's deal in this message of God's wrath. He said, "Thou hast sold thyself to work evil in the sight of the LORD" (v. 20). Ahab had made a terrible bargain. It was a deal which was deadly for his soul. He exchanged the welfare of his soul for cheap, corrupt, temporal gains of this world. Judas sold out for 30 pieces of silver. Achan sold out for some clothes and silver. Ahab sold out for a vineyard. And many in every age allow sin to destroy their sense of values; and, as a result, they bargain away that which is most valuable for that which is a curse.

*The dynasty of Ahab.* The proclamation of God's wrath included an announcement that the dynasty of Ahab would end. His family would not continue long on the throne but would be overthrown, and another family would take over. God said,

"Behold, I will bring evil upon thee, and will take away thy posterity, and will cut off from Ahab every [male] . . . And will make thine house like the house of Jeroboam the son of Nebat, and like the house of Baasha the son of Ahijah, for the provocation wherewith thou hast provoked me to anger, and made Israel to sin" (vv. 21,22). It is the desire and dream of every king that his descendants will ever be on the throne. But Ahab's sin will destroy that dream. Sin ever destroys our hopes and aspirations.

*The dame of Ahab.* Lastly, the proclamation of God's wrath spoke about Ahab's wicked wife Jezebel. It predicted her terrible, dishonorable death. God said, "The dogs shall eat Jezebel by the wall of Jezreel" (v. 23). Judgment would come upon Jezebel near the very scene of her crime against Naboth. And it came as predicted when Jehu took over as king. At his orders, Jezebel was thrown out the palace window in Jezreel and ran over by Jehu's horses and chariot. And then the dogs ate the corpse (II Kings 9:30–37). She was not accorded an honorable funeral but died despicably, unwanted, and despised which was most fitting for the way she had lived.

What a terrible woman Jezebel was for Ahab to have as a wife. She was such a wicked woman and was the one who stirred up Ahab to doing so much evil (v. 25). It is a great warning to be careful about whom one marries. T. DeWitt Talmage said, "By all these scenes of disquietude and domestic calamity [caused by Jezebel], we implore you to be cautious and prayerful before you enter upon the connubial state which decides whether a man shall have two heavens or two hells, a heaven here and a heaven there, or a hell now and a hell hereafter."

## 2. The Effect of the Proclamation

The message of God's wrath spared no punches. It cut deeply. But it was needed, it was appropriate, and it had a good effect upon Ahab. "And it came to pass, when Ahab heard those words, that he rent his clothes, and put sackcloth upon his flesh, and fasted, and lay [slept] in sackcloth [he wore itchy pajamas to bed!], and went softly [walked barefoot says Josephus, walked slowly says Keil]" (v. 27).

Ahab had finally done something commendable! For once he gave some respect to what Elijah said regarding right and wrong. Later in Scripture, however, we will see that his repentance was not very deep. But, nevertheless, it was better than no repentance at all; and it was better than his attacking Elijah and punishing him because he spoke the truth—an attack Ahab was guilty of later in regards to Micaiah (II Kings 22).

Ahab's change of attitude was observed by God and resulted in the manifestation of God's grace. "And the word of the LORD came to Elijah the Tishbite, saying, Seest thou how Ahab humbleth himself before me? Because he humbleth himself before me, I will not bring the evil in his days; but in his son's days will I bring the evil upon his house" (vv. 28,29). God's grace delayed the execution of the sentence of judgment until the days of Ahab's sons. Apart from this grace, the house of Ahab would have been destroyed much sooner.

How marvelous is God's grace. It takes notice of the slightest bit of repentance. It reaches even to the worst of sinners. God is indeed "ready to forgive" (Psalm 86:5). In fact, He is much more ready to forgive than we are to repent. God is so ready to forgive, so ready to manifest His grace, that when He detects the slightest indication of repentance, as in Ahab's case, He immediately opens the door of grace. How this should encourage anyone who have failed, who wonder if God is interested in them anymore. We must never look lightly upon sin because of grace, but we must never deem sin as too much for God's grace. He is not only "ready to forgive" (Ibid.), but He is also "plenteous in mercy" (Ibid.). Therefore, hasten to Him with your sin and seek His forgiveness. He will not drive you away when you come asking forgiveness but will give you a Divine welcome! Ahab's experience is great proof of that wonderful truth.

That the message on the wrath of God resulted in a manifestation of the grace of God ought to help us think more kindly about such messages. As we noted above, many deplore this message on the wrath of God and leave it out of their preaching in favor of preaching about the love of God or some similar message that does not include the stern truths about the wrath of God. But the truth of the matter is, the message on the wrath of God is a message filled with the grace of God. Had no message on the wrath of God been given Ahab, there would have been no grace forthcoming, either. God in mercy sends the severe message about His wrath in order to wake us up to repent so He can show grace. Sending the message on wrath is motivated by grace. Let the critics of judgment messages ponder that one awhile!

### 3. The Witnesses of the Proclamation

Elijah's message on the wrath of God was heard by more than just Ahab on that fateful day in the vineyard of Naboth. We learn from another text of Scripture that two men, Jehu and Bidkar (officers in Ahab's court), also heard the message. They had accompanied Ahab to the vineyard, and so they were there when Elijah delivered his anathema to Ahab. Later Jehu remembered the message. When he killed Joram (sometimes rendered "Jehoram"), the son of Ahab, to pave the way for his (Jehu) becoming the king of Israel, Jehu told Bidkar (who had become Jehu's assistant), "Take up, and cast him [Joram] in the portion of the field of Naboth the Jezreelite; for remember how that, when I and thou rode together after Ahab his father, the LORD laid this burden [prophecy] upon him. Surely I have seen yesterday the blood of Naboth, and the blood of his sons, saith the LORD; and I will requite thee in this plat, saith the LORD. Now therefore take and cast him in the plat of ground, according to the word of the LORD" (II Kings 9:25, 26).

It is too bad Jehu did not continue to remember what Elijah said to Ahab. It could have spared Jehu much trouble, prolonged and purified his reign over Israel. But like many, Jehu soon forgot the Word of God and departed from God's ways—much to his personal loss and much to the nation's loss, too.

# XI.

# THE WOUNDED

## II KINGS 1

ELIJAH'S EARTHLY SOJOURN is nearing its end; but before he leaves the earth, he will have one more dramatic face-to-face confrontation with the wicked house of Ahab. This time, however, it will not be with Ahab but with Ahab's son Ahaziah who has become king. Ahaziah became king when Ahab was killed in battle with the Syrians a few years after Elijah confronted Ahab in Naboth's vineyard. Not surprisingly Ahab died as he lived—rebelling against God—for he went to battle disregarding the warning of the godly prophet Micaiah. "And the dogs licked up his blood" (I Kings 22:38) as they had licked up the blood of martyred Naboth.

With Ahab gone, some might hope for an improvement in Israel's throne. But unfortunately Ahaziah was a "chip off the old block"; for he "walked in the way of his father, and in the way of his mother [Jezebel], and in the way of Jeroboam the son of Nebat, who made Israel to sin; For he served Baal, and worshipped him, and provoked to anger the LORD God of Israel, according to all that his father had done" (I Kings 22:52, 53).

Having lived like his father, it is not surprising that one day Ahaziah found himself face to face with the bold and stern prophet Elijah. That which brought about the meeting of Elijah and Ahaziah commenced with a fall in the palace. Ahaziah fell through a palace window seriously injuring himself. Concerned as to whether he would survive the wounds, Ahaziah sought the false god Baal-zebub to learn his prospects. The seeking of Baal-zebub climaxed his evil deeds, and God ordered Elijah on the scene to confront the wounded king about his evil.

In this study of the encounter of Elijah with the wounded king, we will consider the providence of events, the practice of unbelief, and the pronouncement of judgment.

## A. THE PROVIDENCE OF EVENTS

Nothing happens by chance. God directs all. He works in nature, events, and history to bring about His purpose. But men often look the other way denying and mocking the idea of God's providential involvement. Men prefer to describe many of their experiences in life as things which simply happen without design or purpose. All of this leaves out God, of course. And it is the kind of thinking which espoused evolution, for it would give us a universe without a Designer and a Builder.

But wise men know better. They recognize in the events of life the work of the Master Designer. They do not speak of "luck" or "chance" or "happenstance" in regards to circumstances, but look at events in terms of Divine providence.

In our text, the working of Divine providence is most evident in the inflicting of Ahaziah and the intervening of Elijah into the case.

### 1. The Inflicting of Ahaziah

Ahaziah had been king about two years when he "fell down through a lattice [a window covering of wood or metal strips] in his upper chamber that was in Samaria" (v. 2). Scripture does not say what Ahaziah was doing when he fell through the lattice. All we know is that he fell through it to the ground obtaining serious injuries in the process. The lattice could have been in poor repair or loosely attached; and when Ahaziah leaned or fell against it, the lattice gave way.

Ahaziah's fall, which men would describe as merely an "accident," manifested God's providential dealings with the house of Ahab. Ahaziah was the "son of a doomed house" (J. Orr). Elijah had predicted in Naboth's vineyard the complete destruction of Ahab's dynasty and family. The falling through the lattice was part of the fulfilling of this prediction. More than a body fell through the lattice. Part of a condemned dynasty fell through it. It was another step in the ending of the rule of Ahab's house over Israel. God was at work vindicating righteousness and bringing due judgment upon wickedness.

How easy it is for God to stop the wicked in their tracks. He can order the slightest providence to halt the strongest sinner. Ahab was stopped when an enemy soldier "drew a bow at a venture [at random]" (I Kings 22:34), Haman was stopped by the insomnia of a king which occurred at a most strategic time (Esther 6), and Ahaziah was stopped when he fell through the lattice of a palace window. Oftentimes it seems like the wicked are invincible; but though we "have seen the wicked in great power, and spreading [flourishing] himself like a green bay tree. Yet he passed away and, lo, he was not" (Psalm 37:35, 36). He who despises the precepts of God will find the providences of God working against him. Matthew Henry said, "He is never safe that has God for his enemy."

## 2. The Intervening of Elijah

As a result of his fall, Ahaziah "was sick" (v. 2) and bedridden (v. 6) and so concerned about his wounds that he wondered if he would survive them. This concern about his survival was so great, he decided to inquire of one of his gods to see what his prospects were. He directed his inquiry to Baal-zebub, one of the gods of Baal. "He sent messengers, and said unto them, Go, inquire of Baal-zebub the god of Ekron whether I shall recover of this disease [injury]" (v. 2).

Baal-zebub was "the god of flies, [the] fly destroyer, who was considered the patron deity of medicine" (Jamieson). "'Baalim' was the general epithet for the false gods, each having his own peculiar office and district, hence the distinguishing titles of Baal-zebub, Baal-peor, Baal-zephon, Baal-bireth" (Pink). The idol of Baal-zebub was not located in Israel; nor was it located in Phoenicia, the home base of Baal worship. It was located in Ekron of Philistia. Though Ekron was closer than the country of Phoenicia, it was still forty miles from Samaria, where Ahaziah resided. Being bedridden it would be impractical for him to make the trip to Ekron, so he sent messengers to do the inquiring of the priests of Baal-zebub.

Ahaziah's seeking to inquire of Baal-zebub was an act which greatly dishonored Jehovah God, and this brought Elijah on the scene. The messengers started on their way, but they did not reach Ekron. As they were traveling, they suddenly met up with Elijah. A coincidence? A thousand times no. God had ordered Elijah to meet the messengers. "The angel of the LORD said to Elijah the Tishbite, Arise, go up to meet the messengers of the king of Samaria, and say unto them, Is it not because there is not a God in Israel, that ye go to inquire of Baal-zebub the god of Ekron?" (v. 3). We may not always be as aware of the Divine orders which bring about apparent coincidental meetings as we are here in this incident. But whether we are aware of the orders or not, they are always present in one way or another; for nothing happens by chance. All things are ordered and directed by God. The meeting of Elijah and the servants of Ahaziah was not fate, luck, or happenstance. It was designed by God. His providence guided it all.

Elijah was always showing up at the most unexpected and inopportune times for those on the wrong course in life. Obadiah had a most unexpected and uncomfortable meeting with him when looking for grass for Ahab's horses. Ahab had a most unexpected and unwanted meeting with Elijah when he was looking over the vineyard of Naboth. And here the messengers of Ahaziah are unexpectedly intercepted and interrupted on their journey by the saintly prophet which for Ahaziah would be a most unwanted intervention.

As we noted in Ahab's being "found out" in Naboth's vineyard, so here the same truth is seen. All evil will sooner or later be arrested by God and brought to His court. Men often believe they are getting away with their evil when their arrest is delayed, but eventually God guides providence to bring about the arrest of the wicked one. Evil cannot outwit the providence of God. Lattices give way and Elijahs show up unexpectedly.

It does not have to be that way, of course. Providence can work for one as well as against one. But if you want providence in your corner, you must be in God's corner. "All things work together for good to them that love God" (Romans 8:28) but not for those who do not love God. Ahaziah did not love God. Thus Divine providence became his curse.

## B. THE PRACTICE OF UNBELIEF

Upon intercepting Ahaziah's servants, Elijah ordered them to "Go, turn again unto the king that sent you, and say unto him, Thus saith the LORD, Is it because there is not a God in Israel, that thou sendest to inquire of Baal-zebub the god of Ekron? Therefore thou shalt not come down from that bed on which thou art gone up, but shalt surely die" (v. 6). To their credit the servants obeyed Elijah right to the letter. Their excellent obedience to Elijah, a man they did not know, shames the poor obedience of many to the God they profess to know.

The servants' report to Ahaziah was met with a hostile reaction, for Ahaziah did not believe the message of God. And in his unbelief, he attacked the speaker of the message of God which in this case was Elijah. Attacking the speaker of God's message is an habitual practice of unbelief. Always when the message of God is rejected, the preacher will be attacked. Unbelief in God's Word will be revealed in animosity towards the proclaimer of God's Word. And the greater the unbelief, the greater will be the animosity. This practice of unbelief explains why many pastors are attacked by church members and voted out of their pastorate. It explains why many missionaries have often been treated cruelly and have even suffered martyrdom. In rejecting God's message, unbelief tries to silence those who would proclaim it. So when Ahaziah rejected God's Word, he attacked Elijah, God's messenger, and endeavored to silence him so he would no longer proclaim God's message. To examine this attack upon Elijah, we note the ardent asking about Elijah, the attempted arrest of Elijah, and the awesome action by Elijah.

## 1. The Ardent Asking About Elijah

After the servants had delivered the message to Ahaziah, he immediately sought to know who the man was that gave the servants the message. Ahaziah's ardency to know the identity of the man was not so Ahaziah could seek him for more messages from God. No, his asking about the messenger was with evil intent. He wanted to know who the man was so he could seek him out to arrest and eliminate him. So he asked his servants, "What manner of man was he which came up to meet you, and told you these words?" (v. 7). They said, "He was an hairy man [refers to his garment], and girt with a girdle [belt] of leather about his loins" (v. 8). This description, which the servants gave Ahaziah of the "man," was sufficient for Ahaziah to know that it was Elijah; for he said, "It is Elijah the Tishbite" (Ibid.).

Though there were other prophets around who had intruded uninvited into the presence of royalty with a Divine message (cp. I Kings 20:35–42), we suspect Ahaziah knew it was Elijah before he was described by the servants. B. H. Carroll said, "The message was more impressive than the garb of the one who sent it . . . [but] both are always recognizable by tyrants." Ahaziah was not ignorant of his father's encounters with Elijah, and the intervening here had the trademarks of Elijah stamped all over it. Ahaziah could not help but see that clearly.

Ahaziah's question—"What manner of man was he?"—is an instructive question. It ought to cause every servant of God to search his heart and ponder his ways to see what manner of person he is so he does not cast any bad reflections on the message. Men will criticize God servants whether they have faults or not. But God's servants need to live as spotless a life as possible so the criticism will not gain the strength of fact. People do indeed look at the manner of life of God's servants; yea, they often scrutinize it. If those who serve God want to honor the message they proclaim, they had better see to it that their manner of life corresponds to the message of the Lord. Unfortunately, we have many ministers today whose manner of life is a disgrace to God and curse upon the ministry.

## 2. The Attempted Arrest of Elijah

Upon confirming Elijah's identity, Ahaziah "sent unto him a captain of fifty with his fifty" (v. 9) to attempt to arrest Elijah. We note the aim of the arrest and the arrogance in the arrest.

*The aim of the arrest.* Scripture does not specifically state that this ordered arrest of Elijah by Ahaziah was to kill Elijah, but that aim is readily implied. Edersheim says, "There cannot be any reasonable doubt that this [sending of the captain and his fifty troops to arrest Elijah] was with hostile intent. This appears not only from the words of the angel in verse 15, but also from the simple facts of the case. For what other reason could Ahaziah have sent a military detachment of fifty under a captain, if not either to defeat some hostile force and constrain obedience, or else to execute some hostile act?" Ahaziah, being of the character that he was, would be glad to get rid of Elijah. "Ahaziah may have been long wishing to arrest and imprison him, and now thought he saw this opportunity" (Rawlinson).

*The arrogance in the arrest.* The troops Ahaziah sent to arrest Elijah found Elijah on the top of a hill. The captain of the troops then gave orders for the arrest of Elijah. The orders said, "Thou man of God, the king hath said, Come down" (v. 9). The first part of the statement appeared to show respect ("Thou man of God"), but the orders ("Come down") certainly did not. It showed great arrogance. It was typical government arrogance against religion. It was also the arrogance of unbelief and the flesh which vaunts itself against the work and workers of God and usurps the authority of God in regard to His work. When the second fifty and their captain were sent, the message showed even more of this wicked arrogance; for the orders said, "Come down quickly" (v. 11) instead of just "Come down."

Evil is ever this way with God. It is always demanding. It would dictate to God. It is the spirit of self-will that scorns the precepts of the Word of God and says, "I don't care what the Bible says; I am going to do what I want to do." It is also the attitude which views worldly position as qualification for giving orders spiritually. Many a church has had trouble with members who are executives and leaders in the world, but who spiritually fall far short of qualifying for church office. Yet, these folk with worldly position arrogantly make demands and hesitate not to disrespect and disregard church authority in business meetings and other church services.

**3. The Awesome Action by Elijah**

The attempted murderous arrest of Elijah was foiled by Elijah. To examine Elijah's awesome action in stopping the arrest and in thus saving his life, we note the conflagration in the action and the criticism of the action.

*The conflagration in the action.* When the first captain of fifty sent by Ahaziah spoke to Elijah and said, "Thou man of God, the king hath said, Come down" (v. 9), Elijah responded to this presumptuous command by saying, "If I be a man of God, then let fire come down from heaven, and consume thee and thy fifty" (v. 10). No sooner had he said that, then "there came down fire from heaven, and consumed him and his fifty" (v. 10). How awesome, devastating, and terrifying. What a strong warning to not mistreat God's servants. But incredibly this great fiery warning did not deter Ahaziah one bit. He sent another group of fifty and their captain and, as we have noted above, with even greater arrogance and earnestness of his unbelief by changing the message from "Come down" to "Come down quickly." How insanely persistent is unbelief. It is suicidal in nature. When it grips the heart there is no warning that will affect it. So the second group was also destroyed by Divine fire.

After two groups were destroyed by fire, you would think Ahaziah would soften up and get the message. But he did not. Like Pharaoh of old, who saw his land destroyed by plague after plague, Ahaziah continued in hardened rebellion against God and sent a third group. How tragic and how pitiful it is to see this king hesitating not to do battle with the Almighty even though he is lying on his death bed and is not long for this world. As Matthew Henry said, "No external alarms will startle and soften secure sinners, but rather exasperate them."

Fortunately for the third group, its captain was wiser than Ahaziah and the previous captains; and he did not ignore the warnings of the fiery judgment. He came to Elijah and "fell on his knees . . . and besought him, and said unto him, O man of God, I pray thee, let my life, and the life of these fifty thy servants, be precious in thy sight" (v. 13). This group was spared because they manifested a different attitude entirely towards God's man than what had been seen previously. Instead of arrogance against God's man, there was humbleness before him. And it is humbleness that obtains the ear and help of God. Again we quote Matthew Henry who said, "There is nothing to be got by contending with God [As Ahaziah did]: if we would prevail with him, it must be by supplication . . . never any found it in vain to cast themselves upon the mercy of God."

*The criticism of the action.* The action of Elijah in calling down fire upon the soldiers does not go over well with some folk, and so they become very critical of the action and of Elijah. To examine this criticism, we will look at the exoneration of Elijah and the condemnation of the soldiers.

First, the *exoneration of Elijah*. Elijah is often censored for calling down fire upon the first two groups. Much of this has come from a misunderstanding of the New Testament passage of Luke 9. The incident referred to there is of the time Jesus and His disciples were rejected in a village of the Samaritans. James and John were very upset about this rejection and said to Jesus, "Wilt thou that we command fire to come down from heaven, and consume them, even as Elijah did?" (Luke 9:54). But Jesus scorned the idea and rebuked them. He said, "Ye know not what manner of spirit ye are of. For the Son of man is not come to destroy men's lives, but to save them" (Luke 9:55,56).

There are at least four ways in which this passage in Luke will vindicate Elijah. They concern accusation, application, animation, and approbation. (1) *Accusation*. The passage does not accuse Elijah of evil. Christ rebuked the disciples, but He did not in anyway condemn Elijah. (2) *Application*. This passage shows plainly that the situation with James and John was vastly different than with Elijah. Elijah's life was in danger, but James and John were not in danger. The Samaritans were not coming out to slay James and John but merely did not receive them. Elijah however, was being hostilely approached by a group of soldiers. Therefore, the disciples were wrong to make an application of Elijah's situation to their situation. (3) *Animation*. The passage reveals that the spirit of James and John was much different than the spirit of Elijah. It is obvious James and John were animated by anger and personal resentment more than anything else. Elijah was animated by honor for God. Yes, it may sound as though it was personal vindication ("If I be a man of God, then let fire come down from heaven and consume thee and thy fifty"); but the emphasis in on who is to give Elijah orders—God Almighty or Ahaziah. As Matthew Poole said, "Elijah's desire did not proceed from a carnal and malicious passion; but from a pure zeal to vindicate God's name and honour." (4) *Approbation*. The passage shows that it takes God's approval for fire to come. The disciples could not bring fire down upon the Samaritans, and neither could Elijah on his own bring fire down upon the soldiers. Only God could send such fire down from heaven, and He would do it only if He approved. In Elijah's case He did approve of the fire, and that approval indeed vindicates Elijah's action. But in the disciples' case, God did not approve. And that lack of approval condemns their actions, but it does not in anyway condemn Elijah's actions.

Second, the *condemnation of the soldiers*. Another criticism of the destructive fire needs to be answered here, too. This criticism says the 102 soldiers destroyed by the two fires from heaven were dealt with unfairly because they were only doing their duty in carrying out Ahaziah's orders. But such an argument will not hold water. Nowhere in Scripture will we ever be exonerated for carrying out the evil orders of man. To the contrary, we are exhorted in Scripture to put our first allegiance to God, not to men. Peter said, "We ought to obey God rather than men" (Acts 5:29). Normally it will be proper to obey those of this earth who are over us in authority. But never, never are we to allow this submission to man to take priority over submission to God. Every order man gives us must be acceptable to God's orders, or we have a Divine duty to disobey them. The 102 soldiers got what they deserved. They cooperated with a wicked king and shared in his punishment.

## C. THE PRONOUNCEMENT OF JUDGMENT

The angel of the Lord told Elijah to go with the third group of soldiers. "Go down with him; be not afraid of him" (v. 15). As we noted earlier, the "be not afraid" implied the intended infliction of evil upon Elijah by the first two groups of soldiers. But the third group was different. They did not do evil to Elijah but escorted him safely to King Ahaziah.

When Elijah came to the king and confronted him regarding his sin, he repeated the message of judgment which he had given to Ahaziah's servants earlier. "He said unto him, Thus saith the LORD, Forasmuch as thou hast sent messengers to inquire of Baal-zebub the god of Ekron, is it not because there is no God in Israel to inquire of his word? Therefore thou shalt not come down off that bed on which thou art gone up, but shalt surely die" (v. 16).

This pronouncement of judgment was a courageous pronouncement, a needed pronouncement, but a disregarded pronouncement.

### 1. A Courageous Pronouncement

The truth is seldom easy to proclaim. And it is especially difficult to proclaim when the situation where you proclaim the truth is hostile. Elijah was back in the lion's den so to speak. He was back in Samaria where Ahab and Jezebel had ruled so wickedly and where Ahaziah, Ahab's wicked son, was now ruling. He had to face Ahaziah face to face and deliver the goods.

It was a lot easier to tell the servants what to tell Ahaziah, but now he must tell Ahaziah the anathema of God right to his face. But Elijah did not fail. He spoke the same unwanted truth in the palace which he had also spoken out on the road to Ekron.

Not many have courage to serve like Elijah. They preach vigorously against certain sins but are careful to do it when the crowd is sympathetic. Put them in front of a crowd of common people, before servants of Ahaziah; and they will blaze away against sin. But put them before influential people, before the Ahaziahs; and they get velvet on their tongues and slobber out a much revised message. Now, of course, they call it tact and a few other nice words; but the truth of the matter is they are nothing but cowards. Anybody can speak boldly on the road to Ekron. But it takes a man of tremendous spiritual courage to faithfully speak the truth in the palace of Ahaziah.

**2. A Needed Pronouncement**

Ahaziah's going to Baal-zebub was a terrible deed. It was an act which did great dishonor to Jehovah the God of Israel. "The king's consultation of Baal-zebub, god of Ekron, is a complete and absolute denial of the Divinity of Jehovah. To consult a foreign oracle is equivalent to saying that the voice of God is wholly silent in one's own land" (Rawlinson). So Elijah's rebuking question to Ahaziah was, "Is it not because there is no God in Israel to inquire of his word?" (v. 16). Pink quotes Thomas Scott who said, "When a king of Israel sent to inquire of a heathen oracle he proclaimed to the Gentiles his wont of confidence in Jehovah: as if the only nation favored with the knowledge of the true God had been the only nation in which no god was known. This was peculiarly dishonorable and provoking to Jehovah." Yes, it was a most serious sin. The fact that the pronouncement against it is repeated word for word three times in the first chapter of II Kings (vv. 3,5,16) emphasizes that fact. This evil indeed needed the repeated pronouncement of God's anathema.

We need the same pronouncement repeated again and again

today, for multitudes in our time do just like Ahaziah. When trouble comes they seek everything but God. How seldom do folk "inquire of his word" in such times. More likely they will seek the counsel of the world, such as an Ann Landers, psychiatrists and psychologists, who ignore God and His Word in favor of their Baal-zebub thinking; or even consult witches, and fortune tellers who tread in the cursed waters of demonism.

This practice is not limited to the poor and uneducated. President Kennedy consulted Jeanne Dixon, and the Reagans consulted the astrologers. Even a good many members of Bible-believing churches reflect Ahaziah's habit, for they are slow to seek God in time of trouble but too often prefer to seek help from the Ekrons of the world instead of seeking help from the Word of God. They show a surprising respect for worldly prognosticators and advisors while showing a likewise surprising skepticism of the value and validity of the Word of God. All of this is a gross dishonor of God; for it says He either does not exist or that His Word is unreliable and, therefore, unworthy of our trust. Such an attitude invites severe judgment from God, and our land is surely ripe for such judgment.

**3. A Disregarded Pronouncement**

"So he died according to the word of the LORD which Elijah had spoken" (v. 17). Ahaziah had ignored the warning of the judgment fire upon two companies of his soldiers, and here he continues to reject God's warnings, for the message of doom moved him not. Unlike his father Ahab, who when he heard the anathema of God in Naboth's vineyard "rent his clothes, and put sackcloth upon his flesh, and fasted, and lay in sackcloth, and went softly" (I Kings 21:27), Ahaziah is not recorded as showing any signs of repentance. If he had, God would have acted; for, as we noted earlier about Ahab, God is ever ready to forgive. The slightest effort at repentance does not go unnoticed with God. But Ahaziah, though young, was a hardened sinner. He had not learned from his father's experiences or from the drought or from the Mount Carmel manifestation or from any other demonstrations of Jehovah's might and power. He despised Jehovah-God; and, as a result, he ended up paying the great price of being cut down by God in this life and being consigned to eternal hell fire in the next life.

Tragically, the attitude of Ahaziah abounds all around us. God sends ample warnings, but people give no attention or respect to these gracious warnings. Rather, they go on their way explaining the warnings, the rumblings of nature, and the "accidents" as mere happenstance with no meaning whatever to the soul of man. It is a foolish and fatal game to play as Ahaziah's life attests.

# XII.

# THE WHIRLWIND

## II KINGS 2:1–12

FOR MANY PEOPLE the end of one's journey in life is a morbid subject. The world especially does not like to think or speak about it. And for a very good reason—without Christ they have no hope. Departing from this world is terrifying to them. It is horror, not hope. But the believer looks at leaving this earthly sojourn with a far different attitude. Yes, there may be and often is suffering by the one who is passing to the other side; and there are tears in the eyes and hearts of those who remain. But believers "sorrow not, even as others [unbelievers] which have no hope" (I Thessalonians 4:13). The departure of a believer can be one of triumph and of reward.

And what a triumphant and rewarding departure Elijah had from this world! A whirlwind, accompanied by a chariot and horses of fire, lifted him from the earth and took him straight to heaven. Yes, it is hard to give up Elijah; but for the believer, it certainly is not an unpleasant thing to ponder and study his parting from this earth.

In this study on the ending of Elijah's journey on earth, we will note the pathway of Elijah which led to the place of his exodus by the whirlwind, the parting of Elijah in the whirlwind, and the portrayal of Elijah given by Elisha immediately after Elijah's parting by the whirlwind.

## A. THE PATHWAY OF ELIJAH

Elijah spent his last day on a journey which included visiting some of the schools of the prophets and a miraculous crossing of the Jordan River. Shortly after crossing the Jordan he was whisked away in the whirlwind. We will follow the pathway of Elijah and note the area, authority, associate, attitude, academies, and accomplishment on the pathway.

**1. The Area of the Pathway**

The area covered by Elijah's pathway was a distance of 30 to 35 miles. It was covered in just one day which meant it had to be walked at a good and relentless pace. The pathway was rich with spiritually significant locations. Four of these locations are listed. They are Gilgal, Bethel, Jericho, and the Jordan. We will look briefly at each.

*Gilgal.* This was the starting point of the pathway. There are five or six locations named Gilgal in Scripture. The most famous is the one near Jericho where Joshua and Israel first set up camp after crossing the Jordan River to enter Canaan. The Gilgal from where Elijah's last journey began could not have been that Gilgal, however, as his pathway went "down" (v. 2) from Gilgal to Bethel. Bethel was several thousand feet higher than the famous Gilgal near the Jordan and would require going "up" not "down." Also Scripture implies that Bethel was between this Gilgal and Jericho which is definitely not the case with the famous Gilgal near the Jordan. The Gilgal which fits our text would be the Gilgal near Mount Gerizim and Mount Ebal, "the great trysting-place of the final consecration of the tribes after their entrance into the land of promise" (Edersheim) as noted in Deuteronomy 11:30. This Gilgal was "eight or nine miles" north of Bethel (Ibid.).

*Bethel.* From Gilgal Elijah's pathway led to Bethel. Jacob's vision of the ladder going from earth to heaven made Bethel a special star on Israel's map. And well it should, for the ladder was a type of Christ as Christ Himself testified (John 1:51). The name Bethel means "house of God," and its early history was associated with dedication to God. But in Elijah's day, Bethel was synonymous with apostasy; for when Israel divided after Solomon's death, Bethel was one of the two places (Dan was the other) where the worship of golden calves was instituted by Jeroboam, the first king of the Northern Kingdom. As a seat of idolatry, Bethel became hostile to the truth. An example of this is seen in the mistreatment of Elisha shortly after Elijah's exodus from the earth by the whirlwind.

*Jericho.* From Bethel the pathway went to Jericho. The town of Jericho was famous because of its destruction when Israel entered the land of Canaan under the leadership of Joshua. God put a curse on rebuilding Jericho then. For centuries no one opposed the curse. But it was under Ahab's rule, hence during Elijah's time, that the city was again rebuilt—and not without experiencing the curse (I Kings 16:34).

*Jordan.* After Jericho, the pathway crossed the Jordan. No river is more famous in the world. Though a crooked thing and despised because it was dirty (II Kings 5), it nevertheless was the scene of some great spiritual events which are recorded in the Scripture. The most important of these events up to Elijah's time was the crossing of the Jordan by the Israelites under Joshua's leadership.

Elijah's crossing over the Jordan so he could depart from this world from the east side of Jordan reminds us of Moses, that great emancipator of Israel, who also departed from this world from the east side of Jordan. There are great similarities between Moses and Elijah. Jamieson quotes Bishop Hall's excellent statement regarding these similarities. Hall said, "There must be a parallel betwixt the two great prophets that shall meet Christ at Tabor [during Christ's transfiguration]—Moses and Elijah. Both received visions on Horeb; to both God appeared there—in fire and in other forms of terror; both were sent to kings—one to Pharaoh, the other to Ahab; both revenged idolatries with the sword—the one upon the worshippers of the golden calf, the other upon the four hundred Baalites; both divided the waters—the one of the Red Sea, the other of Jordan; both must be fetched away beyond Jordan—the body of Elijah is translated, the body of Moses is hid."

## 2. The Authority on the Pathway

Elijah's life was characterized by submission to Divine authority. His movements were a result of God's leading. Again and again we read in Scripture of Elijah heeding God's directives on where to go and what to do. "The word of the LORD came unto him, saying, Get thee hence, and turn thee eastward, and hide thyself by the brook Cherith . . . So he went and did according unto the word of the LORD" (I Kings 17:2,3,5); "the word of the LORD came unto him, saying, Arise, get thee to Zarephath . . . So he arose and went to Zarephath" (I Kings 17:8–10); "the word of the LORD came to Elijah . . . saying, Go, show thyself unto Ahab . . . And Elijah went to show himself unto Ahab" (I Kings 18:1,2); "let it be known this day that thou art God in Israel, and that I am thy servant, and that I have done all these things at thy word" (I Kings 18:36); "the angel of the LORD said to Elijah the Tishbite, Arise, go up to meet the messengers of the king of Samaria . . . And Elijah departed [to meet the servants]" (II Kings 1:3,4). On the last day of his earthly sojourn, his submission to Divine authority was still very conspicuous. "The LORD hath sent me to Bethel" (v. 2), "the LORD hath sent me to Jericho" (v. 4), and "the LORD hath sent me to Jordan" (v. 6) were the directives which guided his pathway on his last day. Elijah ended his life the way he had lived it—submitting to the authority of God's will.

When the end comes there is no better place to be than in the will of God. But one is not likely to be in the will of God at the *end* of life if he has not practiced living in the will of God *during* his life. The secret to Elijah's walking his last day in submission to God's authority is that he walked all his days that way, too. May we be encouraged by Elijah's example to walk daily according to the Word of the Lord.

## The Whirlwind

### 3. The Associate on the Pathway

Elijah did not travel alone on this pathway. Elisha, his associate, was right there beside him the whole way. Elisha had been appointed as Elijah's eventual successor some years before when Elijah came back from his Mount Horeb experience. After the appointment, Elisha kept company with Elijah and was groomed by Elijah for his office. Now they take their last journey together.

Two significant things stand out prominently on this journey regarding Elisha as Elijah's associate. They are the persistency of Elisha in following Elijah and the promise for Elisha given by Elijah.

*The persistency of Elisha.* Elisha was very faithful to Elijah, and it was most evident on this journey, for Elisha stayed with Elijah the entire way even though he had repeated opportunities to leave. Three times on the journey Elijah tested Elisha by saying, "Tarry here, I pray thee; for the LORD hath sent me" (vv. 2, 4, 6) elsewhere (Bethel, Jericho, and Jordan). But Elisha passed the test most successfully. "I will not leave thee" (Ibid.) was his persistent response to any suggestion of parting company. Therefore, "*they* went down to Bethel" (v. 2); "*they* came to Jericho" (v. 4); "*they* two went on" (v. 6); "*they* two stood by Jordan" (v. 7); "*they* two went over on dry ground" (v. 8); "*they* were gone over" (v. 9); "*they* still went on" (v. 11).

Such a commitment to companionship is certainly needed in many areas of life today. We think especially of marriage where so many divorces are occurring. Couples often separate at the drop of a hat. Marriage will never succeed, however, unless couples make an Elisha-like "I will not leave thee" commitment. And such a commitment is what God expects couples to make in marriage (Matthew 19:5, 6).

*The promise for Elisha.* After Elijah and Elisha had crossed over the Jordan, "Elijah said unto Elisha, Ask what I shall do for thee, before I be taken away from thee" (v. 9). Elijah gave

Elisha a magnanimous promise. It was Elisha's reward for sticking with Elijah. Faithfulness has its rewards, and Elisha discovered what choice blessings they are.

Elisha's response to the promise was most noble. He did not ask for fame or fortune, nor did he seek material or physical blessings. Rather he wisely sought for spiritual blessings. He requested, "Let a double portion of thy spirit be upon me" (v. 9). The request for a "double portion of thy spirit" was not a request of pride to be twice as great as Elijah. No, this request spoke of an inheritance blessing. The term, "double portion," is used in Deuteronomy 21:17 to describe the portion the first-born received from his father's estate. Thus in principle the term is associated with an inheritance. Specifically, it is associated with the inheritance of one who is taking over the leadership of the estate. When the father died, the first-born took over his father's place. In like manner, Elisha was to inherit Elijah's office when Elijah departed. So Elisha was asking that he might inherit ("double portion") the spiritual power ("of thy spirit") of Elijah which was vital to have if he was going to fill that office.

Would that man would be more conscious of their need of spiritual power today. We get so big and exult in our own strength, our own ability, and our own savvy, and forget that without God's spiritual enduement we are as helpless as can be. But as Pink says, "The work of the ministry is such that no man is naturally qualified for it; only God can make any meet for the same."

Elisha's request was no small request as indicated by Elijah's "Thou hast asked a hard thing" (v. 10). "Hard" in the Hebrew means very difficult. Elijah's use of the word emphasizes the greatness of Elisha's request But great though the request may be, Elijah meant what he said. So Elisha's request would be granted by Elijah—provided Elisha see Elijah when he departed (v. 10), which he did. (For a more detailed study of the promise made to Elisha and his response to it, see the author's book on Elisha.)

## 4. The Attitude of the Pathway

Elijah's attitude on the pathway to the whirlwind is most exemplary. Two attitudes particularly stand out—his tranquility and his humility.

*Tranquility.* His attitude about departing the earth was one which only the righteous can truly possess. Elijah did not show any fear of leaving the earth. He was not in great anxiety about the unseen world. He knew God and faithfully served Him. Therefore he was not worried about what was in store for him in eternity and could look forward to his meeting with God. Anyone who has lived as Elijah can think likewise. As John Knox said on his death bed, "Oh, serve the Lord in fear, and death shall not be terrible unto you."

*Humility.* His attitude about the glorious aspect of his departure was one of great humility. He did not glory in it. He did not seek special attention by it. He remained conspicuously quiet about the whole thing. How commendable.

Elijah's humble attitude here certainly contrasts to the attitude of many saints today. F. B. Meyer said, "Alas! what a rebuke is here for ourselves! . . . when we remember how eager we are to tell men, by every available medium, of what we are doing for the Lord. There is not a talent with which He entrusts us which we do not parade as a matter of self-laudation. There is not a breath of success that does not mightily puff us up." Krummacher spoke similarly when he said, "Let us here blush at ourselves! For how vain are we apt to be of our own little distinctions!" Yes, we would have called a press conference or sent out a press release to all the news media to let them know how we were going to depart. We would have tried to get all the attention and glory we could get out of it. But this was not the attitude of Elijah. He was not thinking of his personal glory, but only of God's glory. Such thinking, however, is seldom evidenced in our self-glorifying age. But let Elijah's attitude on his pathway be more evident in us on our pathway.

Elijah

## 5. The Academies on the Pathway

At Bethel and Jericho were schools of the prophets (the term "sons of prophets" [vv. 3,5,7] means students training to be prophets). Elijah and Elisha encountered these students when they traveled through these towns. Unfortunately, the students in these academies did not conduct themselves very well in this last meeting they would have with Elijah. The students had a conversation problem in both towns, and at Jericho there was also a committee problem.

*The conversation problem.* Students in both schools spoke the same thing to Elisha about Elijah's departure, and on each occasion they received the same rebuke from Elisha. The "sons of the prophets . . . came forth to Elisha, and said unto him, Knowest thou that the LORD will take away thy master from thy head today?" (v. 3). The departure of Elijah was not only known by Elijah and Elisha, but the sons of the prophets also knew. And they even knew the day. But knowledge does not always beget good manners; and the sons of the prophets did what many do when they expand their knowledge—demonstrate a good deal of arrogance, disrespect, and lack of discretion. They knew something, and so they must tell Elisha what they knew (to impress him with their knowledge). Then they questioned if Elisha knew (how folk like to gloat if they know some important thing and can get others, especially a superior as Elisha was, to admit he does not know it). Of course, Elisha knew; and they should have known that. But pride is blind to many obvious things.

Elisha's response to them was terse and stern. "Yea, I know it; hold ye your peace" (v. 3). "Hold ye your peace" can be translated "be still" or "keep silent." Rawlinson amplifies the statement as, "Hush—do not chatter about what is so sacred; do not suppose that you are wiser than anyone else; be a little modest and a little reticent."

Christians can be ever so straight doctrinally and, yet, be very offensive in their deportment because they lack what

Krummacher says we need, "a nice attention to feeling and social decorum which well befits the sons and daughters of Zion." Pastors are sometimes at fault here when they describe illnesses and other problems from the pulpit in rather uncouth and indiscreet ways. Parishioners also need to be careful and kind when inquiring of another's welfare or in telling of their own troubles.

*The committee problem.* This problem occurred only with the students from the academy in Jericho. Jericho was not far from the Jordan; and so some of the students, a committee of fifty, ventured forth to follow Elijah and Elisha at a distance to see the departure of Elijah. "Fifty men of the sons of the prophets went, and stood to view afar off" (v. 7). "Afar off" was indicative of the character of their faith, however. After Elijah's translation, which they witnessed, they insisted Elisha send another committee of fifty strong men into the hills to "seek" Elijah (II Kings 2:16). Their theology was so bad they thought God might have dropped Elijah somewhere in the hills surrounding Jericho. These scholars are like many in every age who can be shown an abundance of evidence regarding truth, yet, still question it. They may have good professors, and the schools may have good curriculums, but these students do not seem to catch on spiritually.

## 6. The Accomplishment on the Pathway

The Jordan River cut across the pathway of Elijah on his last journey on earth. Undaunted by the problem, Elijah "took his mantle, and wrapped it together, and smote the waters, and they were divided hither and thither, so that they two went over on dry ground" (v. 8). What a great accomplishment! In it there is a challenge, a censure, and a consolation.

*A challenge.* This great accomplishment of Elijah was done near the very end of his earthly sojourn. Unlike many senior saints in our churches, he was not ready, at the end of his sojourn, to sit down and twiddle his thumbs and talk about what great things he had accomplished in the past. No, he was going to keep attempting great things through the power of God right to the very end.

Would that the older members of our churches were this way. For the most part, however, these folk have little interest in launching out on any significant new project, such as a building program. Their accomplishments are in the past; and they seem to prefer that their church accomplishments be in the past, too. But Elijah's action at Jordan challenges them to pursue notable accomplishments right to the very end of their lives.

*A censure.* Two words—"dry ground" (v. 8)—really condemn the skeptics who are always trying to explain away this and other miracles by naturalistic explanations. One of their favorite explanations for this miracle, and for the similar miracle which occurred in Joshua's time, is that an earth slide occurred up the river on the Jordan where it runs through a narrow ravine and cut the waters off for a time. But the Bible says Elijah and Elisha, and also the Israelites of Joshua's day, walked over the Jordan on "dry ground" (v. 8; Joshua 3:17). A river bed does not dry up naturally in a short period of time. It takes days to dry. Elijah and Elisha here and the Israelites of Joshua's day did not wait days before crossing over. They crossed over immediately. The explanations the skeptics make, because they cannot believe the miracles, are harder to believe than the miracles.

*A consolation.* This crossing over the Jordan by Elijah and Elisha should encourage all who would walk the path God chooses. Sometimes in walking that path we confront discouraging obstacles which block the way and which seem impossible to move. But as F. B. Meyer said, "Where God's finger points, there God's hand will make the way . . . Step down the shelving bank, and the waters of difficulty shall part before you; and you shall find a pathway where to human vision there was none." God will part all the Jordans that stand in our way if it is His pathway for us. Our concern need not be about His parting the Jordans but rather about our being on the right pathway.

## B. THE PARTING OF ELIJAH

Scripture does not always give length of text to that which is important. Sometimes the most dramatic and most vital events and truths are told in brief sentences, not in lengthy detailed paragraphs. So it is with Elijah's parting. Maclaren said, "Surely never was such a miracle told so quietly. The actual ascension is narrated in a sentence. Its preliminaries take up the rest of this narrative."

In examining this dramatic, but briefly reported, parting of Elijah, we will consider the circumstances, character, and comparisons of his parting.

### 1. The Circumstances of His Parting

In considering the circumstances of Elijah's parting, we have two things in mind—the time of the parting and the place of the parting.

*The time.* The time of Elijah's parting was God's time. It was "when the LORD would take up Elijah into heaven by a whirlwind" (v. 1) that Elijah's parting occurred. God, not Elijah, determined the "when."

How grateful Elijah should be that it was God's time that prevailed and not Elijah's time. Elijah had requested to die earlier when he was under the "juniper tree" in great despair after the warrant from Jezebel (I Kings 19:4). But God refused to answer that request. And how gracious it was of God to refuse the request. What blessing, what reward, and what triumph Elijah would have missed had his prayer been answered.

The same is true with us, too. Many times our requests are not granted by God. That generally causes us to fuss and complain. But if we only knew as God knows, we would cease fussing and complaining. His denials of our requests were for our good. And the denials bring far better blessings than the grantings would. As F. B. Meyer said, "We shall have to bless Him for ever, more for prayers He refused than for those He granted."

*The place.* Elijah's departure took place in an obscure location just east of the Jordan River. Human thinking would have planned for Elijah to leave in a more prominent place and situation such as from Mount Carmel in front of a great audience or from Samaria in front of all his enemies to "show them a thing or two." But it is not whether man sees or not that makes a thing glorious; it is whether God sees. And God had no trouble with the obscure location east of Jordan.

Your location in life may be obscure, but it does not mean you cannot have a glorious home-going. What determines a glorious home-going is your loyalty to the Lord. Your passing from this earth will not be slighted by God just because you have not had a big and famous position in life. Nor does the number of folk at your funeral determine the heavenly glory your home-going receives. Elijah had a tremendous, glorious departure; but Elisha was the only man with him when he departed.

## 2. The Character of His Parting

We want to consider two features regarding the character of the parting of Elijah for heaven. They are the uniqueness of the parting and the appropriateness of the parting.

*The uniqueness.* Elijah's departure was unique in two ways. It was unique in its accompaniments and in its accomplishment.

First, the *accompaniments.* His departure was accompanied "by a whirlwind" (v. 1), and "a chariot of fire, and horses of fire" (v. 11). What an unusual home-going! No other person ever had such a home-going.

In spite of the clarity of the Scripture regarding these accompaniments and the part they played, few people get it straight. Most people assume Elijah was taken to glory in a chariot of fire. Artists, whose religious paintings seldom are in accord with Biblical facts, generally paint Elijah in a chariot riding to heaven. But no where in Scripture does it say he rode a chariot home. Rather the Word of God says a whirlwind took him to glory. "The LORD would take up Elijah into heaven by a whirlwind" (v. 1), and "Elijah went up by a whirlwind into heaven" (v. 11). Most folk are acquainted with how tornadoes pick up things and carry them many miles. In similar fashion Elijah was picked up from the earth and carried to heaven. It was not by a flaming chariot. The chariot and horses only accompanied him.

Notice of this frequent error in people's thinking should prompt us to be more careful in our own Bible study. Too often in our Bible study we pay more attention to such things as tradition and artists' conceptions of Biblical scenes than we do to what the Scripture actually says. Such an approach to Bible study promotes ignorance and doctrinal error.

Second, the *accomplishment.* Elijah entered heaven apart from dying. Only Enoch, of all mankind from Adam until now, had a like accomplishment. He, like Elijah, skirted death's door when being ushered into eternity. But the Scripture's account of Enoch's departure gives no hint that it was accompanied with such dramatic features as Elijah's departure was. Scripture simply says, "Enoch walked with God, and he was not; for God took him" (Genesis 5:24). With Elijah, however, it was a whirlwind and the chariot and horses of fire.

Elijah and Enoch will not be so unique in the accomplishment of their home-going after the Rapture takes place. Multitudes of believers will share with these two giants of the faith in the same accomplishment when they are snatched up from the earth to meet the Lord in the air. If you are alive at that time, will you be among the multitude of those who will be raptured?

*The appropriateness.* The end of Elijah's life on earth certainly fit the character of his ministry. The whirlwind, the chariot and horses of fire all speak of Elijah's work on earth. F. B. Meyer summed it up well when he said, "There was fitness in the method. He had himself been as the whirlwind, that falls suddenly on the unsuspecting world, and sweeps all before it in its impetuous course, leaving devastation and ruin in its track. It was meet that a whirlwind-man should sweep to heaven in the very element of his life . . . nothing could be more appropriate than that the stormy energy of his career should be set forth in the rush of the whirlwind; and the intensity of his spirit by the fire that flashed in the harnessed seraphim."

If our home-going were to characterize the way we have lived for the Lord, would it evidence that we had lived with great earnestness for God? If God adjusted the character of our departure from earth to the way we had served Him, some would indeed have a very dramatic departure. But others would have a very dull departure, for their lives have not evidenced much excitement for the Lord at all. Yes, they were excited about other things, such as sports and making money; but spiritual things seldom gave them an extra heart beat.

**3. The Comparisons of His Parting**

Elijah's exodus from the earth has in it both contrasts and similarities to the passing of others from the earth.

*Contrasts.* What a contrast his leaving the earth was to that of his two worst enemies, Ahab and Jezebel. Ahab was killed in a battle he was told by God's prophet Micaiah not to enter. When he died the "dogs licked up his blood . . . according unto the word of the LORD" (I Kings 22:38). Jezebel died when she was thrown from the window of her dwelling in Jezreel and her body was trodden under by Jehu's horses and chariot. Then dogs came and ate everything except her "skull, and the feet, and the palms of her hands" (II Kings 9:35).

Of course, you do not need a departure like Elijah's to be a contrast to the wicked. In fact, in the eyes of the world you may not have nearly as glorious a parting as some wicked. But that does not change the greatness of the contrast. What gives the greatest contrast is the destiny of the departing. Elijah went to "heaven" (vv. 1,11) when he departed this earth. That contrast was the greatest of all contrasts he had with his wicked enemies. And that is the only one that really matters.

*Similarities.* Elijah's parting speaks of and reminds us of other partings. First, it reminds us of the Rapture. When the Rapture occurs the saints on earth will, like Elijah, enter eternity without going through the valley of death. They, like Elijah, will be "caught up . . . to meet the Lord in the air" (I Thessalonians 4:17). Second, Elijah's parting reminds us of the Lord's ascension. Elijah was talking to his loyal disciple just prior to his parting; and when he was taken, the Scripture says his loyal disciple "saw him no more" (v. 12). In like manner, Christ was speaking with His loyal disciples just prior to His being "taken up" into glory; and when He was taken, Scripture says Christ was then "out of their sight" (Acts 1:9).

## C. THE PORTRAYAL OF ELIJAH

Elijah did not have a funeral, but he did have an eulogy given about him after he left the earth. It was a very short eulogy, but it gave a great portrayal of a great prophet. The eulogy for Elijah was given by Elijah's associate Elisha. When "Elisha saw it [the parting], he cried, My father, my father, the chariot of Israel, and the horsemen thereof" (v. 12). Interestingly, this same eulogy was given of Elisha when he lay on his death bed. King Joash came to visit Elisha; and the Scripture said he "wept over his [Elisha's] face, and said, O my father, my father, the chariot of Israel, and the horsemen thereof" (II Kings 13:14).

This eulogy which Elisha gave of Elijah was a twofold portrayal of Elijah. It portrayed him as a father and as a fortress.

### 1. The Father Portrayal

The cry "My father, my father" is both a term of respect and a term of affection.

*A term of respect.* It was common in those days not only for a son to respectfully call his earthly paternal parent, "Father";

but also for the student to call his teacher, "Father"; for the servant to call his Master, "Father"; and for the younger to call the elder, "Father." Now Elijah was all four to Elisha. He became Elisha's father by virtue of the fact that Elisha, when a young man, left his home and parental father to go with Elijah. Elijah would have to fill in for Elisha's father in giving fatherly advice down through the years. Elijah was also the tutor of Elisha as we have noted previously in this chapter. He trained Elisha in the prophetic office so that when he passed from this world scene, Elisha would be equipped to take over. Furthermore, Elijah was Elisha's master; for Elisha served Elijah. "Elisha the son of Shaphat, which poured water on the hands [task of the servant] of Elijah" (II Kings 3:11). And, of course, Elijah was Elisha's elder, probably twenty or more years older than Elisha. So it is fitting that Elijah be called "My father, my father"; for there was plenty of respect due Elijah from Elisha from those four positions.

Respect was also due Elijah for the great spiritual work he did in Israel. Society in his day gave most of their honors to the wicked rulers and people of the day and had little respect for Elijah. But it was all a great mistake. If ever there was a man in Israel who needed to be given great respect it was Elijah.

What a great thing it would be if we demonstrated respect for that which is representative of Elijah today. Respect for our parents, our employer, our elders, our teachers, and especially for our spiritual leaders. But, alas, little respect is seen anywhere today. Of course, a great many parents, employers, elderly, teachers, and spiritual leaders do little to merit praise. Their lives are often more like an Ahab and Jezebel than an Elijah. But where the performance is good, there ought to be respect. Lack of respect is a reflection of poor character in those failing to show the respect. And any pastor will vouch for the fact that those who show him the least respect at church are often those in the church who have the most trouble with their character.

*A term of affection.* Can anyone read "My father, my father" and not see tremendous affection in the term? This was not only a cry of respect for Elijah, but it was also a heart cry of affection for him. How greatly Elisha had been attached to Elijah.

Elisha's affection for Elijah is a rebuke to the type of people many are attracted to in our day. Young people often drag some piece of trash into a minister's office and say this is what they want to marry. Others take as role models Hollywood stars, rock musicians, and money grabbing professional athletes who prefer to play ball on Sunday instead of being in church. And our churches and Christian organizations are not helping much in this area either; for they are ever parading before the public, at their meetings or in their periodicals, "heroes" of the faith who fit the aforementioned categories. Especially do they exalt the professional athletes and trump them up as "role models." But we reveal our character by whom we are attracted to and by whom we make our heroes. We desperately need a change in all of this today. But that change will only come when we have a change of character and reflect Elisha's values instead of the carnal values of this world.

## 2. The Fortress Portrayal

"The chariot of Israel, and its horsemen" (v. 12) refer to the miliary. "Chariot" here is "war-chariot" according to Keil. The chariot and the horsemen were that in which nations based their power, their protection, their security. So Elisha's statement tells us Elijah was the great protection of Israel. He was the great fortress for the nation which shielded them from destruction. It was not Ahab's chariots and horses but Elijah that gave Israel security. With him gone "The public had lost its best guard . . . Elijah was to them, by his counsels, reproofs, and prayers, better than the strongest force of chariot and horse, and kept off the judgments of God. His departure was like the routing of an army, an irreparable loss. 'Better have lost all our men of war than this man of God'" (Matthew Henry).

The best defense and the best security a nation can have is godly people. A nation may have the best nuclear powered missiles, the greatest number of men in arms, and the best arms but still be as weak as water. Sodom's security was related to how many righteous were in the city (Genesis 18:23–33). Unfortunately for Sodom, it had too few righteous to save it from destruction. Is not our nation perilously close to the same situation? Not only are we having less and less righteous in our nation, but the scorning and mocking of the righteous and righteousness is increasing with alarming speed. However, we cannot despise the Elijahs and what they represent without cursing the land.

# XIII.

# The Writing

## II Chronicles 21

We do not think of Elijah as a writer. We think of him as a man mighty in deeds and in spoken words. And he certainly was a man mighty in deeds and in spoken words. But the Scripture also records Elijah as doing some writing. This fact is found in a text many overlook, for it is not found in the same place in Scripture where the rest of his activity is recorded. It is recorded in Second Chronicles while his other activity is recorded in First and Second Kings.

Scripture does not record Elijah as writing much. It was simply a short letter to Jehoram, the wicked king of Judah, who was the son and successor of Jehoshaphat and the son-in-law of wicked Ahab and Jezebel. But though the letter was short, it still was very long in instruction. And it was forceful, too. It cut to the quick. It dealt with sin and judgment in typical Elijah fashion. And it will furnish us another instructive study from the life of Elijah.

We are making Elijah's writing ministry the last chapter of our study on Elijah even though we have already studied his exodus from the earth. We are doing this because the letter Elijah wrote was not delivered until after his translation. Our text does not state that fact, but a study of the chronology of events in the books of Kings and Chronicles produces this conclusion.

In this study of Elijah's writing we will note the postscript of service the writing was for Elijah, the pursuit of evil by Jehoram which prompted the writing, and the prophecy of judgment which the writing contained for Jehoram.

## A. THE POSTSCRIPT OF SERVICE

Since this ministry of Elijah's was posthumous (B. H. Carroll fittingly calls the writing "a posthumous bolt of lightning"), it becomes a postscript of service; for this service is added to his record after the main body of his service (service performed during his lifetime) had occurred.

We want to note three things about this postscript of service: the questioning of it, the qualification for it, and the quality of it.

### 1. The Questioning of It

Because Elijah's translation took place before the writing was delivered to Jehoram, some question if this was actually Elijah's writing. Those who have questioned Elijah's authorship of the writing have advanced some interesting, but invalid, explanations regarding the text. We will look at some of these explanations in order to show their weaknesses and to show why it was indeed Elijah's postscript ministry.

One of the main explanations given by those who do not accept our text as speaking of Elijah is that there is a manuscript error in the text and that it really refers to Elisha, not Elijah. However, this explanation has no support from the manuscripts. "The word [Elijah] occurs in all existing Hebrew manuscripts and in all the Oriental versions" (Thomas Whitelaw).

Another explanation says the letter was written in heaven by Elijah and supernaturally delivered. This explanation is harder to believe than the conclusion that Elijah wrote the letter before he died and had it delivered by another later on. Furthermore, there is no textual suggestion to support such a conclusion.

Still another explanation says that the Elijah in our text is not the same Elijah we have been reading about in First and Second Kings. Not many embrace this conclusion; for it, like the previous explanation, has no textual support and creates more problems than it solves.

Then there are those who view this text as just another case of the inaccuracy of the Bible which, they say, means we cannot trust the Scriptures. There are always those who seem very quick to disbelieve and discredit the Scripture. These critics hesitate not to discredit a passage of Scripture at even the slightest appearance of a difficulty in it. As soon as they see such a passage, they quickly announce that the Scripture is simply not reliable, that it is full of errors, is contradictory, etc. They do not try to reconcile the text, nor do they allow for Divine miracles or prophetic revelation to enter the picture. Their one obvious aim is to discredit the Scripture and to discourage belief in it. It is dishonest scholarship and has no merit whatsoever.

All the critics of the conclusion that this text was a postscript ministry of Elijah, the great prophet from Tishbe, seem to make no allowances for the view that Elijah could easily have written the letter in his lifetime, then given it to Elisha or another person to see to it that it was delivered at the appropriate time. The critics, of course, do not accept that view. After all, they argue, how could Elijah know about Jehoram's conduct before he was king? But they do not argue against the fact that the letter contained a prediction of Jehoram's death two years before he died. And if Elijah could know that fact in advance, why could he not know of Jehoram's conduct in advance?

To accept the prediction of Jehoram's death in one breath and to reject Elijah's knowing of his conduct in advance in another breath is most inconsistent thinking and without value. It also ignores the fact that Elijah was given revelation of other events which also happened years after his home-going such as Jezebel's death, Jehu coming to the throne, and Hazael becoming king in Assyria. The critics also ignore the fact that some of the writing prophets, such as Isaiah, delivered prophecies many years before they were fulfilled. As an example, Isaiah's prediction of Cyrus delivering the Israelites from Babylonian captivity was made before the Babylonian captivity even began and while Assyria, not Babylon, was in power. And it was made a hundred years before Cyrus was born! Also the prophet Micah predicted the location of Christ's birth some four hundred years before it happened! What, therefore, would be so difficult about Elijah being informed of God a few years in advance regarding Jehoram's behavior and then told what to write? Absolutely nothing! It is the most sensible, the most logical, the most exegetically correct, and the most Scripturally supported conclusion.

**2. The Qualification for It**

The writer of Hebrews said of Abel, "He being dead yet speaketh" (Hebrews 11:4). Why did Abel's life speak well for God *after* he died? Because it spoke well for God *before* he died! So it was with Elijah, and so it will be with anyone. Before anyone can have a postscript added to a letter, they must first have written a letter. A postscript implies and demands that something went before it. It is no different in service. The qualification for having a postscript of service after you have died is to have performed some service, as Elijah, Abel, and others did, while you lived.

For a good many there are no postscripts of service, but instead there are many postscripts of sin. During the lifetime of these folks, they did not serve the Lord, but served sin. So when they died they left behind a legacy of trouble which haunts and hurts lives of people for generations. Evil acts come to light and sometimes years after a person has died. And these evil acts bring shame and disgrace to many still living, and sometimes they also bring lawsuits and other great problems to society.

But for Elijah and others who have served God well, there are often many postscripts of service. They have left behind such things as books, writings, organizations, institutions, converts, disciples, and money which continue to perform great service for the Lord after they have passed from this earthly scene. But none of this would have happened if they had not performed well during their lifetime.

All of this should cause us to do some real heart searching of our own lives to see what sort of postscripts will be added on to them after we pass from this world. Are we serving the Lord faithfully with what we have in this life, or are we living for self and pursuing evil pleasures? After we die it will be disclosed what we have left behind. And this is not related just to our wills, either. It will show up in an abundance of ways and will reveal how we have lived and what sort of person we really were during our lifetime on earth.

### 3. The Quality of It

It is not surprising that the quality of Elijah's postscript service is of the same excellent quality of his service while he was still on earth. His writing emphasized the Word of God and the Way of God. Anything which emphasizes the Word of God and the Way of God will have quality to it.

*The Word of God.* The Word was prominent in Elijah's postscript service. The very first thing said in the letter to Jehoram was, "Thus saith the LORD God" (v. 12). Right away Jehoram is directed by Elijah to God's Word. The Word of God is made the authority, the guide, the rule of life. It is declared plainly and forcefully. Thus the writing of Elijah had great value, great quality to it. But without the Word his writing would be of little worth.

This truth is ignored in a host of our churches, however. Our churches have many pastors who run here and there, institute all sorts of socially oriented programs, are back-slappers, and denominational officers; but they do not major on preaching the Word. Also our churches have many services and meetings and get-togethers in which the Word of God plays no part at all, or if it is included it is a very minor part. You do not need to take a Bible to most of the meetings the average church has because you will not need it. Therefore, what is done is of little eternal value. But if our service as individuals or as a church is to have any quality to it, then the Word of God must be front and center. It must be most prominent.

*The Way of God.* Elijah's writing rebuked Jehoram for not walking in God's way. "Thou hast not walked in the ways of Jehoshaphat, thy father, nor in the ways of Asa king of Judah, But hast walked in the way of the kings of Israel" (vv. 12,13).

Jehoshaphat and Asa, for the most part, walked in the ways of God. But Jehoram did not. He walked in the ways of evil, for that is the way in which all the kings of Israel (the northern kingdom) walked.

We seem so prone to hedge on speaking out on the right way and wrong way today. Unlike Elijah, we do not delineate right and wrong very clearly. We play politics in the church and in the pulpit. We do not want to offend anyone, so we hesitate to correct anyone. But a preacher who has lost his courage to speak out plainly in the honoring of God's way and in condemning the world's way is a preacher who needs to get right or get out of the ministry. The job of the man of God is to guide people in the right way, in God's way. But many muddle the message and water down the Word to such an extent that you have a hard time knowing what is right and wrong. People can listen for years to some men and never know the right way. There is no quality in such a ministry.

## B. THE PURSUIT OF EVIL

That which prompted Elijah's letter was the great evil of Jehoram. Jehoram pursued evil like those in the prophet Micah's day, "with both hands earnestly" (Micah 7:3). In fact, it seemed like it was about all he pursued. And to live so evilly begged for a confrontation with Elijah. And Jehoram got it—in the form of a letter.

Elijah's letter cites the evil of Jehoram and describes it in very plain and pungent terms. Today the description would be too strong for our society, for it tolerates so much sin and opposes calling sin by its right names. Elijah, however, was not in the business of appeasing sinners but in apprehending them. He did not mince his words in denouncing evil. He called a spade a spade.

We note three things from Elijah's writing about the evil pursued by Jehoram: the inventory, the instigator, and the inexcusableness of his evil.

# The Writing

## 1. The Inventory of His Evil

When we inventory Jehoram's evil deeds, we will discover that the list of his evil deeds can be put into two categories: his evil regarding religion, and his evil regarding relatives.

*Evil regarding religion.* Elijah's letter said Jehoram had "made Judah and the inhabitants of Jerusalem to go a whoring, like to the whoredoms of the house of Ahab" (v. 13). This refers to the promoting of Baal worship by Jehoram. The use of the terms "whoring" and "whoredoms" not only speaks of the unfaithfulness of the people to Jehovah when they worshiped other gods, but it also speaks of the awful immorality and licentiousness associated with Baal worship.

Jehoram went after Baal unlike his father Jehoshaphat who "sought not unto Baalim" (II Chronicles 17:3). And worse, he forced Judah to do likewise. He "*made* Judah and the inhabitants of Jerusalem to go a whoring." What a terrible blight Jehoram brought on the theology and morals of Judah. What a corrupt influence Jehoram was upon the people. He corrupted the people by example and by edict.

We influence others whether we realize it or not. Jehoram used his powers as king to evilly influence people. But you do not have to be a king with great power in order to influence others to evil. You can be a nobody and still do it. "None of us liveth to himself" (Romans 14:7). And you, like Jehoram, have to answer as to how you have influenced people.

*Evil regarding relatives.* The writing of Elijah also mentioned the murderous deed of Jehoram in which he had "slain thy brethren" (v. 13). Jehoram had seven brothers. When he became king this was seven too many as far as he was concerned. "Now when Jehoram was risen up to the kingdom of his father, he strengthened himself, and slew all his brethren with the sword" (v. 4).

Elijah's writing not only cited this awful deed, but it also gave the reason for it. Elijah wrote, "Thy brethren . . . were better than thyself" (v. 13). His brothers being better than he was would produce much jealousy in a character like Jehoram. It would give him concern that one of them might replace him as king, and it would definitely crimp his evil actions. So he murdered his brothers.

Jehoram's attack upon his brothers reminds us of Cain's attack on Abel. Why did he kill Abel? "Because his own works were evil, and his brother's righteous" (I John 3:12). Abel was better than Cain. And evil hates good and will attack it if it can. So Cain and Jehoram attacked and killed their brothers.

Much attack on the godly by the wicked is because of this very reason. The righteous need to remember that their life is a continual rebuke to the ungodly; and, therefore, it provokes the ungodly. And if the ungodly can, they will attack in vicious ways. Even church troubles are often rooted in this very problem. Members living in sin cannot stand a godly pastor and his righteous message; so they strike back and attack the pastor and sometimes succeed in getting him voted out of the church.

**2. The Instigator of His Evil**

Elijah's writing compared Jehoram's conduct to that of the kings of Israel and in particular to "the house of Ahab" (v. 13). There was a very good reason why Jehoram's conduct would especially compare to the house of Ahab. Jehoram's wife Athaliah was the daughter of Ahab and Jezebel; and she was like her mother Jezebel in that she was a great instigator of her husband's evil pursuits. Jehoram "walked in the way of the kings of Israel, like as did the house of Ahab; *for* he had the daughter of Ahab to wife" (v. 6; cp. I Kings 21:25 which records Jezebel as the instigator of Ahab's sin).

The marriage of Athaliah to Jehoram would look like a great political match to the world. It looked like it would really help to unite Judah and Israel and bring these two divided nations together, if not as one nation then at least as two nations working harmoniously together. But when character is ignored, the peace and unity sought will only be a mirage. Athaliah had no character. She was a curse, not a blessing, to Jehoram and to the nation of Judah.

What a curse ungodly women are to mankind. R. G. Lee said, "Search the pages of the Bible all you will; study history all you please. And you will find one truth that stands out above some other truths. What is that truth? The truth that the spiritual life of a nation, city, town, school, church, home never rises any higher than the spiritual life of women." How true. And you will find that the real leaders of such things as abortion, women's lib, and other unholy movements are often women of the most unsavory character.

Again we see in Scripture the great warning against marrying the wrong person. This truth was taught so plainly and forcefully regarding Ahab's marriage to Jezebel. Here it is seen just as plainly and just as forcefully in the marriage of Jehoram. Yet, are we learning from the Word? Do we pay attention to what the Word is teaching? From the looks of what some people bring into a minister's office as the one they want to marry, it does not seem so. The lessons of Jehoram's marriage to Athaliah and of Ahab's marriage to Jezebel seem to be almost universally ignored.

### 3. The Inexcusableness of His Evil

Jehoram was not without examples of good conduct which showed him the right way to live. His father and grandfather, who served as kings before him, gave him good examples of conduct. Elijah's writing pointed this out when it said, "Thou hast not walked in the ways of Jehoshaphat thy father, nor in the ways of Asa [his grandfather] king of Judah" (v. 12). Jehoshaphat and Asa were far from perfect, but they gave Jehoram a far better example of how to live and how to rule than what Jehoram was doing. He could not excuse his evil by claiming ignorance of the right way. He "walked in the way of the kings of Israel" because he chose to do it. He let his evil wife Athaliah influence him rather than the good examples of his father and grandfather. God had shown him a better way, but he ignored it. His evil was therefore inexcusable.

We have to answer for the advantages we are given to do right. And we have more advantages than we realize. Today we have more spiritual advantages in our country than any people in any age have ever had. Yet, like Jehoram, we often despise our advantages and live a vile life. That only makes our sin worse, for the greatness of our sin is not only determined by the evil done but by the advantage we had to do better. Jehoram's evil was very bad in itself, but it was so much worse because of his advantages to do better.

## C. THE PROPHECY OF JUDGMENT

Elijah had the unenviable task of announcing to people the doom of their ways. These confrontations with the corrupt, in which he plainly and forcefully denounced their sin and then predicted their judgment, was a significant part of his recorded ministry. He announced to Ahab that there would be a drought because of the evil of the land. He also announced to Ahab that he (Ahab) and Jezebel would both die in disgrace, that his sons would be slain, and that his dynasty would be overthrown because of the sin of the royal couple. He announced to Ahaziah that he would die because he had gone after pagan gods. Here he wrote to Jehoram about the curse on his life because of his sin. The curse was a severe one. "*Because* thou hast not walked in the ways of Jehoshaphat . . . nor in the ways of Asa . . . But hast walked in the way of the kings of Israel . . . Behold, with a great plague will the LORD smite thy people, and thy children, and thy wives, and all thy goods; And thou shalt have great sickness by the disease of thy bowels [intestines], until thy bowels fall out by reason of the sickness day by day" (vv. 12–15). Jehoram's evil ways had already caused much trouble in his land. "In his days the Edomites revolted from under the dominion of Judah . . . The same time also did Libnah revolt from under his hand; *because* he had forsaken the LORD God of his fathers" (vv. 8,10). But Elijah's writing here predicted more trouble—lots more trouble—for him because of his sin.

# THE WRITING

Evil deeds bring trouble. The devil likes to advertise evil in such a way that it looks like all it will bring is good things. But, of course, the devil is a liar and tells it exactly the opposite of the truth. Truth says evil curses. The world foolishly wants us to forget that fact, however. So they dare anyone to suggest that homosexuals are the prime cause of AIDS. They reason away the problems of gambling, alcohol, and the psychological effects of abortion, and they explain them as anything but the cause of evil. Furthermore, the world reasons away the cause of the devastating storms and problems of nature as being unrelated to our behavior. But the Word of God will not teach us to think that way. It tells us plainly that evil causes trouble, that you cannot live in disregard to God's way and come up a winner; for the judgment of God will doom the sinner.

We note the area in which the judgment of God was predicted upon Jehoram for his evil and the attitude of Jehoram to the announced judgment.

## 1. The Area of Judgment

The curse upon Jehoram was twofold, Elijah wrote that God would send destruction to Jehoram's family and disease to his body. Both Jehoram's home and health would suffer greatly because of his sin.

*Judgment on his home.* Elijah's writing prophesied the curse on Jehoram's home when it said, "Behold, with a great plague will the LORD smite thy people, and thy children, and thy wives, and all thy goods" (v. 14). And it came to pass just as Elijah had predicted. "The LORD stirred up against Jehoram the spirit of the Philistines, and of the Arabians, that were near the Ethiopians; and they came up into Judah, and brake into it, and carried away all the substance that was found in the king's house, and his sons also, and his wives [except Athaliah unfortunately]" (vv. 16,17).

The curse on the home, particularly his sons, caused Jehoram to experience judgment in the coin in which he had sinned.

What grief of heart it must have been for Jehoram to see his sons being carried away captive. But Jehoram was only reaping what he had sown. When Jehoram took over the kingdom he killed his brothers, an atrocious deed which we noted earlier. Jehoram had removed his father's sons from the land, but now his own sons are removed from the land. One son was not captured (v. 17), however; not because God was being merciful to Jehoram, but because "The LORD would not destroy the house of David, because of the covenant that he had made with David, and as he promised to give a light to him and to his sons forever" (v. 7).

*Judgment on his health.* Not only did God curse his home, but he also cursed Jehoram's health. Elijah's written prophecy said, "Thou shalt have great sickness by disease of thy bowels [intestines], until thy bowels fall out by reason of the sickness" (v. 15). It was a loathsome disease and doubtless explains why he "departed without being desired" (v. 20).

We get a good idea of how repulsive and disgraceful Jehoram's disease was by noting the death of Antiochus Epiphanes and of one of the Herods who both had afflictions which sounded much like Jehoram's affliction. The death of Antiochus Epiphanes, the great persecutor of the Jews a few centuries before Christ, is described in the apocryphal book of Second Maccabees. "So that the worms [probably intestinal worms] rose up out of the body of this wicked man, and while he lived in sorrow and pain, his flesh fell away, and the filthiness of his smell was noisome to all his army" (II Maccabees 9:9). In the New Testament we are told of one of the Herods who, after he gave a speech in Caesarea and was acclaimed "the voice of a god, and not of a man" (Acts 12:22), was "immediately" smote by an angel of the Lord "because he gave not God the glory; and he was eaten of worms, and gave up the ghost" (Acts 12:23). Vincent says the Greek word used in Herod's affliction "is used by medical writers of intestinal worms."

If the sickness of Jehoram was not the same sickness as that of Antiochus Epiphanes or Herod, it certainly was similar; and it could easily disenchant people with him so that when he died, he died "without being desired" (v. 20). Without our modern medical helps, he would have become a terrible stench, a person nobody would want to be near.

Oh, how easily God can touch man and strip him of his boasted glory and power. One cannot sin against God without a "because" coming upon him sooner or later. As Krummacher said, "The Divine curse, like a growing storm, soon discharges itself." You behave counter to God's ways and the day will come when a bolt from heaven will find its mark, and you will be stopped in your tracks. "It is a fearful thing to fall into the hands of the living God" (Hebrews 10:31). But our generation, like so many preceding it, has very little fear of the holiness of God. And this lack of fear has promoted gross unholiness which dooms to great judgment.

## 2. The Attitude About Judgment

Jehoram's attitude concerning Divine judgment was fatally poor. He disregarded both Elijah's written prophecy of judgment and his own actual experience of it. His poor attitude revealed a heart that was as hard as stone.

Regarding Jehoram's attitude about the written prophecy of judgment, Krummacher said, "Doubtless it [the writing] must have occasioned momentary terror and alarm; but we read of no contrition, much less of true repentance on his part . . . instead of repenting, he makes his face harder than a rock, and his neck as an iron sinew . . . Well might he shudder at reading such a writing. But it [the reading] did not end in humiliation; and whatever will not bend must break."

When judgment came upon him, as predicted, it did not affect Jehoram, either. The invasion of Jerusalem which resulted in the sacking of his palace and the carrying off of his family did not move him. The fatal disease which attacked his body when he was only thirty-eight did not move him, either. The disease lasted for two years (v. 19) which would give him plenty of time and incentive to think things over, but he would not bow to God's chastening hand. He did not evidence one bit of contrition over his evil. Oh, the hardness that sin brings upon the soul. God can smite ever so severely and give ever so many chances for repentance, but the hardened sinner ignores them all and goes to hell.

What a warning this is to us. God sends us writings, too. He has sent us the greatest writing ever sent to man, namely, the Bible. It warns of sin and the judgment it can bring. But too often we scorn the Word and, instead, pursue with abandon a life of sin. Then when judgment begins to strike us down, we still refuse to bow to the Almighty and His ways. If periods of grace come during His dealings with us, we only use them as more opportunities to pursue our sinful ways. But one thing we learn from Elijah's ministry is that God's judgment is sure to come upon unrepenting sinners. He will in due time strike down the rebellious soul.

Yes, Elijah sends a clear message to every rebellious, disobedient soul. His last writing sums it all up—sin brings judgment! We cannot afford to toy with sin and let it numb us to the place where we are insensitive to God's Word and God's chastening hand upon us. Sin will make us extremely unattractive in the end, and it will make us especially unattractive to God. Sin pursued and unrepented of will always result in departing "without being desired" (v. 20) by heaven. What a terrible epitaph of a life. But it does not have to be that way. We can heed the ministry of Elijah, repent of our evil, turn from our wicked way, and thus escape the justified wrath of a holy God.

# Quotation Sources

The person listed is the author of the book which follows his name unless an asterisk (*) appears after the book title. In this case the person is a contributor to the book or is quoted in the book. Our quoting a person does not mean we necessarily endorse all the beliefs, practices, or associations of that person.

Cardous, J. A. *The Biblical Illustrator (Vol. 4).**
Carroll, B. H. *An Interpretation of the English Bible (Vol. 2).*
Cook, F. C. *The Bible Commentary (Vol. 1).*
Edersheim, Alfred. *The Bible History, Old Testament.*
Haldeman, I. M. *Bible Expositions (Vol. 1).*
Hammond, J. *The Pulpit Commentary (Vol. 5).**
Havner, Vance. *Road to Revival.*
Henry, Matthew. *Commentary on the Whole Bible (Vol. 2).*
Jamieson, Robert. *A Commentary (Vol. 1).*
Keil, C. F. *Commentary on the Old Testament (Vol. 3).*
Keller, W. Phillip. *Elijah: Prophet of Power.*
Krummacher, F. W. *Elijah the Tishbite.*
Lee, R. G. *"Pay-Day—Someday" Sermon.*
MacDonald, J. A. *The Pulpit Commentary (Vol. 5).**
Mackintosh, C. H. *Miscellaneous Writings (Vol. 5).*
Maclaren, Alexander. *Expositions of Holy Scriptures (Vol. 2).*
Merson, D. *The Biblical Illustrator (Vol. 4).**
Meyer, F. B. *Elijah and the Secret of His Power.*
Orr, J. *The Pulpit Commentary (Vol. 5).**
Parker, Joseph. *Preaching Through the Bible (Vol. 4).*
Pink, Arthur W. *The Life of Elijah.*
Poole, Matthew. *A Commentary on the Holy Bible (Vol. 1).*
Rawlinson, G. *The Pulpit Commentary (Vol. 5).**
Scroogie, Graham. *The Unfolding Drama of Redemption.*
Smith, James. *Handfuls on Purpose (Vol. 5).*
Spurgeon, Charles. *The Treasury of the Bible, O. T. (Vol. 1).*
   *Lectures to My Students.*
Talmage, T. DeWitt. *The Biblical Illustrator (Vol. 4).**
Urquhart, J. *The Pulpit Commentary (Vol. 5).**

Vincent, Marvin. *Word Studies in the New Testament (Vol. 1)*.
Watkinson, W. L. *The Biblical Illustrator (Vol. 4).*
Whitelaw, Thomas. *The Pulpit Commentary (Vol. 6).*
Wilson, William. *Old Testament Word Studies*.